D1564258

ALL BECAUSE OF A MORMON COW

ALL BECAUSE

OF A

MORMON COW

Historical Accounts of the
Grattan Massacre, 1854–1855

EDITED BY
John D. McDermott, R. Eli Paul,
and Sandra J. Lowry

UNIVERSITY OF OKLAHOMA PRESS : NORMAN

Library of Congress Cataloging in Publication Control Number: 2018017415

Contents

Illustrations

Figures

Map

Preface

The Grattan Massacre occurred near Fort Laramie, Nebraska Territory, on August 19, 1854. Lieutenant John L. Grattan, U.S. Army, led a detachment of twenty-nine soldiers and a civilian interpreter to a large Lakota encampment to arrest an Indian man accused of killing a Mormon emigrant's cow. Tense negotiations turned into brazen demands, and the situation rapidly deteriorated to the point that soldiers fired into the village. Chief Conquering Bear was mortally wounded, and the enraged villagers turned on Grattan, killing him and his entire command. Considered the first shots fired in the First Sioux War (1854–56), the Grattan Massacre came to be regarded as a seminal event in the history of the Plains Indian wars.

The 1854 fight and its aftereffects endangered the survivors at Fort Laramie, threatened the closure of the overland trail, and drew a storm of national debate over whom to blame: the inexperienced army officer fresh from West Point; his inebriated, provocative interpreter; Mormon passersby on their way to Utah; conniving French traders; their Lakota customers and kinsmen by marriage; or the appointed head chief, who had kept an unsteady peace since the Horse Creek Treaty of 1851. The federal government rushed to judgment and answered with a punitive expedition against the Sioux tribes in 1855. Four decades of intermittent conflict between the Lakota nation and the United States ensued. That so much death and destruction followed the loss of an emigrant's cow still possesses the power to leave one stunned.

In looking for scapegoats, attracting a great deal of national attention, and mounting a punitive expedition, military leaders seemed, inexplicably, to have learned little from the Grattan debacle. Shocking defeats continued: Fetterman's near Fort Phil Kearny in 1866, that of Custer's immediate command at the Little Bighorn in 1876, and the rout of Perry's troops at White Bird Canyon in 1877. Ethnocentrism, ignorance of Indian cultures, distrust of a

large standing army, insufficient forces and resources, lack of military train-
ing, unfamiliar landscapes spanning huge distances, inability to effectively
engage in irregular warfare, and rampant fraud and corruption, especially
in the purchase and distribution of military and agency goods—all of these
factors contributed to the problem.

For this volume we have brought together all known contemporary accounts
of the Grattan fight and its immediate aftermath. Many are newly discovered
or come from obscure sources. All were recorded in the period 1854–55, when
the events were fresh in narrators' memories, and they supply a sense of
immediacy to the story. The accounts by Indian leaders Little Thunder and
Big Partisan, who counseled unsuccessfully with Grattan, have never been
published in their entirety. Those by members of Mormon emigrant trains
in the form of diary entries have been largely absent from previous historical
studies. They join better-known accounts that government officials formally
gathered as part of an impromptu investigation of the affair.

Here are versions by those who were triumphant that day, by those who
were near-participants, and by others who were affected directly by the fight's
consequences. Because of their military or civilian background, many provided experienced, eyewitness insights. A few who left contemporary, hearsay
accounts are included as well in order to reflect the general tenor of the
times. Together they portray the event from many individual and cultural
perspectives, present the broadest picture possible, and illustrate many of
those aforementioned contributing factors as they played out in large or small
part at Fort Laramie in 1854. Because of their understanding of military and
Indian affairs on the northern Plains, several individuals represented here
provide experienced, specific, on-the-ground insights that reflect the issues
of the day and the biases of the times.

Our long-standing interests in this part of the American West—Fort
Laramie, the overland experience, the frontier army, the Lakota people, and
the history of their first war—are all reflected in this book. This first volume
presents a detailed summary of the story by the senior editor, a new look
that benefits from the previously unpublished sources found and presented
here. A compendium of the historical accounts from 1854–55, each prefaced
with an editorial comment, follows this summary. Arranged in chronological
order and presented in two distinct parts, these narratives encompass the
event and those that immediately followed, particularly the important role
that Oscar Winship played in recording the facts in the case. The second,

forthcoming volume will include an almost equal number of later accounts, reminiscent and reflective, that span the ensuing decades. The memory and legacy of this event lasted well into the twentieth century, a stimulus to historical inquiry that continues to the present. The character of the later reminiscent accounts is strikingly different, and they need to be introduced and evaluated separately. That effort requires a closer examination of the nature of oral history and Indian testimony, their strengths and weaknesses, and the mechanisms for recording and remembering the Plains Indian wars.

The First Sioux War that waged episodically between the years 1854 and 1856 on the central and northern plains settled little, its few battles and skirmishes comparatively minor in number and scale to those that followed and its negotiated conclusion more a temporary armistice that a lasting peace. It served as mere prelude to later, greater conflicts between the Lakota peoples and the U.S. Army, but of course, that would only become clear after the passage of more decades of struggle. The twentieth- and twenty-first-century historians who have dealt with all or parts of the First Sioux War largely treated the conflict as preamble, its resolution readily apparent to all who knew how this story eventually ended.

This route taken by scholars has been down the path of least resistance, although their narrative vehicles have differed. Four works in particular relating to the Grattan fight provided an overland trail perspective, or more accurately, an *overlander* perspective: a 1954 *Nebraska History* article by Lloyd E. McCann, titled simply "The Grattan Massacre"; a portion of one chapter in Merrill J. Mattes's 1969 tome, *The Great Platte River Road*; John D. Unruh Jr.'s 1979 synthesis, *The Plains Across*, which supplanted the Mattes book; and Michael L. Tate's more recent *Indians and Emigrants: Encounters on the Overland Trails* (2006). In these studies the August 19, 1854, conflict was based on an almost inevitable clash when two cultures literally collide with one another, although to their credit Mattes, Unruh, and especially Tate battled long-held popular stereotypes to stress just how rare such emigrant-Native conflicts were. McCann's study of the Grattan fight, the most detailed of the lot, depended considerably on Indian testimony, the usage of which set the standard for all serious studies of the First Sioux War.

Offering another perspective, that of *place*, were four histories: LeRoy R. Hafen and Francis Marion Young's 1938 *Fort Laramie and the Pageant of the West, 1834–1890*; Remi Nadeau's 1967 popular history *Fort Laramie and the Sioux Indians*; David Lavender's 1983 National Park Service guidebook

Fort Laramie and the Changing Frontier; and Douglas C. McChristian's more recent, in-depth study, *Fort Laramie: Military Bastion of the High Plains* (2008). Their titles make obvious that they focused on the history of an individual military outpost and the military men who garrisoned Fort Laramie. Less obvious were how these works portrayed all the individuals and communities who lived and interacted within that space. Although drawing on many of the same historical sources as the first group of trail histories, these studies depended on the staggering amounts of government paper that the frontier army generated to provide the contextual fodder for this part of the fort's life history. Exploiting this abundance of riches the best was McChristian, the only military historian of this group, who added considerably to the Grattan story by emphasizing the 1853 skirmish at Platte Bridge, the ominous foreshadowing of the 1854 tragedy.

Military leaders, especially those above the rank of brevet second lieutenant, seem to inspire modern biographers as much as, if not more than, those they led, and another vast number of words has been expended on documenting their lives and careers. The familiar names to follow, particularly for a Civil War enthusiast, include these biographical examples: *General William Selby Harney* by George Rollie Adams (2001); *General John Buford* by Edward G. Longacre (1995); *The West of Philip St. George Cooke, 1809–1895* by Otis E. Young (1955); and the intriguingly titled *"Happiness Is Not My Companion": The Life of General G. K. Warren* by David M. Jordan (2001). For these historical figures and their Boswells, the Sioux Expedition of which they were members merited a chapter or less, used largely to prepare the reader for later achievements on the eastern battlefields.

The historian who delved deeper into the subject was the academic and editor Ralph P. Bieber, with his extensive 1932 introduction to expedition participant and enlisted man Eugene Bandel's *Frontier Life in the Army, 1854–1861*. Nevertheless none of these military histories paid much attention to the Grattan fight that prompted the involvement of these military men. That was left, more or less, to Carolyn M. McClellan, Bieber's Washington University student, whose 1945 master's thesis on the Sioux Expedition drew heavily from surviving Missouri newspapers of the time.

Placing the Grattan and Blue Water Creek fights—and the Sioux Expedition and the aforementioned military participants—in their proper contexts was the purpose of two important studies of the frontier army, Robert M. Utley's *Frontiersmen in Blue* (1967) and Durwood Ball's follow-up synthesis *Army*

Regulars on the Western Frontier, 1848–1861 (2001). This military campaign, one of many in the American West, fell neatly in the middle of their timelines, and both authors provided succinct accounts in their respective military histories. This pair of authors, along with John D. McDermott and his *A Guide to the Indian Wars of the West* (1998) easily offered the incentive for a book-length study of the campaign. This was fulfilled somewhat redundantly by two works in 2004, Paul N. Beck's *The First Sioux War* and R. Eli Paul's *Blue Water Creek and the First Sioux War, 1854–1856.* For the latter author the opportunity to present new sources on Indian history proved irresistible, the result being his 2004 narrative and his work on this complementary volume.

Placing the First Sioux War in the context of the histories of the Native peoples involved was largely the province of George E. Hyde and his two narrative histories, *Red Cloud's Folk* (1957) and *Spotted Tail's Folk* (1961). Both were written less from the Indian perspective than their titles might imply, a condition largely remedied by more recent studies, particularly Catherine Price's *The Oglala People, 1841–1879: A Political History* (1996), Jeffrey Ostler's *The Plains Sioux and U.S. Colonialism from Lewis and Clark to Wounded Knee* (2004), and Kingsley M. Bray's *Crazy Horse: A Lakota Life* (2006). The latter, a comprehensive "life-and-times" biography of the Oglala war leader, could have been easily and appropriately titled "Crazy Horse's Folk" in the Hyde tradition. For all these studies, though, the Grattan and Blue Water episodes, and the war in general, serve more as prologue, whatever Native-centric view is employed.

The leads and supporting cast in all these scenarios, however, have remained essentially unchanged, no matter the broader emphasis, interest, or approach. One has the young, brash, headstrong, incompetent Lieutenant Grattan, who takes his woefully outmanned command to an Indian village, demands the surrender of the disrespectful killer of an anonymous emigrant's footsore ox, and "goes all in" when those foolish demands are not immediately met. You have the star-crossed victim Conquering Bear, the Lakota leader who tries unsuccessfully to defuse the situation and dies tragically at the hands of Grattan's soldiers when they fire on the camp. You also have Little Thunder, another unlucky leader at the scene, who tried to prevent bloodshed and who later suffered the further indignity of having his village punished in retribution. And finally, you have the old, brash, headstrong, dangerously competent Colonel Harney, who played the role of avenging angel of death with his devastating attack on Little Thunder's village at Blue Water Creek.

That small cast can now be significantly enlarged. With this volume of eyewitness accounts of the tragedy at Fort Laramie these few main characters are now joined by a much larger and more diverse cast of supporting players, each given the opportunity now to speak their respective lines.

As the publications of the aforementioned historians and authors have been of incalculable help to this publication, so too has the assistance of many friends, colleagues, historical institutions and their staff members, as well as those progressive organizations making their collections increasingly accessible through digital means. Invariably this is where a lengthy list of names and places would ensue, but we will forego the exercise, primarily because two of the editors sadly cannot participate in that tradition. Therefore, our thanks will be confined to Will Bagley and Paul Hedren, the outside readers for the University of Oklahoma Press, who made this work measurably better both in content and quality, and to the past and present editorial staff members with whom we worked, starting with Chuck Rankin and ending with Steven Baker, Robert Clark, Erin Greb, Amy Hernandez, Adam Kane, Bethany Mowry, and Kerin Tate.

Sandra Joy Lowry died on September 19, 2016, and John Dishon McDermott on December 31, 2016. Both were blessed by loving families, who may feel some comfort from their loss by the appearance of this book. Although Sandy and Jack did not see the final, revised manuscript, they were there for virtually the entire journey, and of course, this book could not have been done without them. More importantly for all the scholars they assisted over the decades, they were instrumental in the growth and development of the Fort Laramie Library, which stands today as a great testament to their dedication in preserving and interpreting the site's history. Their lives should be celebrated by all whose paths they crossed. This book, therefore, can serve as its own acknowledgement for their contributions as "friends" of Fort Laramie.

Editorial Procedures

The format of this volume requires some explanation. The presentation of the historical accounts, arranged in chronological order following the introduction, conforms to a template developed by the editors. Each entry begins with a telling epigraph, excerpted from the account, and is followed by a concise, one- or two-paragraph editorial introduction. The original historical account relating to the Grattan fight follows. The entry ends with the source of the document given. Additional comments, asides, and observations, along with relevant sources, may appear with the source. This has obviated the need to insert explanatory notes within the text.

The historical accounts are meant to be read, not deciphered. Punctuation and capitalization have been added or deleted where needed with no loss or change in meaning. Extraneous portions of the original document that have no relevance to the subject have been deleted. The use of brackets within an account indicates an addition or emendation by the editors, usually for the sake of clarity. The use of [sic] has been kept to a minimum, preserving the original authors' spelling and grammatical errors unless they are unclear. The editors' goal has been to provide the right amount of set-up and lively annotation without burying the manuscript in notes or overwhelming the individual historical account. The result makes for a linear, logical, and quite readable narrative, more so than other such compendia of first person historical accounts.

ALL BECAUSE OF A MORMON COW

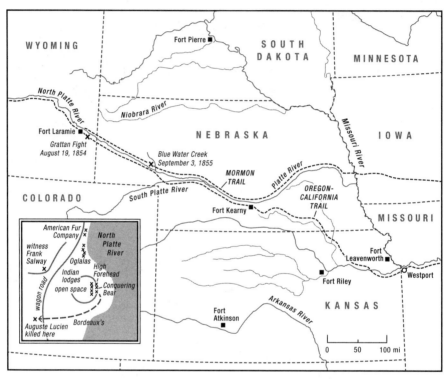

Fort Laramie and the West, 1854–1855, with Grattan fight inset.
Courtesy Wild West *Magazine. Redrawn by Erin Greb.*

Introduction

The Story

In many respects, progress marked the coming of midcentury. In July 1853, the USS *Susquehanna* and its sister ships *Mississippi* and *Saratoga* sailed into Tokyo Bay, only one day away from Japan's largest city, Edo, a place that had been free from foreign contact for nearly 250 years. In 1854 Samuel Colt fought with lawyers, not pistols, in his duel with the U.S. Congress to extend the patent on the revolver that took his name. A milestone in world literature occurred the same year when Charles Dickens gave the first reading of *A Christmas Carol* at the Birmingham Town Hall. American letters were also coming of age with Henry David Thoreau's *Walden* seeing print in 1854 and proclaiming, "Eastward I go only by force; but westward I go free." In the same year, Scottish adventurer William Drummond Stewart, who lived those words, published to great acclaim his novel *Edward Warren*, a thinly veiled autobiography. Stewart had lived the life of a gentleman fur trader in present Wyoming, having made three sojourns into beaver country since 1833. His words stirred the blood of adventurous young men living on the edge of the frontier.

By 1854 the region about which Stewart wrote had been experiencing an invasion of sorts. Following the Platte River across Nebraska and the North Platte into Wyoming, thousands of home-hungry emigrants moved on to Utah, Oregon, and California. The year 1843, the first one of significant westward migration, saw nearly a thousand persons, guided by Marcus Whitman, headed for Oregon. A new destination was added in 1847 when Brigham Young and 2,200 Mormons traveled to the Great Salt Lake. In 1848 gold was discovered in California, and the following year at least 25,000 forty-niners passed by Fort Laramie. Travel on the Oregon-California-Mormon Trail doubled in 1850, its peak year, with more than 50,000—maybe 70,000—emigrants wending their ways west. To protect and aid these travelers, the United States government funded the construction of three small military posts, Fort Kearny in present Nebraska, Fort Laramie in Wyoming, and Fort Hall in Idaho.[1]

The second of these little garrisons, Fort Laramie, became the catalyst in the conflict to come.[2] Located 327 miles west of Fort Kearny by the established, well-traveled route, it was, more importantly, 639 miles west of Fort Leavenworth, its source of supply. Without walls, it spread out on the banks of Laramie Creek, a stream that flowed into the North Platte about one and a half miles from the outpost. Looming above the frame buildings that the military garrison constructed was old Fort John, the adobe-walled trading post built by the American Fur Company in 1841. Sagging and decrepit, it served as the last bastion of defense in case of trouble, a role it would sadly play in 1854.[3] Maj. Winslow F. Sanderson of the U.S. Mounted Riflemen had purchased the American Fur Company trading post on June 26, 1849, for $4,000, and the first garrison consisted of two companies of Mounted Riflemen and one company of the Sixth U.S. Infantry. The Mounted Riflemen remained there until ordered to move elsewhere on July 23, 1851. This left only Company G, Sixth Infantry, to control a mounted adversary in a vast region of sagebrush and buffalo grass. Commenting on the lack of troops stationed along the Oregon Trail, Commissioner of Indian Affairs John Wilkins Whitfield declared: "The military posts located in this agency are perfect nuisances. The idea that one company of infantry can furnish aid and protection to emigrants who pass through this agency is worse than nonsense. They can protect themselves no further than their guns can reach; they have no effect upon the Indians so far as fear is concerned; [the Indians] neither respect nor fear them; and as to protecting the traveler on the road, they are of no more use than so many stumps."[4]

The Plains Indians, particularly the Lakota tribes, also known as the Teton Sioux, became more and more restless as the tide of emigration swelled. Overlanders had to start in the late spring as soon as the grass was up in order to make the long trip before winter set in. Moreover, most emigrants began at the same time, their wagons sometimes traveling a dozen abreast, cutting a large swath, sometimes a mile wide, through the semiarid Great Plains, scaring away game and exhausting wood resources. To defuse a volatile situation, government officials negotiated a treaty with the region's tribes, focusing on the western Sioux, Cheyenne, and Arapaho, a loose alliance that could prove the most troublesome if provoked. Their ranges covered large sections of the overland trail. The 1851 Fort Laramie Treaty, sometimes called the Horse Creek Treaty, established general boundaries for the Sioux, Cheyenne, Arapaho, Arikara, Assiniboine, Crow, Gros Ventre, Mandan, and Shoshone tribes and promised an annual payment of $50,000 in trade goods for fifty years for the use of the overland trail. Each tribe agreed to the appointment of a single chief to act in government matters. Conquering Bear, whose name in Lakota appeared phonetically as "Mah-toe-wha-you-whey" on the treaty, led the Wazhazha band of the Brulé Lakota tribe and was selected by his peers as chief of all the Western Sioux.[5] The U.S. Senate subsequently cut the number of years for annuities to ten with a proviso for a possibility of five more years.[6] If this appears as a one-sided decision far removed from the brokers of the original deal—as it did to the native groups at the time—it proved to follow a pattern that would repeat itself during the history of Indian-white relations.

To anticipate and comprehend the conflict to come, an act of violence that disrupted overland travel, one must first understand the social and economic milieu of Fort Laramie at midcentury: how the fort came to be, how it changed during its early history, and how its diverse inhabitants shaped what happened on August 19, 1854. There were in effect four communities living and interacting at Fort Laramie: traders, Indians, soldiers, and emigrants.

The first Euro-Americans to penetrate the wilds of what is now present Wyoming were the fur traders who came looking for beaver pelts and the skins of buffalo, deer, and elk beginning in the mid-1830s. They drew their Indian customers to the immediate area and continued to arrive and thrive in the following decades. To obtain furs and hides and send them to the States, these forerunners of white conquest developed practical transportation routes, from horse trails to wagon roads, which later served land seekers who migrated westward. The places where rivers joined were havens to those who worked in the wilderness. Fresh water, good grass growing from water-permeated soil, trees for shelter from the heat and the wind, and poles and branches for tipis and makeshift lodges were some of the reasons why trappers sought confluences, and they returned to them time and time again.

The first permanent settlement in Wyoming was a trading post built near the confluence of the Laramie and North Platte Rivers. In 1834 William L. Sublette and Robert Campbell constructed a cottonwood log stockade there. Dubbed Fort William, the post became the center of trade with the Lakota, who had recently migrated onto the northern plains. Having obtained both horses and firearms in the late eighteenth and early nineteenth centuries, these Sioux had become nomadic, following the great herds of buffalo that roamed the region. Moving into Nebraska and Wyoming as a vanguard and pushing their competitors out were the Oglala and Brulé, two of the seven Western Sioux tribes. After the establishment of Fort Laramie in 1834, Bull Bear, the leading Oglala chief, moved about four thousand of his kinsman there, and Smoke, an Oglala counterpart, followed with others, creating a year-round Fort Laramie community. The post became the locus of Oglala activity for the next forty years. Together these "Southern Lakota," the southernmost expansionist groups that favored such hunting ranges of the Plains as the White River, Platte River, and Smoky Hill watersheds, were the people most involved in the nearby events two decades later.[7]

During the winter of 1841–42, after the killing of Bull Bear, the Oglalas split into two factions. About half the tribe, Bull Bear's faction, moved and occupied lands in present Kansas and Nebraska between the Platte and the Smoky Hill Fork. The other half, Smoke's followers, went north and occupied the headwaters of the Powder River in northern Wyoming. The tribe continued, however, to trade at Fort Laramie, as did the Brulés who ranged farther east.[8]

Some of the first traders on the scene married Indian women, strengthening their business ties with the Sioux, and fathered children who became tribal members.[9] Author Sylvia Van Kirk has pointed out that in the fur trade, "white and Indian met on the most equitable footing that has ever characterized the meeting of 'civilized' and 'primitive' people." The purpose was not to subjugate the Indian, take his property, or change his basic way of life or beliefs. It was to trade for mutually useful items.[10] Later these same men took on new duties, serving as interpreters when treaties were made and offering advice on many subjects, thus gaining influence over the chiefs.[11] Called "squaw men" by local travelers, most of these early adventurers who gravitated to the Fort Laramie area were French Americans who came from St. Charles, Missouri. They included Joseph Bissonette, James Bordeaux, Dominique Bray, Sefroy Iott, Nick and Antoine Janis, Joe Larrabee, Auguste Lucien, Leon Pallardy, Baptiste "Big Bat" Pourier, John, Peter, and Joseph Richard, and the Sublette brothers. Two of these St. Charles Frenchmen—Bordeaux and Lucien—played major roles in the Grattan episode.

Born on August 22, 1814, James Bordeaux began his full-time career as a trader in 1830 as a hunter for the American Fur Company at Fort Union on the Missouri River. Bordeaux remained in the employ of the powerful firm during most of the next two decades, gradually working his way up the ladder to assume positions of trust and responsibility. By 1840 he was the chief trader at Fort Laramie. In that year he cemented ties with the Brulés by marrying Huntkalutkawin, the daughter of Lone Dog of the Red Lodge band. Known as Marie, she was the sister of Swift Bear (sometimes translated as Quick Bear), who later became chief of the Corn band. Bordeaux later took a second wife, Supiwin, a cousin of Marie, also known as Annie. By his first wife he had six children, by his second, three. Bordeaux continued as one of the principals of Fort Laramie, actually managing operations of the post for long periods of time in the absence of superiors. He remained at Fort Laramie until the army purchased it in 1849, then moved eight miles east to establish his own trading post. This became the setting for the Grattan fight.[12]

The soldiers stationed at Fort Laramie had their own community but especially in the early years forged significant ties with certain Indian families. As one might expect, lacking women of their own race, some young men soon entered into liaisons with Indian maidens. Chief among these was First Lt. Richard Brooke Garnett, an 1841 graduate of West Point, who arrived at Fort Laramie on June 22, 1852, and commanded the post from July 19 to May 18, 1854.[13] One day as Garnett rode through a camp of Indians waiting for their agent to arrive, he met a beautiful Indian girl named Looks-at-Him (Looking Woman), whose friendliness contrasted to that exhibited by the other Indian women, and in June 1853 he made the girl his mistress. Garnett left his command in May 1854 to return east, leaving behind his Indian cohabitant. Some months later she gave birth to a baby boy, William, who grew to become one of the great army scouts of the nineteenth century.

Liaisons such as this one probably made relations between the two races less contentious, and the cultural knowledge obtained on both sides helped to broaden perspectives.[14] Second Lt. Hugh Brady Fleming, who commanded Fort Laramie after Garnett, realized pragmatically the value of fostering close ties with the Indians when he later wrote to his superior that "we must remember that with so few troops as were stationed at Fort Laramie, so far in the Indian country, surrounded by thousands of Indians, it becomes absolutely necessary to rely on the good faith of some of them even for the safety of the garrison itself."[15]

The fourth segment of the Fort Laramie community was the emigrant, who came not to settle but to pass through. His use of the natural resources on the way, however, was devastating to native peoples. Increased travel antagonized the Indians; they complained of disappearing game, the lack of grass for their ponies, the loss of sheltering trees from the riverbanks, and the lack of wood for their campfires. Some of these impacts were life threatening in a nomadic society functioning in a semiarid environment.

Evidence of Lakota unrest appeared in early 1851, two years after the great hordes of initial gold-seekers had passed by. On January 13, Fort Laramie's commander ordered First Lt. Washington Lafayette Elliott and nineteen Mounted Riflemen to proceed to Sitting Bear's village and arrest a brave who had stolen a horse from Edwin A. Abbey, a civilian. The outcome of the visit is unknown, but because no other mentions of the incident appear in the post records, one assumes that no violence ensued. In early October 1852, an Indian imperious in his demands for provisions drew a gun on a soldier and threatened to shoot if food was not given to him; the Indian was arrested and put in irons.[16]

Violence came the following year on June 15 when Company G of the Sixth Infantry skirmished with Indians near Fort Laramie. Early in the travel season the only bridge over the Laramie had been carried off in high water, requiring a ferry to provide a river crossing.[17] On April 25 the ferry sank, and two days later a swamping nearly caused two more deaths. Finally on May 9 the army contracted with Enoch W. Raymond and Company to provide a "good flat boat," operated by not less than two men. The articles of agreement prohibited the firm from selling liquor or goods at the site, and the army collected 5 percent of the gross tolls received.[18] Trouble began on June 15 when a party of Miniconjou Lakotas wanted to cross the North Platte River in the skiff. More interested in the ferrying of paying emigrants, the keeper refused the request, and the angry warriors took the boat by force. Consequently the contractor went to the fort for redress, and a sergeant and three enlisted men later swam the river and retrieved the boat. While returning to the other side, the soldiers became the target of Miniconjou irritation in the form of musket fire when a ball passed near the ear of the sergeant. Upon reaching the fort, commander Richard Garnett ordered Lieutenant Fleming and twenty-three men to proceed to the village and arrest the tribesman who had shot at the sergeant. In case the Indian was not forthcoming, Garnett directed Fleming to take two prisoners, using force if necessary.

Fleming and his men left just before dark that evening, crossed the river in two little boats, making multiple trips, and arrived at the Indian village located on the north bank of the North Platte River. Perhaps as many as one thousand Miniconjous were camped there. Fleming told Auguste Lucien, his interpreter, to go to the tipi of Chief Little Brave, the acknowledged head of the band, and tell him that he must have the Indian who shot at one of his men or the chief would be made a prisoner. However, the chief was absent, so Fleming formed a protective circle and began to search the lodges, while the Indians became more and more agitated. As the soldiers drew near, some of the warriors withdrew to a ravine in the rear of the village and began firing their guns and arrows. Fleming's troops charged the ravine, returned fire, and forced the warriors to flee. They killed three of the Miniconjous and took two prisoners.[19] Fleming formed his troops into a hollow square, the so-called "phalanx movement," and the victors returned to the fort. They reached Fort Laramie about dawn and reported the engagement, Fleming observing that his "men behaved creditably both to themselves, and the Regiment to which they belong."[20]

After the fight the Miniconjous broke camp and headed for the Black Hills, but a messenger from Fort Laramie overtook them, asking Chief Little Brave to come back for a talk and adding that he might bring as many men with him as he wanted. A few days later Little Brave came to Fort Laramie with sixty warriors where leaders parleyed with Lieutenant Garnett. The officer told the men that he was willing to forget what had passed between them provided that they promised to behave in the future. Little Brave replied in the affirmative, Garnett released the two prisoners, and the Miniconjous departed. While peace continued, many of the Lakotas, including some of the Oglalas and Brulés, remained resentful. When Thomas "Broken Hand" Fitzpatrick, government agent for the Upper Platte Agency, arrived at Fort Laramie on September 10 to present the amendments to the 1851 Treaty to the Sioux tribes for their approval, he found them in a nasty mood and learned that the Miniconjou relatives of those killed in Fleming's raid had been in the camps circulating demands for vengeance.[21] The 1853 fight set the stage for a repeat performance the following year, one with far more tragic consequences.

———

In 1854 the Regular Army of the United States numbered 10,329 officers and men.[22] Of this number approximately seventy-five foot soldiers were stationed at Fort Laramie, hardly a force to strike fear into the hearts of thousands of mounted warriors. In fact, the force was so small as to be considered ludicrous. Thomas Fitzpatrick, a respected frontiersman as well as an influential Indian agent, observed: "So small is the forces usually at their disposal that they maintain their own position in the country more by the courtesy of the

Indians than from an ability to cope with the numbers that surround them. Instead of serving to intimidate the red man, they rather create a belief in the feebleness of the white man." He recommended that Fort Laramie have three hundred mounted troops for duty.[23] David D. Mitchell, the former Indian superintendent who had presided over the 1851 treaty, remarked that a company of infantry could be of no more use in protecting travelers or chastising Indians than "so many head of sheep."[24] Common sense aside, this little handful of frontier regulars had a duty to perform. The purpose of the Fort Laramie garrison was to guard the Oregon-California Trail and protect those who used it, albeit with a small group of infantrymen.

Beginning in the summer of 1854, troops had a new type of traveler for which to assure safe passage. The government had awarded a new transcontinental mail contract to William M. F. Magraw and John E. Reeside, and joined by the Hockaday brothers, the firm provided limited passenger service along with carrying the mail. By July, Magraw had opened six stations between the Big Blue River in Kansas and Fort Bridger, one of these located about a mile below Fort Laramie.[25] On July 24 the Sixth Military Department issued an order reminding officers commanding posts along the trail of their mission, and this was constantly on their minds during this season's emigration.[26]

Now in command of Fort Laramie was Lieutenant Fleming, who had been in charge since May 18, 1854, when Garnett left on recruiting duty and would conveniently miss the year's events. Fleming had entered West Point on July 1, 1848, and graduated twenty-nine in a class of forty-three. Attached as a brevet second lieutenant to the Sixth Infantry on July 1, 1852, until a regular assignment became available, he made second lieutenant on June 9, 1853.[27] His attack on the Miniconjou village six days later and its apparent success earned him a certain amount of respect from his peers, perhaps even a measure of authority on Indian matters.

Serving under Fleming was twenty-four-year-old Bvt. Second Lt. John Lawrence Grattan, a young man not yet permanently attached to a regiment and one whose ambition was obvious to all who knew him. Born in Vermont in 1830, Grattan was the son of a prominent New England businessman and political enthusiast. Of Irish heritage, the Grattans probably came to the United States by way of Canada in the early nineteenth century. John Grattan grew up in Lisbon, New Hampshire, situated near the Ammonoosuc River in the foothills of the White Mountains, where he attended public school. Peter, his father, ran a wheelwright shop and was a strong supporter of U.S. Representative

Harry Hibbard, also from Lisbon.[28] It was undoubtedly through the latter that young Grattan obtained an appointment to West Point. Robert E. Lee was the commander of the military academy when Grattan entered in 1848, and when he graduated in 1853, having been kept back for a year for having failed mathematics on his first try, he ranked thirty-six out of fifty-five. Two steps above him was Philip H. Sheridan, and above both and finishing seventh was John M. Schofield. Both of these classmates eventually rose to the rank of commanding general of the U.S. Army. First in the class was James B. McPherson, later a Civil War general and noted fatality at the Battle of Atlanta. Grattan's best standings were in French (17th) and his worst in infantry tactics (41st), both skills that soon figured dramatically and somewhat ironically in his short life. Residents of his hometown described the young lieutenant about this time as "fine looking" and noted for his honesty and intelligence.[29]

Lieutenant Grattan arrived at Fort Laramie on November 18, 1853, shortly before garrison strength was reduced to only one company. Grattan had with him at the fort all the books that he had studied while at West Point and a number of works of ancient and modern history. His other possessions included a fifty dollar gold watch, a military cloak, a pistol, a musket, and several horses.[30] Besides his intellectual growth, the young officer's social life took an interesting turn. He was temporarily engaged to marry Victoria Vaux, the oldest daughter of post chaplain William Vaux.[31] Reverend Vaux was born at Lewes in the county of Sussex, England, in 1807, immigrated to the United States, and entered the service on September 29, 1849; he had served as the chaplain at Fort Laramie since May 21, 1850.[32] Grattan exhibited an artistic side as well; he owned a half-interest in a melodeon, a small reed organ, while at Fort Laramie and probably played it when courting Victoria.[33] After the departure of Capt. William Scott Ketchum, Sixth Infantry, Grattan became the acting commissary of subsistence and the acting quartermaster, which gave him access to a ready supply of government liquor. Grattan drank to excess on occasion, and Reverend Vaux decided to break off the engagement to Victoria after seeing him drunk.[34]

Besides these facets of his character, Grattan also possessed some preconceived—and dangerous—notions about Indians. According to Post Surgeon Charles Page, he was very friendly with the Lakotas but always determined to punish promptly any transgression. He often expressed the opinion that "with thirty men, he could whip the combined force of all the Indians of the prairie." Page stated in a deposition after the August 1854 debacle that

Grattan "considered them arrant cowards, and thought the discharge of a piece of artillery would scare them into a precipitate flight." Having thus slandered Grattan as arrogant and rash to the point of stupidity, Page politely and rather pointlessly added that he was "a brave young man" who with age and experience would have eventually distinguished himself.[35] Vaux, on the other hand, was thoroughly disapproving of Grattan's conduct in retrospect, "Mr. Grattan, I know, had an unwarranted contempt of Indian character, which frequently manifested itself in my presence and at my quarters, and often, at the latter place, have I reproved him for acts which I conceived highly improper, such as thrusting his clenched fist in their faces, and threatening terrible things if ever duty or opportunity threw such chance in his way."[36]

Other interesting personalities served at the post. A fixture at the post was Leodegar Schnyder, the ordnance sergeant. Born in Sursee, Switzerland, on April 29, 1814, Schnyder's family had immigrated to Pittsburgh, Pennsylvania, from where he enlisted in 1837. After spending some time in Florida fighting the Seminole Indians as a member of the First U.S. Infantry, he had reenlisted in the Sixth Infantry in 1840, marched west with the unit in 1849 to garrison Fort Laramie, and received his appointment to ordnance sergeant on December 1, 1852. Ordnance sergeants were assigned to posts rather than units, and most spent their careers at just a few places, as would Schnyder.[37]

Another character was the post interpreter. Auguste Lucien had married Ena Tiglak, one of the Oglala women of the Laramie "Loafer" band, and had two daughters by her.[38] Born on May 4, 1814, he had worked for David Adams at Fort Platte in 1842 and Sir William Drummond Stewart, the English sportsman, as a hunter and guide in 1843.[39] Before being employed by the army he had been in partnership with Leon Pallardy, who had come from St. Charles to the Fort Laramie area in 1848.[40] On August 31, 1853, Lucien had been one of the witnesses to the signing by the Cheyenne and Arapaho leaders of the amended Treaty of 1851. Sometimes mistakenly referred to in the historical record as "Lucien Auguste," he was known to the Sioux as "Wayus" or "Yuse."[41] Both ordnance sergeant and post interpreter would play critical roles on August 18, 1854.

———

By necessity a warlike group, always needing horses and competing for buffalo, the Lakotas continued in their old ways. According to Vaux, a number of depredations had been committed after emigrant travel began in early

1854.[42] Conquering Bear told Fleming about depredations committed by the Miniconjou band at John Richard's Bridge, 130 miles above the fort, and that their hearts were bad toward the whites.[43] However, other groups seemed friendly, and on July 23, Indians around Fort Laramie arranged a dance for the Kinney party of overlanders. Elle Kinney Ware described the performance, evidencing an attraction often apparent in writings of young white women about Indian men:

"While at Fort Laramie an Indian-war dance was gotten up especially in honor of my father and his party. It was held out of doors of course and at night, still the Indians carried lighted torches, making it a scene much more spectacular. Mother and I looked from a short distance, seated in our carriage. The Indians, about twenty in number, danced as is their custom in a circle. They were naked except for the breechcloth, their supple bodies shone like polished bronze, their harsh voices chanted a weird war song, their grotesque motions as they leaped in the air were full of vigor and rhythm. Sometimes their wild song rose to a howl of lamentation for their dead, sometimes it changed to a monotonous drone, as by voice and gesture springing into the air, they expressed exultation over victories won, the dusky forms in the flickering torch light, uttering strange sounds and going through stranger motions, made a picture that was barbaric, repellent, yet fascinating."[44] Clearly, social interactions between Indian and whites on the overland trail could be eye-popping, yet peaceful.

In early August some Cheyennes killed two head of cattle from interpreter Lucien's herd and captured a number of horses grazing within two miles of the fort. A traders' posse chased them, and the Indians stopped and lined up for a fight. The traders demurred, and the Cheyennes continued on unmolested. Lieutenant Grattan ridiculed the traders for their actions, labeling them as cowards. Troops sent after the raiders were unable to catch them.[45]

A direct result of the growing troubles near Fort Laramie was the egress of many white residents of the area. On August 15, one hundred fifty miles south of Fort Laramie, traveler Paul Carrey met a group of men who had ranged around the post for years. They were leaving the country, they said, because "the Sioux were too bad; there was no longer any security among them for their stock or families; that since the day some Sioux had been killed by the troops, they were speaking of nothing else but revenge, and were determined to kill all the soldiers residing on their lands." Furthermore, "all this would end in war; that the trade would be ruined—so they preferred leaving the county."[46]

Adding to the unrest was the delay in the Indians receiving their promised annuities. By August the Sioux were encamped along the North Platte River several miles below Fort Laramie. They awaited the arrival of Maj. John W. Whitfield, Fitzpatrick's successor and their new Indian agent, to distribute the goods. Contracts had been let to Messrs. Baker and Street, and the firm had already delivered the foodstuffs, clothing, and other annuities, all stored in the American Fur Company trading post, called Gratiot's House after its previous manager.[47] John Baptiste Didier, chief clerk, looked after the store, aided by Charles Gereau, who would later become a government interpreter at Fort Laramie. The establishment stood about five miles east of Fort Laramie.

The huge village ran east from this point to the trading post of James Bordeaux, three miles distant. First were the Oglalas, comprising the biggest delegation. With them as guests were some Northern Cheyennes and white traders. Then came a small grouping of Miniconjous and next the Brulé camp, stretching almost two miles along and parallel to the river and standing between the emigrant road and the North Platte. The Brulés had arranged their tipis in a semicircle, its convexity toward the river. In the rear was a slight but abrupt depression in the ground, partially covered with bushes. The total numbered about six hundred lodges with perhaps as many as eighteen hundred men of fighting age and a few thousand dependents. Finding enough food to sustain such a large group was a difficult task. Fort Laramie area trader Seth Ward remembered that the big game had left the area, and the warriors could only shoot small game nearby, leaving the villagers generally hungry, disgruntled, and prone to excitement.[48]

The peak months for those traveling past Fort Laramie and nearby Indian villages were June and July, as those heading west had to start from Missouri jumping-off places in May in order to have good grass for their animals all the way to the Pacific Coast. Bringing up the rear of the 1854 migration were Mormon groups headed for Salt Lake City. The Mormon caravan that reached Fort Laramie on August 18 and figured into the Grattan story had disembarked from Missouri River boats at Westport Landing, then made its way due south four miles to their staging ground. On June 15 this group of 550 Latter-day Saints left Westport, Missouri, in sixty-nine wagons.[49]

This emigrant group was a participant in the Perpetual Emigrating Company, created on September 11, 1850, to assist the poor in relocating to the Great Basin. Persons receiving assistance from the fund were required to reimburse it by labor or other means. By 1854 groups of converts from

Denmark had arrived at the Missouri River camps and were waiting for transportation. An "outfit" serving ten emigrants consisted of one wagon, two yoke of oxen, two cows, a tent, and $250 to $500 worth of consumable goods. Because emigrants were held financially responsible for the resources assigned to them, the loss of any animals, equipment, or foodstuffs would likely elicit a "hard-nosed" response. When a lame cow belonging to the Hans Peter Olsen Company strayed into the Brulé village below Fort Laramie and was killed by High Forehead, one of a few Miniconjou Lakotas camped there, it prompted a complaint.[50]

The animal's owner reported the incident to Lieutenant Fleming, the Fort Laramie commander.[51] Fleming later stated that according to the cow's owner, the Indian rode up to the emigrant train passing along the road and "tried to kill" one of the party; failing in the attempt, he shot one of the cattle of the train.[52] A convalescing civilian, J. H. Reed, who had been at the post since July 10 and who was staying with Grattan, also reported this story. He stated that "an emigrant informed Mr. Fleming . . . that on the road below, an Indian had shot at him, and afterwards had killed a cow, or an ox, belonging to him." According to Reed, the story later derived from the Indians was that High Forehead had lost some relatives in the skirmish that took place in the summer of 1853 and told his companions, because his relatives were dead, he wanted to die also, but not until he had avenged himself upon the whites. The Indians reported that the Miniconjou man approached the cow's owner with three arrows in hand—one of which he shot at the emigrant but missed. High Forehead then said, "I have missed you; you are in the hands of God Almighty, but I will kill your cow," which he did.[53] Hearing about the incident, Conquering Bear went to Fort Laramie and reported the facts to Fleming, adding that the Indian should be punished. But since he, Conquering Bear, was a Brulé and not a Miniconjou, the soldiers ought to arrest the offender; he reassured Fleming that High Forehead would give himself up.[54]

Acting in accord with Article 4 of the 1851 treaty, which "required restitution or satisfaction of any wrongs committed . . . by any band or individual of their people on the people of the United States," Fleming ordered Grattan to gather a group of volunteers to go to the Indian village and secure High Forehead.[55] Soon assembled were Sgt. William P. Faver, Cpl. Charles McNulty, twenty-seven privates, and interpreter Auguste Lucien. Remembering Schnyder's experience, Grattan suggested that the ordnance sergeant accompany the force, but the veteran wisely declined; he later recalled that he had questioned the lieutenant's judgment and felt the detachment was headed for trouble. When the group departed, this left about ten enlisted men at the fort; thirty-two more had been detailed to guard the post herd and the government farm, the latter some twelve miles north.[56]

The twenty-nine men of Grattan's command were representative of the mixed heritage of those who served in the American army in the 1850s. Ten were Irish, six were Germans, and the rest came from France, Great Britain, and Poland. Most of the troops were in their mid-to-late twenties, mature men by nineteenth-century standards. Pvt. John McNulty, a former clerk from Liverpool, was the youngest at age nineteen, and Pvt. John Williams, a deserter who had just returned to duty, was the oldest at age thirty-six. Nearly half the enlisted men had been in the army more than three years. Only eight, privates Charles Burkle, James Fitzpatrick, David Hammill, Patrick Murley, Patrick O'Rourk, Adolphus Plumhoff, Edward Stevens, and John Sweetman, had served less than one year. Their previous occupations also reflected diversity, including clerk, druggist, farmer, laborer, and shoemaker. Pvt. Stokely Rushing had been a painter, and recent recruit Pvt. Charles Burkle a tailor. Few of these skills were applicable to military service, farming perhaps being the most transferable because it suggested a previous familiarity with livestock and firearms. Grattan's noncommissioned officers were competent and experienced. Sergeant Faver, a twenty-six-year-old, six-foot-tall farmer from Alabama, had made sergeant in three years. Corporal McNulty of Pennsylvania had a prior enlistment and listed his occupation as "soldier."[57]

Grattan was instructed to "go and receive the offender" and "in case of refusal to give him up after ascertaining the disposition of the Indians, to act upon his own discretion, and to be careful not to hazard an engagement without certainty of success." Fleming also told Grattan to inform the chief that the Indian would not be injured in any way and that he would be kept at the fort until "his father" (the agent) arrived.[58] Fleming, Grattan, and Lucien, the interpreter, talked about the journey to the Indian camp. According to Man Afraid of His Horses, the Oglala leader and friend of the whites who had joined the party, the interpreter said, "I am ready but must have something to drink before I die." The officers gave him a bottle, and he drank while his horse, borrowed from the post sutler, was being saddled for him.[59] Earlier Lucien had told his wife he was afraid she would be a widow before nightfall.[60] Grattan playfully prodded Lucien with his sword and told him to get moving. Filling out the group, although unofficially, was Obridge

Allen, an experienced emigrant guide who had arrived the day before. As the four men—Grattan, Lucien, Man Afraid, and Allen—rode away to the Sioux camp, those nearby heard Grattan proclaim in mock heroic voice that he would "conquer them or die."[61]

The little detachment left the post sometime between 2 and 3 P.M. on Saturday, August 19, with most of the infantry riding in a mule-drawn wagon. They took with them two twelve-pounder howitzers, one a mountain gun and the other a larger field piece.[62] Grattan carried two six-shot revolvers.[63] The infantrymen carried the standard weapon of the period, the .69 caliber U.S. Musket, Model 1842. The smoothbore, percussion musket had given good service during the Mexican War, the best and last of its line. However, it had a significant weakness: when fired, an undersized ball ricocheted along the barrel, resulting in an unpredictable trajectory and limiting the effectiveness of the arm to about 75 to 100 yards against individual targets and an efficient volley fire to about 200 yards.[64] A year later the new minié ball cartridge would replace round ball ammunition as the infantryman's standard issue to devastating effect at a place called Blue Water Creek.

Thus equipped and led by a man who needed to prove himself, the little column left Fort Laramie on its ride to destiny. Stopping at Gratiot's House to load weapons and make final preparations, the detachment continued on to the Indian village near Bordeaux's trading post and approached the tipi of High Forehead. With Lucien shouting imprecations, Conquering Bear proving unable to persuade High Forehead to surrender, and Grattan demanding the warrior's capitulation, the war of words ended in cannon shots, gunfire, and the loosing of arrows. The details of that final, fatal confrontation form the bulk of this book.

In the ensuing retaliatory fight led by Spotted Tail, a noted Brulé warrior, Grattan and his command perished immediately, except for one man. Red Cloud, another war leader, and his Oglalas who arrived on the scene as the conflict began, did nothing to save the soldiers, and some may have participated in the chase that ended in the deaths of the last few.[65] Grattan's body bristled with twenty-four arrows, one of which passed entirely through his head; he was later identified by his pocket watch.[66] Pursued and shot from his mount by a warrior named Blue Horse, Lucien was soon dispatched. Family lore has it that the interpreter and his horse were so full of arrows that, observed from a distance, they looked like a giant pincushion. Conquering Bear also received a mortal wound, apparently from the only soldier volley.[67]

After killing Grattan and his men, some Indians charged Bordeaux's house. Obridge Allen, who wisely witnessed the fight from the roof of Bordeaux's, entered at the same time as a warrior who shouted, "Let us wipe out the whites here," and seized trader Antoine Raynall (also appearing as Reynall or Reynald). Bordeaux's Indian relatives who were also inside replied that if the intent was to kill the whites, to begin with themselves. One of the friendly Indians tried to shoot the man who struggled with Raynall, but Bordeaux pushed the gun up, and the ball went into the ceiling. Then the trader threw the warrior out the door.[68] Little Thunder, a Brulé chief who had helped try to get High Forehead to surrender, soon showed up and reported that some of the warriors had stated that since they had killed all the soldiers at the camp, they now intended to kill all at the fort and burn it. Little Thunder then left the building to speak against the attack to his fellow Brulés.[69] Other Indians came to the establishment throughout the night, still at a fever pitch, and Bordeaux wisely gave them the goods they demanded.[70]

Meanwhile the village had started to pack up and move off, crossing to the left bank of the Platte. About midnight some villagers returned to the site of the old camp and shortly thereafter came to Bordeaux's place. Swift Bear, a Brulé chief also present at the clash, then came into the house with a severely wounded soldier, Pvt. John Cuddy. The former farmer from Tip- perary, Ireland, had escaped immediate slaughter by hiding in the brush. About twenty other Indians were present, some friendly and some not. Swift Bear told those around him, "If you kill this soldier, you kill me, for I shall die with him." Bordeaux told his Indian brother-in-law to take Cuddy to the road and start him off in the direction of the fort. The Indian took him about a mile and a half toward the garrison.[71]

The Indians struck camp at daybreak on August 20 and started their families toward Rawhide Creek, several miles north. On their way they destroyed the houses, farming implements, and equipment belonging to the government farm of Fort Laramie.[72] Fifteen minutes after the Indians left Bordeaux's trading post, Private Cuddy reappeared like Jacob Marley's ghost, and some individuals started him for the fort in a buggy, which broke down on the way. Allen finally took him on his horse the rest of the way.[73]

On this same day the Indians raided Gratiot's House to get their annuities, because they believed that their action against Grattan and his men would preclude them from getting any goods from the Indian agent. Also they had nothing to eat.[74] A spokesman for the party informed the employees that the warriors would take what goods they wanted and advised them all to keep away and give them no trouble. The employees carefully heeded the warning.

About two hundred horsemen returned on August 21. As they gathered before the store, Red Leaf, Conquering Bear's brother, and the Man Who Hates Women appealed to the assembled throng not to raid the stores, but to no avail. By the time Red Leaf finished speaking, a mob of people had pressed around him. The latch gave way, the door flew open, and the men rushed in. The goods rolled out—literally! Indians tied whole bolts of calico to horsetails and drove the horses until calico flew in the wind. Every type of good that moved in the Indian trade came flying out the door—boxes of crackers, bags of dried fruit, coils of rope, strings of beads, and scores of shawls. In their haste the party overlooked a box of flintlock guns and several casks of powder. Instead they found the clothing and took all the vests but left the pants and coats, having no immediate use for them. They also left all of the whisky, only because it was so well hidden. Up to now the presence of illicit alcohol in the house had been a secret withheld even from the employees, who now had good occasion to reward themselves. The Indians finally departed by 10 o'clock, and peace reigned.[75]

On the same day one mile west of Fort Laramie on the road to Salt Lake City, the mail station kept by the United States mail contractors came under attack. Destroyed were the station and its corral, and the raiders escaped with a herd of horses and mules.[76] Meanwhile other warriors raided the trading post of Ward and Guerrier at Sandy Point, nine miles west of Fort Laramie, taking goods with an estimated value of $10,000. The Indians killed clerk Eugene Montalow, one of the unsung casualties after the Grattan fight, and his colleagues took flight. This store, too, was plundered and the blacksmith shop burned. Montalow's body was found a few hundred yards from the store. Later the Miniconjou took the horses and mules.[77]

The Mormons in the Fort Laramie vicinity soon heard about the event, and emigrant John Johnson Davies described the scene: "The Danish Captain told our Captain to wait until his train came along and said that the Indians were on the war path. The trappers also were coming towards us, for dear life. We all crossed the river all right. We had a large camp. That night we thought we would have to fight, but the Indians had had their revenge. We camped together for a few nights then separated."[78]

News crisscrossed the region. James Bordeaux sent an express to Fleming early Sunday morning, about 1 A.M., informing him of the disaster, and the remaining men and women of the post took refuge in old Fort John, where they spent an understandably uneasy night.[79] Fleming assessed the damage and the dire situation. Gone were Bvt. Second Lt. John Grattan, Sgt. William P. Faver, Cpl. Charles McNulty, Musician Henry A. Krappe (also spelled Crabbe), Musician Henry E. Lewis, Pvt. Anthony Boyle, Pvt. Charles Burkle (also spelled Burke), Pvt. William Cameron, Pvt. Michael Collins, Pvt. John Courtenay (also spelled Courtney), Pvt. John Cuddy, Pvt. John Donahoe (also spelled Donohoe), Pvt. James Fitzpatrick, Pvt. John Flinn, Pvt. David Hammill, Pvt. John Mayer (also spelled Meyer), Pvt. John McNulty, Pvt. John Meldron, Pvt. Patrick Murley, Pvt. Walter Murray, Pvt. Patrick O'Rourk (also spelled O'Rourke), Pvt. Charles Platenius, Pvt. Adolphus Plumhoff, Pvt. Stokely H. Rushing, Pvt. Stanislaus Saniewski, Pvt. Thomas Smith, Pvt. Edward Stevens, Pvt. John Sweetman, Pvt. William Whitford, Pvt. John Williams, and post interpreter Auguste Lucien.[80] The total was thirty-one: one officer, two noncommissioned officers, twenty-seven privates, and one civilian interpreter. Whether Fleming tallied the Indian killed and wounded is not known.

The next day Fleming sent a report to his superiors that the Indians were menacing the fort, but all his men were on duty; he believed that he would be able to hold out.[81] According to Reverend Vaux, alarms for the safety of the fort and its remaining residents came frequently throughout the day and night. Fort inhabitants huddled together for mutual defense in the ruins of the old adobe walls, fortifying their position as well as they could. Because of the garrison being short-handed, even the chaplain had to stand guard.[82]

Vaux reported later that there were no more than fifty soldiers at the fort, a pitiful force. Fleming had sent couriers to two camps—one to the government farm and the other where the beef herd grazed—with instructions for the men to return immediately to the post. Another messenger went east to Fort Kearny on the Platte River to notify authorities of the fight and to acquaint Washington with the details. On August 22, a traveler passing Fort Laramie noted, "The soldiers were fortifying the fort and Lieut. Fleming was satisfied that he could withstand any attack the Indians might make."[83] A trader also wrote to a Missouri newspaper, "The old American Fur Company Fort is fixed up for the last resort." The writer added, "A small block house is being erected, which held by ten men will add greatly to the strength of the post and protect the frame building from being fired."[84] While the men worked, one of their own, Private Cuddy, died of his wounds. Because of his delirious condition since his arrival to the relative safety of the post, he had been unable to tell his "sole survivor" story.[85]

At Fleming's request Bordeaux and Allen went to the battle site. They found the large howitzer on the ground where it had been dismounted. Grattan and two men lay near the large gun, and the rest of the men were scattered along the road for a mile or more, all dead, mostly killed by arrows and their bodies mutilated.[86] Bordeaux saw to the interment of the little detachment, although the burial was hasty. The Mormon emigrant Robert Campbell reported that on September 14, 1854, he had visited the common grave "and some of the men's heads are not even covered."[87] A pile of stone about two feet high covered the grave, which protected it somewhat from scavengers and served as a rough marker for the dead.[88] Much later Sergeant Schnyder led a detachment that transported Grattan's remains to Fort Leavenworth, Kansas Territory, and their unintended final resting place since the Grattan family made no arrangements to return the remains to New Hampshire.[89] Conquering Bear, whose loss to his people far outweighed that of the upstart lieutenant to his, died on the way to a healing spring at the head of Deer Creek in present northwestern Nebraska. His stricken followers raised his scaffold on the bluffs overlooking the Niobrara River.[90]

Parties of Sioux continued to raid in the area for more than a week. Something apparently happened on August 28 near Fort Laramie that was not fully reported by either military or civilian witnesses. In fact, the incident and its consequences seem to have been repressed. For many years rumors circulated that Schnyder had taken charge of the fort due to the incapacity of Lieutenant Fleming. Some even suggested that the officer was too inebriated to serve, others that the lieutenant had wanted to surrender the post.[91] A hint of something amiss at Fort Laramie, although neither credited to drunkenness or cowardice, exists as a short reference in Fleming's personnel file; the officer had received a wound on August 28, 1854.[92] The event may be a reference to an occasion when approximately two hundred Cheyennes rode into the post at about 10 o'clock at night and fired three shots. Did one strike the commander?[93]

Whatever the reason, the aura of invincibility created by Fort Laramie's young, upstart officers had disappeared in the roar of two cannons. As Lewis Bissell Dougherty, the post sutler, prophetically put it, "All feeling of security is now destroyed, nor will it be restored until the Indians get a good drubbing from the Government."[94] As a first step in recovery and given the great distances involved, Fort Laramie became a two-company post, with companies B and D of the Sixth U.S. Infantry, 111 men, arriving relatively soon on November 12. William Hoffman, major and commander of the Fort Laramie relief column, would figure significantly as an astute student and vocal critic of the actions of Lieutenant Grattan.

Following the Grattan Fight, the Brulés continued to raid along the Oregon Trail. One party in particular consisted of fifteen warriors and was led by Red Leaf, Conquering Bear's brother. Included in the group were Red Leaf's two brothers, his half-brother Long Chin, and Spotted Tail, his cousin, all bent on revenge. On November 13 near Horse Creek, twenty-two miles east of Fort Laramie, the war party attacked the eastbound U.S. mail wagon traveling from Salt Lake City. The warriors killed three men, including the conductor, Jamison, and wounding a passenger, Charles A. Kinkead. The raiders took more than $10,000 in gold coin from the latter and destroyed the mail.[95]

On December 7 the Brulé leaders attempted to arrange peace talks with Fort Laramie's commander and wrote a letter to him from Bordeaux's place, with Seth Ward acting as stenographer. Hoffman declined to see them. The letter included the following plea: "We concluded if you would allow us to come up and see you, we feel that you will do us justice, and we could then explain to you our feelings. If at any time you may conclude to see us, we will willingly come in as we are willing to throw ourselves on the mercy of our great Father."[96]

Raiding continued in 1855. In February Sioux drove off sixty-five head of horses and mules from the Ward and Guerrier trading post. Thomas S. Williams reported that a large war party also stole stock from his group near Devil's Gate, as well as all the animals belonging to the mail company and two other road ranchmen at the same point. Miniconjou raiders subsequently ran off four army mules just west of Fort Laramie early in May. Then in June at Deer Creek Crossing, Sioux warriors killed Robert Gibson, leader of a wagon train from Missouri, as he was shaking hands with them. The same party attacked another group of emigrants at about the same place a few days later, lancing a man and a woman and running off some stock.[97]

Before many of these depredations occurred, though, Secretary of War Jefferson Davis had decided to avenge Grattan's death, and in October 1854 he and General of the Army Winfield Scott made plans to retaliate.[98] Thus, the Grattan fight resulted in the first punitive military campaign in the West.

Chosen to head the expedition was Col. William Selby Harney. Known in his youth as the fastest footracer in the army and subsequently as one of its most relentless pursuers, Harney exacted revenge on September 3, 1855, when he caught Little Thunder's band of Brulés in camp on Blue Water Creek near Ash Hollow, Nebraska Territory. His six hundred troops killed eighty-six and took seventy as prisoners. Harney let it be known that there would be no peace until those who had killed the mail party near Horse Creek were in custody. On October 18, 1855, Spotted Tail and others from the war party surrendered at Fort Laramie to prevent further bloodshed. Expecting to be executed, the captives were surprised to learn that they would be sent east. They were incarcerated at Fort Leavenworth but received their freedom from President Franklin Pierce in early 1856.[99] Spotted Tail's reputation among his peers elevated to a heroic level because of his self-sacrifice for the good of his people. He did not witness, therefore, the March 1856 council convened by Colonel Harney at Fort Pierre on the Missouri River, where the army commander dictated terms to the Lakota nation, and the First Sioux War, one that began near Fort Laramie because of a cow, came to an end.

Notes

1. John D. Unruh Jr., *The Plains Across: The Overland Emigrants and the Trans-Mississippi West, 1840–60* (Urbana: University of Illinois Press, 1979), 120, 122; Merrill J. Mattes, *Platte River Road Narratives: A Descriptive Bibliography of Travel over the Great Central Overland Route to Oregon, California, Utah, Colorado, Montana, and Other Western States and Territories, 1812–1866* (Urbana: University of Illinois Press, 1988), 2; J. T. Dorris, "Federal Aid to Oregon Trail Prior to 1850," *Oregon Historical Quarterly* 30 (Dec. 1929): 322–24; Edward H. Hale, *Kansas and Nebraska: The History, Geographical and Physical Characteristics, and Political Position of Those Territories* (Boston: Phillips, Samson, 1854), 77.

2. Three histories of Fort Laramie are pertinent to this study: LeRoy R. Hafen and Francis Marion Young, *Fort Laramie and the Pageant of the West, 1834–1890* (Glendale, Calif.: Arthur H. Clark, 1938); Remi Nadeau, *Fort Laramie and the Sioux Indians* (Englewood Cliffs, N.J.: Prentice-Hall, 1967); and Douglas C. McChristian, *Fort Laramie: Military Bastion of the High Plains, 1849–1890* (Norman, Okla.: Arthur H. Clark, 2008).

3. First Lt. Daniel P. Woodbury of the Corps of Topographical Engineers measured Fort John after its acquisition: 157 feet on an east-west axis and 111 feet wide, with blockhouses on the northeast and southwest corners, and about 15 feet high. Gordon S. Chappell, "The Fortifications of Old Fort Laramie," *Annals of Wyoming* 34 (Oct. 1962): 148, 152.

4. *Annual Report of the Commissioner of Indian Affairs, Transmitted with the Message of the President at the Opening of the Second Session of the Thirty-Third Congress, 1854* (Washington, D.C.: A. O. P. Nicholson, 1855), 95.

5. Charles J. Kappler, ed., *Indian Affairs: Laws and Treaties*, vol. 2 (Washington, D.C.: Government Printing Office, 1904), 594–96; Nadeau, *Fort Laramie and the Sioux Indians*, 78–86.

6. Harry H. Anderson, "The Controversial Sioux Amendment to the Fort Laramie Treaty of 1851," *Nebraska History* 37 (Sept. 1956): 202.

7. Kingsley M. Bray, "Teton Sioux Population History, 1655–1881," *Nebraska History* 75 (Summer 1994): 172, 174; Kingsley M. Bray, "The Oglala Lakota and the Establishment of Fort Laramie," *Museum of the Fur Trade Quarterly* 36 (Winter 2000): 11–15; Raymond J. DeMallie, "Teton," in *Handbook of North American Indians*, vol. 13, *Plains* (Washington, D.C.: Smithsonian Institution, 2001), 794.

8. Luther Bradley, Notebook, citing William Hoffman, pp. 110–11, Luther P. Bradley Papers, U.S. Army Military History Institute, Carlisle, Pa.

9. Harry H. Anderson, "Fur Traders as Fathers: The Origins of the Mixed-Blooded Community Among the Rosebud Sioux," *South Dakota History* 3 (Summer 1973): 241–44; George E. Hyde, *Red Cloud's Folk: A History of the Oglala Sioux Indians* (Norman: University of Oklahoma Press, 1957), 3, 14, 31, 55; George Colhoff winter count, Elmo Scott Watson Papers, Newberry Library, Chicago; Louis L. Simonin, *The Rocky Mountain West in 1867*, translated and annotated by Wilson O. Clough (Lincoln: University of Nebraska Press, 1966), 135.

10. Sylvia Van Kirk, *Many Tender Ties: Women in Fur-Trade Society, 1670–1870* (Norman: University of Oklahoma Press, 1980), 9.

11. Clark Wissler, "The Enigma of the Squaw-Man," *Natural History* 41 (Mar. 1938): 186.

12. For biographies of James Bordeaux see John D. McDermott, "James Bordeaux," in *The Mountain Men and the Fur Trade of the Far West*, vol. 5, edited by LeRoy R. Hafen and Ann W. Hafen (Glendale, Calif.: Arthur H. Clark, 1968), 65–80; Charles E. Hanson Jr., "James Bordeaux," *Museum of the Fur Trade Quarterly* 2 (Spring 1966): 2–12; and Charles E. Hanson Jr., "James Bordeaux—Chapter Two," *Museum of the Fur Trade Quarterly* 27 (Winter 1991): 2–7. For more on the Swift Bear family, see Josephine Waggoner, *Witness: A Hunkpapa Historian's Strong-Heart Song of the Lakotas* (Lincoln: University of Nebraska Press, 2013), 468–70, 694.

13. Richard B. Garnett was born on the "Rose Hill" estate in Essex County, Virginia, on November 21, 1817. He had some experience with Indian peoples, fighting the Seminoles in the Florida War of 1841–42 and spending time on the frontier at Fort Towson, Indian Territory, and Fort Smith, Arkansas. George W. Cullum, *Biographical Register of the Officers and Graduates of the U.S. Military Academy at West Point, N.Y.*, vol. 2 (New York: D. Van Nostrand, 1868), 25; Valentine T. McGillycuddy, statement, September 13, 1922, William Garnett File, HRG7A D26,

Records of the U.S. House of Representatives, Record Group (hereafter RG) 233, National Archives and Records Administration (hereafter NARA), Washington, D.C.

14. At the time Garnett arrived at Fort Laramie, he apparently had a wife and child in Virginia. During the early years of the occupation of the post, the mention of cohabitation of Fort Laramie soldiers with Lakota women is frequent. It seems to have reached its peak in the 1860s when volunteer troops garrisoned the fort. Eddie Herman, "Couple Credited With Heroism Lie Buried in Unmarked Graves," *Rapid City Journal* (S.Dak.), Nov. 26, 1950; John C. Burns, "Dick Garnett's Boy," in *Looking Back: Footnotes from an Old Fort*, Jan. 3, 1986, item FLNHS C12–184, Fort Laramie Collections, Fort Laramie National Historic Site; John Bratt, *Trails of Yesterday* (Lincoln: University Publishing, 1921), 106–21. Over the decades the historians, librarians, and other National Park Service personnel affiliated with or stationed at Fort Laramie have compiled a vast number of primary and secondary source materials on its history, including letters sent and received, orders, post returns, and more. Drawn largely from the military and Indian records of the National Archives, preserved in the fort's library, and available to the public for research, these materials are hereafter cited collectively as "Fort Laramie Collections."

15. Second Lt. Hugh B. Fleming, Fort Laramie, Nov. 19, 1854, to Maj. William Hoffman, Letters Sent, Fort Laramie, Fort Laramie Collections, reprinted in "Letter from the Secretary of War, Transmitting Information Relating to an Engagement between the United States Troops and the Sioux Indians near Fort Laramie," in *House of Representatives Reports*, No. 63, 33rd U.S. Congress, 2nd session, 1854–55, Serial 788 (hereafter *House of Representatives Reports*, No. 63); also in "Report of the Secretary of War, in Compliance with a Resolution of the Senate of the 1st Instant, Calling for Copies of the Correspondence Respecting the Massacre of Lieutenant Grattan and His Command by Indians," in *Senate Executive Documents*, No. 91, 34th U.S. Congress, 1st session, 1855–56, Serial 823 (hereafter *Senate Executive Documents*, No. 91).

16. Order No. 32, headquarters, Fort Laramie, Jan. 13, 1851, Orders, Fort Laramie Collections; "Indians at Fort Laramie," *Missouri Republican* (St. Louis), Nov. 8, 1851.

17. First Lt. Richard B. Garnett, Fort Laramie, July 24, 1853, to Col. Samuel Cooper, Fort Laramie Collections.

18. Articles of Agreement between Enoch W. Raymond and Company and First Lt. R. B. Garnett, May 9, 1854, Letters Received, Fort Laramie Collections.

19. Correspondent of the *Republican*, Fort Laramie, June 28, 1853, "Trouble with the Sioux Indians," *St. Joseph Gazette* (Mo.), Aug. 3, 1853; "Diary Kept by Mrs. Maria H. (Parsons) Belshaw, 1853," Paul and Helen Henderson Collection, Box 4, American Heritage Center, University of Wyoming, Laramie; Basil Nelson Longsworth, "The Diary of Basil N. Longsworth, Oregon Pioneer," typescript, Division of Women's

Professional Projects, Works Progress Administration, Portland, 1938; copy in John D. McDermott Collection, Rapid City, S.Dak.; Big Partisan, statement, Dec. 7, 1854, and Man Afraid of His Horses, statement, Feb. 13, 1855, Letters Received, Department of the West, Records of the U.S. Army Continental Commands, RG 393, NARA; R. Eli Paul, *Blue Water Creek and the First Sioux War, 1854–1856* (Norman: University of Oklahoma Press, 2004), 15–17.

20. Fleming to Garnett, June 16, 1853, Letters Received, Fort Laramie Collections.
21. McChristian, *Fort Laramie*, 66–68; Anderson, "Controversial Sioux Amendment," 217.
22. *Official Army Register for 1854* (Washington, D.C.: Adjutant General's Office, Jan. 1, 1854), 31.
23. Nadeau, *Fort Laramie and the Sioux Indians*, 90.
24. Albert Watkins, ed., "Notes of the Early History of the Nebraska Country," in *Publications of the Nebraska State Historical Society*, vol. 20 (Lincoln: Nebraska State Historical Society, 1922), 260–61.
25. John S. Gray, "The Salt Lake Hockaday Mail, Part 1," *Annals of Wyoming* 56 (Fall 1984): 12. See also William P. MacKinnon, "The Buchanan Spoils System and the Utah Expedition: Careers of W. M. F. Magraw and John M. Hockaday," *Utah Historical Quarterly* 31 (Spring 1963): 127–50.
26. Order No. 19, July 24, 1854, Sixth Military Department, Fort Laramie Collections.
27. Francis B. Heitman, *Historical Register and Dictionary of the United States Army*, vol. 1 (Washington, D.C.: Government Printing Office, 1903), 424.
28. Mary R. Cummings, "School History," *Littleton Courier* (N.H.), June 21, 1901; A. A. Woolson, *Reminiscences of Lisbon, N.H.* (Littleton, N.H.: Courier Printing, 1912), 7.
29. Cullum, *Biographical Register* 2:358; *Official Army Register for 1853* (Washington, D.C.: Adjutant General's Office, Jan. 1, 1853), 7–8; Post Returns, November 1853, Fort Laramie Collections; W. W. Morrison, "Grattan Massacre," *Annals of Wyoming* 27 (Oct. 1955): 174.
30. Peter Grattan, Lisbon, N.H., to Harry Hibbard, Dec. 9, 1854, Letters Received, Office of the Adjutant General, Main Series, 1822–1860, Records of the Office of the Adjutant General, RG 94, Microfilm Publication No. 567, roll 498, entries G342-H338, NARA.
31. Mrs. H. B. (Vaux) Peyton, Seabright Station, Santa Cruz, Cal., to Grace Raymond Hebard, Laramie, Wyo., item B-V469-w, Grace Raymond Hebard Papers, American Heritage Center. There is a reference to a "Miss Allen," a Grattan "fiancee" in W. W. Morrison, "Grattan Massacre," *Annals of Wyoming* 42 (Apr. 1970): 86. This is probably a misunderstood reference to "Alpha," a name Vaux often called his daughter Victoria, she being the firstborn. His second daughter he called "Omega." When an officer asked him how he knew she would be the last child, he replied that "should Providence rule otherwise, he would commence on the diphthongs." Owen Wister's diary, Frontier Notes, May–Aug. 1894, Owen Wister Collection, American Heritage Center.

32. Post Returns, May 1850, Fort Laramie Collections; Peyton to Hebard, Grace Raymond Hebard Papers. After his death Vaux's body was preserved in the Santa Cruz Episcopal Church, where it remains today. "Intelligence," in *The Spirit of Missions*, vol. 8 (New York: Board of Missions of the Protestant Episcopal Church, 1843), 141; "Chaplain Vaux," *Wyoming Churchman* (n.d.): 20–21, Fort Laramie Collections.

33. Grattan to Hibbard, Dec. 9, 1854, Letters Received, Office of the Adjutant General.

34. Rev. Sidney Hoadley, interview by John D. McDermott, Wheatland, Wyo., July 1992, McDermott Collection. A Fort Laramie correspondent—with no irony—described Grattan and Fleming as "gentlemen in their deportment. . . . They know how to appreciate a stranger's wants and show a ready disposition to supply them. They are both young, but many an older officer would do well to imitate them in their intercourse with strangers and the discharge of their duties in a military capacity." Letter from "Stella" to "Ebony," Fort Laramie, Aug. 10, 1854, in *St. Joseph Gazette*, Sept. 6, 1854.

35. Assistant Surgeon Charles Page to William Hoffman, May 28, 1855, in *Senate Executive Documents*, No. 91.

36. Vaux to Hoffman, Oct. 4, 1855, in *Senate Executive Documents*, No. 91.

37. John D. McDermott, "Fort Laramie's Silent Soldier, Leodegar Schnyder," *Annals of Wyoming* 36 (Apr. 1964): 5–8. For the date of Schnyder's appointment to ordnance sergeant, see Fort Laramie Collections.

38. Emily H. Lewis, "Shadow of the Brave," *True West* 10 (Sept. 1962): 28–29, 55–57, in item RGD949, S1.543, Clifford Family, Paul D. Riley Collection, Nebraska State Historical Society (hereafter NSHS); George E. Hyde, *Spotted Tail's Folk: A History of the Brulé Sioux* (Norman: University of Oklahoma Press, 1961), 50n9.

39. Dan L. Thrapp, "Auguste Lucier [sic]," in *Encyclopedia of Frontier Biography*, vol. 2 (Glendale, Calif.: Arthur H. Clark, 1988), 883–84; Charles E. Hanson Jr., and Veronica Sue Walters, "The Early Fur Trade in Northwestern Nebraska," *Nebraska History* 57 (Fall 1976): 303.

40. Nicholas Janis, statement in the claim of Leon F. Pallardy, Oct. 13, 1892, Indian depredation claims, no. 8266, Records of the United States Court of Claims, RG 123, NARA. Indian depredation claims and their testimony continued for decades after the massacre, and the eyewitness accounts found therein will be fully discussed in the next volume of Grattan-related accounts.

41. The present usage is prompted by the fact that the name appears as Auguste Lucien in James Bordeaux's correspondence (Bordeaux and Lucien both came from St. Charles, Missouri); in the amended 1851 Fort Laramie Treaty document signed by Cheyenne and Arapaho leaders on August 31, 1853; and in the official report of the men killed in the Grattan Fight. Also, Lucien's mixed-blood granddaughter in an interview gave the last name as "Lucia," which is a fairly close English equivalent for the French pronunciation. See Kappler, *Indian Affairs* 4:1080; "Indian Battle," *New York Times*, Oct. 23, 1854; Lewis, "Shadow of the Brave," 28; Capt. Ed. Johnson, Fort Laramie, Oct. 10, 1855, to Hoffman, in

Senate Executive Documents, No. 91, S.823: 23; Lloyd E. McCann, "The Grattan Massacre," *Nebraska History* 37 (Mar. 1956): 11n.

42. William Vaux, "Report from Fort Laramie, Oct. 1, 1854," in *The Spirit of Missions*, vol. 20 (New York: Board of Missions of the Protestant Episcopal Church, 1855), 40.

43. Fleming to Hoffman, Nov. 19, 1854, in *House of Representative Reports*, No. 63, and in *Senate Executive Documents*, No. 91.

44. "Crossing the Plains in 1854 as Told by Elle Kinney Ware," typescript, Hall-Kinney Family Collection, microfilm roll MS618:51, NSHS.

45. Fleming to Col. Lorenzo Thomas, Aug. 20, 1854, in *House of Representatives Reports*, No. 63; Page to Hoffman, May 28, 1855, in *Senate Executive Documents*, No. 91; Johnson to Hoffman, Oct. 10, 1855, in *Senate Executive Documents*, No. 91; Nadeau, *Fort Laramie and the Sioux Indians*, 90; George Bird Grinnell, *The Fighting Cheyennes* (Norman: University of Oklahoma Press, 1956), 106.

46. Paul Carrey, extract from his journal, Oct. 2, 1854, in *House of Representatives Reports*, No. 63.

47. John B. Didier, deposition, Aug. 3, 1855, Chouteau Miscellany, Pierre Chouteau Collection, Missouri History Museum, St. Louis, Mo.; copy in Fort Laramie Collections.

48. Capt. Oscar F. Winship to Capt. Frank N. Page, Sept. 1, 1854, Letters Sent, Fort Laramie Collections, also found in *House of Representatives Reports*, No. 63; Nadeau, *Fort Laramie and the Sioux Indians*, 91; McCann, "Grattan Massacre," 5. Seth Ward's story was told by John Hunton in the *Goshen County News and Fort Laramie Scout* (Torrington, Wyo.), Apr. 4, 1928.

49. Lulla Hansen Peterson, "The Life of Johanna Marie (Domgaard) Hansen," 2013 digitization of 1938 typescript, FamilySearch, https://familysearch.org/photos/stories/3754570; B. H. Roberts, *A Comprehensive History of the Church of Jesus Christ of Latter-day Saints*, vol. 4 (Salt Lake City: Deseret News Press, 1930), 51.

50. Peterson, "Life"; James Bordeaux, "Sarpy's Point, Nebr.," Aug. 21, 1854, in *New York Daily Tribune*, Sept. 8, 1854, also in Watkins, "History of the Nebraska Country," 259–60; James Bordeaux per Sam Smith to John Wilkins Whitfield, Fort Laramie, Aug. 31, 1854, Letters Received, Upper Platte Agency, Records of the Bureau of Indian Affairs, RG 75, NARA (hereafter cited as LR, Upper Platte Agency, RG 75, NARA); Roberts, *Comprehensive History*, 4:5. Some accounts referred to the animal specifically as an ox, and not all agreed as to its disposition. For example, American Horse, an Oglala leader who was fourteen years old at the time, said it was an ox with sore feet, too old to be good to eat, so they took only the intestines. American Horse, interview by A. E. Sheldon, July 30, 1903, Addison E. Sheldon Collection, NSHS.

51. *New York Daily Tribune*, Sept. 8, 1854; Bordeaux to Whitfield, Aug. 31, 1854, LR, Upper Platte Agency, RG 75, NARA.

52. Fleming to Winship, Aug. 30, 1854, in *House of Representatives Reports*, No. 63.

53. J. H. Reed, statement, Nov. 19, 1854, in *House of Representatives Reports*, No. 63, and in *Senate Executive Documents*, No. 91.

54. Carrey, journal, Oct. 2, 1854, in *House of Representatives Reports*, No. 63; Reed, statement, Nov. 19, 1854, ibid.

55. Page to Hoffman, May 28, 1855, in *Senate Executive Documents*, No. 91; Fleming to Thomas, August 20, 1854, in *House of Representatives Reports*, No. 63.

56. Johnson to Hoffman, Oct. 10, 1855, in *Senate Executive Documents*, No. 91; McChristian, *Fort Laramie*, 63; Nadeau, *Fort Laramie and the Sioux Indians*, 92.

57. Regimental Returns of the Regular Army, Sixth U.S. Infantry, 1849–1854, Microfilm Publication No. 665, roll 67, NARA; Paul N. Beck, *The First Sioux War: The Grattan Fight and Blue Water Creek, 1854–1856* (Lanham, Md.: University Press of America, 2004), 44; John D. McDermott, *A Guide to the Indian Wars of the West* (Lincoln: University of Nebraska Press, 1998), 26.

58. Fleming to Hoffman, Nov. 19, 1854, in *House of Representative Reports*, No. 63, and in *Senate Executive Documents*, No. 91.

59. Man Afraid of His Horses, statement, Feb. 13, 1855, Letters Received, Records of the Department of the West, RG 393, NARA.

60. Julia Clifford to Lulu Brown, Feb. 16, 1926, in Bayard H. Paine, *Pioneers, Indians and Buffaloes* (Curtis, Neb.: Curtis Enterprise, 1935), 36–37, 75–76.

61. Johnson to Hoffman, Oct. 10, 1855, in *Senate Executive Documents*, No. 91; McCann, "Grattan Massacre," 11n21.

62. Lewis B. Dougherty, "The Massacre at Fort Laramie," *Liberty Weekly Tribune* (Mo.), Oct. 6, 1854; Obridge Allen, statement, late August 1854, in *House of Representatives Reports*, No. 63; "Indian Battle," *New York Times*, Oct. 23, 1854.

63. James Bordeaux, statement, Nov. 19, 1854, in *House of Representatives Reports*, No. 63, and in *Senate Executive Documents*, No. 91.

64. The musket had a percussion lock instead of a flintlock ignition system, a .69 caliber barrel, 42 inches in length (57 and 3/4 inches overall), and fired a .64 spherical lead projectile that weighed about 390 grains. With a standard charge of 110 grains of powder, it had a velocity of 1,500 feet per second. The powder and ball came in a paper cartridge, with the percussion caps supplied separately. Robert A. Murray, "Military Firearms at Fort Laramie, 1849–1890," typescript, Apr. 1977, Fort Laramie Collections; Louis A. Garavaglia and Charles G. Worman, *Firearms of the American West, 1803–1865* (Albuquerque: University of New Mexico Press, 1984), 110–13.

65. Red Cloud, interview by Eli S. Ricker, November 24, 1906, in *Voices of the American West*, vol. 1, *The Indian Interviews of Eli S. Ricker, 1903–1919*, ed. Richard E. Jensen (Lincoln: University of Nebraska Press, 2005), 346; R. Eli Paul, *Autobiography of Red Cloud: War Leader of the Oglalas* (Helena: Montana Historical Society Press, 1997), 4; McCann, "Grattan Massacre," 17n30.

66. *New York Daily Tribune*, Sept. 8, 1854; William Kenceleur, "Horrible Outrage: Twenty Soldiers Murdered by the Sioux Indians," *Fremont County Journal* (Sidney, Iowa), Sept. 16, 1854; "Rocky Bear's Story," *Sheridan Enterprise* (Wyo.), Oct. 1, 1907.

67. Edgar Fire Thunder, interview by Merrill Mattes, Oct. 20, 1942, Fort Laramie Collections; Lewis, "Shadow of the Brave," 28–29, 55–57; Allen, statement, in *House of Representatives Reports*, No. 63; *New York Times*, Oct. 23, 1854.

68. Allen, statement, in *House of Representatives Reports*, No. 63.

69. Bordeaux, statement, ibid.

70. Allen, statement, ibid.; *Liberty Weekly Tribune* (Mo.), Oct. 6, 1854.

71. Allen, statement, in *House of Representatives Reports*, No. 63; W. H. Powell, "Fort Laramie's Early History," in *Collections of the Wyoming Historical Society*, vol. 1 (Cheyenne: Wyoming Historical Society, 1897), 178.

72. Allen, statement, in *House of Representatives Reports*, No. 63; Winship to Page, Sept. 1, 1854, ibid.; Nadeau, *Fort Laramie and the Sioux Indians*, 91.

73. Allen, statement, in *House of Representatives Reports*, No. 63; *New York Times*, Oct. 23, 1854.

74. Edward Claudey, John Savard, J. B. Didier, and Joseph Turgeon, statement, Fort Laramie, September 1, 1854, LR, Upper Platte Agency, RG 75, NARA; John Baptiste Didier, statement, August 5, 1855, ibid.

75. Didier, statement, ibid.; Francis (Frank) Salway, interview by Addison E. Sheldon, July 31, 1903, Sheldon Collection, NSHS; Frank Salaway [Salway], interview by Eli S. Ricker, Nov. 3, 1906, in Jensen, *Indian Interviews* 1:332–37; *Liberty Weekly Tribune* (Mo.), Oct. 6, 1854.

76. Jesse A. Jones, Samuel Rider, and N. A. Mitchell, affidavit, Nov. 1, 1854, LR, Upper Platte Agency, RG 75, NARA.

77. John Soissons, Oct. 23, 1889, Seth Ward, Nov. 28, 1885, and Dec. 5, 1889, and George T. Tackett, Nov. 29, 1889, statements in claim of Ward and Guerrier, Indian depredation claims, no. 712, RG 123, NARA.

78. John Johnson Davies, "Historical Sketch of My Life," *Utah Historical Quarterly* 9 (July–Oct. 1941): 161–62. See also a similar account by S. R. Parkinson in Lydia D. Alder, "The Massacre at Fort Laramie," *Improvement Era* 12 (June 1909): 636–38.

79. Bordeaux, statement, in *House of Representatives Reports*, No. 63.

80. Second Lt. Hugh B. Fleming, Sixth Infantry, commanding Fort Laramie, Oregon Route, to Col. Samuel Cooper, adjutant general, Washington, D.C., Sept. 14, 1854, McDermott Collection; *New York Times*, Oct. 23, 1854; Paul Henderson, "Nearly 100 Years Have Passed Since Massacre West of Lingle," *Guide-Review* (Lingle, Wyo.), Mar. 1, 1951.

81. Fleming to Thomas, Aug. 20, 1854, in *House of Representatives Reports*, No. 63.

82. Vaux, "Report from Fort Laramie, Oct. 1, 1854," 41; Peyton to Hebard, Grace Raymond Hebard Papers.

83. Mr. McConnell, "Late from the Plains," *Omaha Arrow* (Neb. Terr.), Oct. 13, 1854.

84. *Liberty Weekly Tribune* (Mo.), Oct. 6, 1854.

85. Col. William P. Carlin, "Before the War," *National Tribune* (Washington, D.C.), Jan. 22, 1885. Some reported much later that Cuddy could not tell his story because he had been shot through the mouth by an arrow. Another account

described him simply as "speechless." *Goshen County News and Fort Laramie Scout*, Apr. 4, 1928; John Taylor to Brigham Young, "On the Platte 75 Miles to Fort Kearny," Oct. 6, 1854, Brigham Young Office Files, 1832–1878, reel 56, box 43, fd. 2, Church History Library, Church of Jesus Christ of Latter-day Saints, Salt Lake City.

86. Fleming to Bordeaux, Aug. 20, 1854, in *Missouri Republican*, Sept. 13, 1854; Allen, statement, in *House of Representatives Reports*, No. 63; *New York Times*, Oct. 23, 1854; Vaux, "Report from Fort Laramie, Oct. 1, 1854," 40.

87. Thomas Sutherland, "Robert Campbell Company Report, 1854 August 22," Robert L. Campbell Company, Mormon Pioneer Overland Travel, 1847–1868 (database), Church of Jesus Christ of Latter-day Saints, Salt Lake City. https://history.lds.org/overlandtravel/sources/4931/. Harvey Jones, a merchant who passed by on his return to the states, described the killing field "as looking . . . like a butcher's yard." "Arrival of a 'Prairie Merchant,'" *St. Joseph Cycle* (Mo.), Sept. 29, 1854, reprinted in *Missouri Republican*, Oct. 4, 1854.

88. Government contractors removed the remains of the enlisted men in 1891 and reinterred them at Fort McPherson National Cemetery in Maxwell, Nebraska, where they reside today. Maj. Daniel Robinson, "Reminiscences of Fort Laramie," typescript, Fort Laramie Collections; *Goshen County News and Fort Laramie Scout*, Apr. 4, 1928; Eugene F. Ware, *Indian War of 1864*, introduction to the Bison Book edition by John D. McDermott (Lincoln: University of Nebraska Press, 1994), 218–19; *Sheridan Enterprise*, Oct. 1, 1907.

89. In February 1855, a general court-martial found Pvt. Simeon Covington, Company D, Sixth Infantry, guilty of having stolen some of Grattan's personal effects after his death, including a shawl, two pairs of shoes, and—almost ironically—two volumes of Winfield Scott's *Infantry Tactics*. Covington's punishment was to walk in front of the guardhouse for seven days, from Guard Mounting to Retreat, wearing a sign proclaiming him a "thief," and then to serve twenty-three days at hard labor while wearing a ball and chain. The court also fined him a month's pay. Order No. 13, Feb. 27, 1855, Fort Laramie Collections.

90. Mari Sandoz, "The Look of the West—1854," *Nebraska History* 35 (Dec. 1954): 247–48.

91. James H. Cook to C. G. Coutant, Mar. 20, 1898, Charles G. Coutant Collection, H74–9, fd. 57, Wyoming State Archives, Cheyenne; James P. Nolan, interview by David L. Hieb, n.d., Fort Laramie Collections.

92. The post returns do not record a skirmish on that day. See Lloyd E. McCann, Butler University, Indianapolis, to David L. Hieb, Nov. 9, 1953, Fort Laramie Collections. An attack on Fort Laramie is mentioned for August 28, 1854 in Heitman, *Historical Register* 2:401, but post records do not contain any such reference.

93. Jno. W. [John Wilkins] Whitfield, Indian agent, Platte Agency, Westport, Mo., to A. [Alfred] Cumming, superintendent, Indian affairs, St. Louis, Sept. 27, 1854, in *Annual Report of the Commissioner of Indian Affairs, 1854*, 94; McChristian, *Fort Laramie*, 90n2.

94. *Liberty Weekly Tribune* (Mo.), Oct. 6, 1854. The Dougherty letter and additional biographical information appear in Mark William Kelly, *Lost Voices on the Missouri: John Dougherty and the Indian Frontier* (Leavenworth, Kans.: Sam Clark, 2013), 644–46.

95. "Correspondence," Mar. 12, 1855, in *Missouri Republican*, Dec. 12, 1854, and Apr. 13, 1855; Hoffman to Page, Nov. 19, 1854, in *House of Representatives Reports*, No. 63, and in *Senate Executive Documents*, No. 91; Francis (Frank) Salway interview, Sheldon Collection, NSHS; Paul, *Blue Water Creek*, 32. C. A. Kinkead's name appeared with various spellings in the historical literature, including Kinkhead, Kinkade, and Kinkaid. His firm later sought relief from the U.S. Government for their monetary loss. *Congressional Globe*, Mar. 3, 1860, 966–67.

96. Little Thunder and Big Partisan to "Father" (Fort Laramie commanding officer), "Sarpies [Sarpy's] Point," Dec. 8, 1854, in "A True Copy: O. F. [Oscar F.] Winship, A. A. G.," Jan. 8, 1855, Letters Received, Department of the West, RG 393, NARA.

97. Hafen and Young, *Fort Laramie*, 237–39; Antoine Bordeaux, interview by Walter M. Camp, Walter Mason Camp Papers, Lilly Library, Indiana University, Bloomington; Thunder Bear, interview by Walter M. Camp, Walter Mason Camp Papers, Harold B. Lee Library, Brigham Young University, Provo.

98. For a full discussion of the Harney campaign, see Paul, *Blue Water Creek*, chaps. 3–7.

99. *Missouri Democrat* (St. Louis), Dec. 14, 1855; *Missouri Republican*, Aug. 13, 1855, and Feb. 13, 1856. See also Thomas S. Twiss, Fort Laramie, to the commissioner of Indian affairs, Oct. 18 and Oct. 28, 1855, LR, Upper Platte Agency, RG 75, NARA; Hoffman, Fort Laramie, to Winship, Fort Pierre, Nov. 4, 1855, Letters Sent, Fort Laramie Records.

August 20–September 20, 1854

1. Hugh B. Fleming, army officer, August 20, 1854
the bodies of those who have been killed

The succinct reply of Second Lt. Hugh B. Fleming to trader James Bordeaux's as-yet-undiscovered message begins a succession of rich primary sources that form this compendium of the Grattan massacre. Fleming's note, penned a day after the disaster, reflected a combination of polite decorum—for example, the use of the term "unfortunate transaction"—and maddening obtuseness. His request for Bordeaux to risk his own life to pick up the soldier dead can only be described charitably as naive.

Your letter of the 19th has been received by me, and in reply I say that I am unable to take further notice at present of this unfortunate transaction, and I wish you to speak to the Bear [Conquering Bear] and other chiefs with reference to the matter. Make the best terms with them you can for the present, for your own safety and the safety of others likewise unprotected in the country. I wish you to use all means in your power to procure the restoration for the bodies of those who have been killed.

Second Lt. Hugh B. Fleming, Sixth Infantry, commanding, Fort Laramie, to James Bordeau[x], Sarpy's Point, Nebraska, Aug. 20, 1854, in *Missouri Republican*, Sept. 13, 1854. The "Bordeau" spelling appears throughout some of the accounts in this book.

2. Hugh B. Fleming, army officer, August 20, 1854
I have the honor to make a report of an engagement.

By the time Fleming penned the report that follows, he had learned that Conquering Bear had been mortally wounded, and the expressman who took it to Fleming's superiors undoubtedly dropped off the lieutenant's note to Bordeaux. Once the overland messenger reached Fort Leavenworth and made his delivery, modern communication took over in the form of a telegraph network that stretched from Kansas Territory to the East Coast. Details from the report soon became national news. In retrospect the helpless, almost embarrassing Fleming-to-Bordeaux plea seems an unlikely document for military officials to release to the press; therefore, Bordeaux himself must have seen fit to get it to the St. Louis newspaper via a team consisting of the same anonymous expressman, an unknown recipient, and an obliging telegrapher.

For Hugh Brady Fleming this may have been the ultimate exploit of his military career. Born in Pennsylvania in 1827, Fleming graduated from the U.S. Military Academy in 1852, was assigned immediately to Fort Laramie, and served there until 1855. Frontier service before and after bracketed his routine administrative duties during the Civil War. His military record indicated no dramas equal to the one in 1854.

I have the honor to make a report of an engagement between a detachment of company G, 6th regiment of infantry, and the Sioux Indians.

The Indians have been committing depredations upon emigrants and traders in this section of the country all summer and those of the most daring kind. A few days since they came within two miles of the fort and killed two head of cattle out of the interpreter's herd; pursuit was immediately made, but the troops were unable to overtake them. On the 18th instant one of the Sioux went to an emigrant train, passing along the road, and shot down one of the oxen in the train, which left the poor emigrant in a very destitute condition. This occurred close to the fort, and I was compelled to take notice of it or give up entirely all protection to emigrants. The head chief of the Sioux came and reported the fact to me and expressed a willingness to give up the offender. Accordingly I sent Brevet 2nd Lieutenant J. L. Grattan, 6th infantry, with the interpreter, Sergeant Faver, Corporal McNulty, and twenty [later determined to be twenty-seven] privates, to receive the offender, and the whole detachment were massacred without exception. How this occurred I am at present unable to state, as there are so many different reports. I have no reliable information as to the number of Indians killed and wounded, but the Bear[,] Head chief[,] is reported among the killed. The Indians are hostile, menacing the fort, but all my men are on duty, and I think we shall be able to keep possession of it.

We stand much in need of more troops and hope they will be sent as soon as possible. I have sent this by express to the commanding officer of Fort Leavenworth and requested him to telegraph the same to you without delay.

Provision must accompany the troops, as we have only sufficient for those now at the post.

Second Lt. H. B. Fleming, Sixth Infantry, Fort Laramie, commanding, to Col. Lorenzo Thomas, assistant adjutant general, New York, N.Y., report, Aug. 20, 1854, in "Letter from the Secretary of War, Transmitting Information Relating to an Engagement between the United States Troops and the Sioux Indians near Fort Laramie," in *House of Representatives Reports*, No. 63. The express from Fort Laramie arrived in town on September 5. "Frightful Massacre by the Sioux," *Herald of Freedom* (Lawrence, Kans.), Sept. 15, 1854. Fleming sent his report to New York, and not to Washington, D.C., because, in a fit of pique, Commanding General Winfield Scott, a Whig, had removed his headquarters from the capital and its intolerable Democratic administration. For more on the impact of the telegraph on the Kansas frontier, see Randy Mullis, *Peacekeeping on the Plains: Army Operations in Bleeding Kansas* (Columbia: University of Missouri Press, 2004). Fleming's early record can be found in Cullum, *Biographical Register* 2:322, entry no. 1564, and in his obituary by James Sill, "Necrology—Hugh Brady Fleming," in *Twenty-Sixth Annual Reunion of the Association of Graduates of the United States Military Academy at West Point, New York, June 10th, 1895* (Saginaw, Mich.: Seemann and Peters, 1895), 92–97.

3. Lewis B. Dougherty, trader, August 20, 1854

I must thank providence I was not here when the troops started down.

Lewis Bissell Dougherty's letter home joined the other August 20 accounts in the expressman's mailbag, a mix of civilian and military correspondence that reached a mass readership by mid-September. His father, John Dougherty, a long-time trader, businessman, and government official operating from the Missouri frontier town of Liberty, owned the sutlerships of Forts Kearny and Laramie, and Lewis ran the store at the latter. Their hometown newspaper's Whig politics were clearly at odds with those of the Democratic administration and its secretary of war, Mississippi resident Jefferson Davis, whom the editor handily chastised.

From the young Dougherty we have a time when the detachment left Fort Laramie —2:00 P.M.—and the proper pronunciation—*GRAT-tun*—of Grattan's name from its misspelling ("Gratton"). He underreported the loss of both men and materiel, although both would be corrected later.

We publish below an extract from a letter from Lewis B. Dougherty to his father, Major John Dougherty, of this county [Clay County, Missouri], giving an account of the killing of Lieut. Grattan and twenty-two [later found to be twenty-seven] soldiers near Fort Laramie by the Indians. Will not our government awake to the dangers that threaten our emigrant trains to the Pacific, and so augment our military forces on this frontier as to prevent such occurrences?

Why is not the [1853] murder of Lieut. [John Williams] Gunnison avenged, and why this apathy on the part of government to the protection of emigrants and the Inland Commerce of the plains? Their neglect is treasonable under the circumstances. Will not our members of Congress speak out, trumpet tongued, when Congress meets and demand greater protection? The truth is we need a Secretary of War who lives in and knows the West and knows the peculiarities of Indian character. Unless we have more posts in Kansas, Nebraska, and Utah, we shall be appalled with the murders and robberies that will take place when emigrants begin to pour into those territories and when travel to and from them is increased. We shall mark this article and send it to the War Department at Washington. We hope the officer filling that department needs only to be informed of the dangers that exist here to use the preventing remedy.

The following is Mr. D's letter:

Fort Laramie, Aug. 20, '54.
Dear Father:

On yesterday about 2 o'clock, P.M., Lt. Gratton [sic] and twenty-two soldiers, with the interpreter, went about eight miles below this to take an Indian of the Bruly [Brulé] band for killing some cattle for an emigrant train. The Indian refused to be taken alive, and the fracas commenced. All the whites were killed and are still lying on the ground. They captured one cannon, twelve mules, and all the guns, pistols, &c. The Indians are all moving off. James Ellis is here with us waiting for an opportunity to go down. I must thank providence I was not here when the troops started down or perhaps now I would be among the dead. The express starts now for the States. Your son, L. B. Dougherty.

Lewis B. Dougherty, "Murder of U. States Troops by Indians," *Liberty Weekly Tribune* (Mo.), Sept. 15, 1854. This article appeared the same day his uncle William noted in his diary the news of the massacre. William Wallace Dougherty, *Doctor on the Western Frontier: The Diaries of Dr. William Wallace Dougherty, 1854–1880, Practicing in Liberty, Clay County, Missouri, and Iatan, Platte County, Missouri* (Liberty, Mo.: Clay County Archives and Historical Library, 2004), 22. Secretary of War Jefferson Davis shared the editor's outrage and coincidentally cited the Gunnison, Grattan, and other killings in his stern annual report of December 4, 1854. "Report of the Secretary of War," in *House Executive Documents*, No. 1, 33rd U.S. Congress, 2nd session, 1854–55, Serial 778. James Ellis has not been identified. See also Marilyn Irvin Holt, "Joined Forces: Robert Campbell and John Daugherty as Military Entrepreneurs," *Western Historical Quarterly* 30 (Summer 1999): 183–202.

4. Hezekiah Mitchell, Utah emigrant, August 14–21, 1854
We came in sight of a Sioux camp.

Englishman Hezekiah Mitchell, born in 1810 in Simmondley, Glossop, Derbyshire, was a Methodist preacher and teacher living in Liverpool, England, before converting in 1844 to the Church of Jesus Christ of Latter-day Saints. It took several years to save the money for him and his family to immigrate to America, and after reaching St. Louis in 1850, more years of saving to leave for Utah. They set out on their overland trek in mid-1854 and reached the Great Salt Lake valley on September 29.

Here begins a series of enlightening accounts kept by Mormon emigrants and officials that dot the compendium and whose words have been used sparingly in retelling the Grattan story. Fortunately several accounts from the "pioneer companies" survive in the church archives and, as excerpted here, offer a fresh, albeit somewhat detached perspective of the passerby. Not all Mormon diarists, including Mitchell, knew at the time that it was the property of a fellow believer that figured so prominently in the August 19 calamity.

Monday [August] 14th. Set out at 5 o'clock in the morning, passed the other two camps, met several wagons from Fort Larimie [*sic*], stopped for dinner; the other two camps came up and corraled. We put out again and made our days journey 20 miles, where there was very good grass and plenty with water and buffalo dung for the fire. Rained sharply.

Tuesday 15th. Turned out after the necessary preparations, found the road rather heavy in places, set down near some water for dinner, after which we journey again about 4 or 5 miles; we came in sight of a Sioux camp of Indians, about 4,000 in number; we had to pass right through them; however, as we were making headway, we had intelligence that they were our friends, as such we turned to the right and camped amongst them. They gathered in their horses and oxen to make room for ours to feed. Excellent horsemen and women, the women riding as the men do; several come up to us; one Chief came and told us where we could get wood, after which another person of distinction came and told us where we could camp and guarded our camp from the Indians own nation. He shot an arrow at one who was coming on horseback at a galloping speed; at another he fired his gun just at his feet; he would not allow any of his natives to molest or come near. Went up to the store, saw several, shook hands with one or two of them, went down to their large temple, or what so every name they may give it, and saw them dancing, singing, playing music, etc.; the sounds are not very harmonious; they had a fire in the mouth or entrance of the place; it is a large round tent. It looks well inside. Very unceremonious in their manners. Apt to take what is not theirs, left them for I did not like their ways, neither did my wife.

Wednesday 16th. Set up at 4 without breakfast in order to get some grass for the cattle, collected a little flour in camp for the person who had kept guard (over the Indians his party) for his trouble. Journ[ey]ed on until we got near the fort; then we put down for dinner, etc. After which we passed on. Job Smith's Company came on, and we forded the river at the Fort Larimie both at one time. The fort is a tolorable good looking place for its location. Wednesday 16th continued. Two Elders buried in this grave yard. Very heavy traveling until we got to higher ground, came to the river by descending down a ruff [rough] road and camped, traveled [——] miles. On guard 3 hours.

Thursday 17th. The camp was divided into four divisions, that is each captain of ten was to go out with his ten and lead them the rest of the journey to the Valley because the feed is scarce; ultimately there are only three companies because Captain [George Philander] Stiles was not supported in his office. After traveling all day we camped where there was little feed, but water and wood. Some little difficulty with the cattle belonging to the Smith Company and ours because they had camped too near us; on watch through the night, traveled 17-½ miles.

[Apparently no Friday, August 18, entry exists.]

Saturday 19th. Just as we were starting an Indian came to the camp, and as we passed on for several miles, we met droves of Indians; I should think not less than 500. [They] appeared very friendly till the last company of them were passing us when they spread a blanket and pointed an arrow at Captain Booths lead steer. We expected a fuss, but we gave them a little bread, and all was right; they are of the Cheyenne tribe. The road is very uneven in the first place having to assend a steep hill a quarter up; then we passed Hebers Spring a little on the right, which brought us to a bluff 3/4 of a mile up; we had to double teams then; it was bad to get up, but we accomplished it. Traveled ten and a half miles.

Sunday 20th. The road is a continuation of hills and hollows; otherwise it is good today. We met more Indians, not so many as the day before; we passed on till we came to the La Bonte River near which the [William] Fields [Field] Company and Captain [Alondra De Lafayette] Bucklands [Buckland] were out of repair. I was appointed Boss. On Monday we did the repairs.

Monday 21st. Commenced repairing the wagons, put two new fellows and one new spoke in one wheel that had been broken, put ark on others and heated the tires so that they were tight when cold. In the after part of the day President [James] Brown was taken ill of the cholera. I administered to him, but he appeared no better; he was much cramped in the bowels and legs. He requested us to lay hands on him and I to be mouth; while speaking a flow of Heavenly Light came into me which manifested that he would get better. He felt the same. Carried him into his tent and waited on him for a while. Then he requested me to see about the wagons again. After retiring to bed, President Brown sent Captain Booth to call me up with a few more, when were informed the Indians were coming in the morning to destroy the trading post. We did not know but their intentions were to molest us too. In consequence after mature deliberation we deemed it wisdom to fix our wagons as soon as possible in the night and put out on our journey as soon as it was daylight and avoid them if possible.

Hezekiah Mitchell journal, June–Sept. 1854, James Brown Company, in Mormon Pioneer Overland Travel, 1847–1868 (database), Church of Jesus Christ of Latter-day Saints, Salt Lake City, https://history.lds.org/overlandtravel/. Family genealogical information can be found in Sidney F. Mitchell, "Chronology of the Life of Hezekiah Mitchell and Sarah Mallinson Mitchell," Darrin and Andrea Lythgoe's Genealogy Pages, http://lythgoes.net/genealogy/history/HezekiahMitchell2.php. For more on this epic emigration season of the Latter-day Saints, see Fred E. Woods, "The 1854 Mormon Emigration at the Missouri-Kansas Border," *Kansas History: A Journal of the Central Plains* 32 (Winter 2009–10): 226–45.

5. William Athol MacMaster, Utah emigrant, August 21–23, 1854
The ind[i]ans and the sold[i]ers at the fort had a fight.

Unlike his contemporary Mitchell, William Athol MacMaster knew the general details of the Grattan fight, particularly the loss of the cow to the Indians. This was probably due to his train approaching from the east (and thence more dangerous) side of Fort Laramie and from hearing the news from the expressman rushing to the States for military reinforcements. The MacMaster wagon train reached Salt Lake City on October 1.

Although MacMaster mentioned several people in his brief account, the one of whom to take especial note is Ezra T. Benson, who at the time was a member of the Quorum of the Twelve Apostles, Church of Jesus Christ of Latter-day Saints. Benson left a brief account that appears later in this section.

Monday [August] 21st. We came to a house about 19 mil[e]s from the fort, and we was there informed that the indans [Indians] and the sold[i]ers at the fort had a fight. 28 solders was kil[le]d and one wou[n]ded. We was orderded [*sic*] to load our guns and make ready for an at[t]ack from the indans, and we camped 18 mil[e]s from the fort, and all the row began because one of the indans taking a cow from the Danes and killing it and not giving up the indan that did it. In the evening two men on horse back came to our camp on their way to Fort Le[a]venworth for help. It would take them eleven days or nine. We placed armed men round the camp and cattle all night. I headed the first guard.

Tuesday 22nd. We came about 3 miles and camped, put[t]ing our wagon in a carall [corral] and our tents inside of it. As we were afraid that the indans was storming the fort, so we thought that it was best to stope [*sic*] behind till Elder E. T. [Ezra T.] Benson of the Twelve came up as he had the charge of the camp as O. P. [Orson Pratt] went on to the valley. And our captain D. Carans [Daniel Garn] thought it wright to stop on him, i.e. E. B. We are camped on the bank of the river Platt[e]. Day verey hot.

Wednesday 23rd. We left and treaveled about 5 miles past Fort Laremoore [Laramie] and camped for the night.

William Athol MacMaster, diary, 1848–1887, Daniel Garn Company, in Mormon Pioneer Overland Travel (database), https://history.lds.org/overlandtravel/. A biographical note accompanies the William Athol MacMaster Papers at the J. Willard Marriott Library, University of Utah, Salt Lake City.

6. James Bordeaux, trader, August 21, 1854

I accordingly sent for the chiefs to go with the Lieutenant and make the arrest.

James Bordeaux astutely provided an early, detailed, and almost dispassionate eyewitness account to the press, an act—"my duty"—that only enhanced the frontiersman's credibility. Bordeaux downplayed his central role in the on-site negotiations, focusing on the events that immediately followed. He also assigned no blame in his first of several accounts of the "bad situation." That would come when pressed.

An affair has happened here between the soldiers and the Indians, which ought to be properly noticed by the United States Government. Having been an eye-witness to the battle, I consider it my duty to furnish a strict account of it and its causes. In the first place, on the 17th of August a train of Mormons passed this place. The Indians, who were encamped here waiting for their payment from [the] government, had no provisions and were of course anxious for something to eat. As the Mormons were passing, a lame cow, belonging to a man in the rear of the Mormon train, became frightened and ran into the Indian camp. The Mormons left the cow behind, and so one of the Indians, a Minnecosha [Miniconjou], shot it down, and with his companions ate it up. The Mormons then went to the fort and reported that the Indians had killed one of their cows.

On the 19th about 2 o'clock in the afternoon, Lieut. Grattan, with a command of twenty-seven soldiers and Auguste Lucien, interpreter, arrived here to arrest the Indian who had killed the cow. I accordingly sent for the chiefs to go with the Lieutenant and make the arrest. They accompanied him, but the Indian was not willing to give himself up, saying that he would die first.

While the Bear Chief of the Wazazies was standing with three other chiefs, the Little Thunder, the Big Partizan, and the Man who is afraid of his Horses, among the soldiers, the Lieutenant ordered his men to fire. They did so and wounded the Bear Chief and his brother. But one round was fired, when the Indians in turn charged and succeeded in routing the soldiers and killing all of them with the exception of one private, who is not expected to recover.

Lieut. Grattan and two of his men were killed while standing by their cannon, the Lieutenant receiving twenty-four arrows, one of which passed through his head. As soon as the soldiers saw their commander fall, they took to flight but were all killed within a half a mile of this place. The Ogalallah camp was about one mile distant, and a white man named Seyfroy [Sefroy] Iott was staying there at the time. Being a Sioux interpreter, the chiefs requested him to stay between the camps to prevent the young men from charging on the soldiers, but he could not succeed and barely escaped with his life.

At my house we were placed in a bad situation. There were with me Mr. Antoine Reynal [Raynall] and Mr. Samuel Smith, with five others, and all we could do was to stay in the house and try to keep the Indians out. As Mr. R. was standing in the doorway of the house, an Indian rushed on him and tried to kill him, when another Indian, the Quick Bear [Swift Bear], tried to kill the first Indian for rushing on a white man, but some one caught Quick Bear's gun, and its contents went into the wall of the house.

By this time a party had collected outside of the house, who tried to force their way in, but some of my friends, the Quick Bear and others, stopped them. After the battle the chiefs came in my house and said that, as the young men had killed all the soldiers that had come to fight them, they would now go and slaughter the rest of the soldiers at the fort, burn all the houses, and kill all the whites on the river, but I told the chiefs to stop them from so doing, assuring them that, since the soldiers had commenced the quarrel, it would be overlooked by [the] government. But they then rushed in the house and demanded of me to give them every thing that they wanted. To save our lives, I gave them every thing that I had in my store, to the amount of two thousand dollars.

The next day they went to the post of the American Fur Company, took all the goods that were sent to them by [the] government, and pillaged the store. The situation of the traders and of Fort Laramie is perilous in the extreme. I was requested by the commander of the fort to bury the dead soldiers since he had not men enough to detach a party for that service, and I succeeded in doing so.

As far as I know anything about Indians, I think that our government ought to send five hundred mounted men, veteran troops, to keep the Indians in subjection and one company of infantry to guard the fort. The Indians in the recent battle, after killing all the soldiers, broke their cannon to pieces and carried off their muskets and animals. As for placing the infantry on a prairie to fight with Indians, it is just the same as putting them up as targets to be shot at. There were about one thousand Indians in the battle. Yours truly, James Bordeau, per Samuel Smith.

Witness that the above is correct, the undersigned being eye-witnesses: Antoine Reynal [Raynall], Tofiel Graph [Groph], Peter Pew [Pugh], Sam'l Smith, Paul [Pedro] Vial, Antonio Lahonn [also spelled Le Whone].

"Authentic Details of the Battle at Sarpy's Point, Defeat of the Troops from Fort Laramie, Government Goods Captured, Bordeau[x]'s Store Pillaged, Sarpy's Point, Nebraska Territory, 8 miles E. of Fort Laramie, Aug. 21, 1854," *Missouri Republican*, Sept. 13, 1854, reprinted in *New York Daily Times*, Sept. 18, 1854.

7. "S," anonymous correspondent, August 26, 1854
the report of friendly Indians who were eye witnesses

This anonymous source—"S"—appears to write from a trader perspective, possibly from the geographic vantage of the American Fur Company house, but that still leaves several individuals in the Fort Laramie community as potential authors. More importantly he was not an actual eyewitness to the running fight, otherwise he would have known that his "friendly Indian" sources had failed to distinguish between Grattan's sergeant as the fleeing horseman who had temporarily escaped the melee and the lieutenant himself. Nevertheless, "S" democratically scoured the area for sources—Indians, traders, refugees, and Mormon travelers—to fill out his lengthy account.

On the 19th inst., Lieutenant Fleming, commanding at Fort Laramie, sent out a detachment of twenty-eight men under Lieutenant Grattan, with two pieces artillery and a mule wagon, accompanied by Mr. [Auguste] Lucien, the interpreter, and a Mr. [Obridge] Allen, recently from California, to make prisoner of an Indian, who had killed some cattle belonging to a Mormon train. The Indian belonged to the Brule band of the Sioux nation, who numbered about two hundred and fifty lodges, comprising over one thousand fighting men, besides the women and children, and encamped about nine miles below the fort, near the store of Mr. Bordou [Bordeaux], a trader. The Ogallalas, another branch of the Sioux, together with other Indians, amounting to upwards of two thousand five hundred men, were encamped in the neighborhood. They had been assembled some time, waiting for the arrival of Col. Whitfield, United States Agent, to distribute the annuity goods and provisions, which had arrived and were stored at the American Fur Company's post, about 4 miles nearer the fort.

The soldiers marched into the Brules' camp, where Lieutenant Grattan called on the chief—Matteoyouwan—to deliver up the Indian who had killed the Mormon's cattle. The chief, who had always been very friendly to the whites, replied that he would surrender the culprit, who was then in camp willing to give himself up, and begged Lieutenant Grattan would not shoot him there but take him away a prisoner. An unconditional surrender was required, which the chief demurred to, as he was advised by the principal men of the band that he had made a "good talk" to the officers, and, if he would not listen to it, they would not give up the Indian because he was much esteemed by the tribe and it would disgrace them all if he were shot in their sight.

The interpreter spoke angrily to the Indians and was riding about much excited, threatening them and declaring that Lieutenant Grattan insisted that the Indian must be instantly shot on the spot, and finally, growing impatient at the delay, shot an Indian in the mouth, killing him. Lieutenant Grattan shot the chief and bade the men fire; both he and the interpreter, immediately after firing, galloped off, pursued by mounted Brules and were overtaken and killed. The soldiers, some of whom fired off the cannon without effect, took to the wagon and started off full tilt towards the fort; several got away afoot, but all were overtaken and killed, except three who were found still alive by some friendly Indians, taken care of, and hid in neighboring lodges; the Brules subsequently found and killed them.

It is stated that Mr. Allen escaped to a friendly lodge, where some squaws wrapped him up in blankets to conceal him from pursuit. This statement of the tragedy is made up from the report of friendly Indians who were eye witnesses, confirmed in part by some traders, who anticipated some trouble when the detachment reached the American Fur Company's post, where a short halt was made, and from the top of a neighboring hill saw through spy glass much of what afterwards passed.

The Brules were highly exasperated by the assault, and, after they overtook Mr. Lucien, they accused him of bringing on the trouble, and altho' he begged them to spare his life and offered to pay a ransom of eight horses, his captors said he must die, and they killed him.

The party that pursued Lieutenant Grattan, after killing him, cut off his legs. It is to be feared this officer acted hastily and wrongly in the whole affair and imprudently chose a position in the midst of the lodges, exposed to the fire of the whole band of warriors, instead of halting near the camp and requesting an interview with the chief. About a week before, at the store of Ward and Guerre [Guerrier], 9 miles this side of the fort, he expressed the wish to have a "muss" with the Indians. I am so informed by a respectable trader who was present, or I would not state it. Lieutenant Grattan might have been prompted throughout by a vindictive feeling which illy qualified him for the duty assigned to him. He has paid the forfeit of his life.

The interpreter was highly censurable, and he was disliked by the Indians. They had a grudge, too, against the soldiers for killing three of their tribe last year. The chief died two days afterwards and just before his death told his people to war only with the soldiers and not trouble other whites or emigrants. No other Indians took part in the melee.

Afterwards the Cheyennes offered their services to Lieut. Fleming to aid in clearing the country of the Brules. The Ogallalas took away their women who had married among the Brules and gave back such of the women they had got of the Brules as they did not want to keep. On the next day the Brules pillaged the store of Mr. Bourdou and distributed his goods among their band.

They afterwards took the road to the American Fur Company's post, which had been left in charge of Mr. Moncrevier [Moncravie] by the company's agent Mr. Gratiot, gone to St. Louis. Mr. M. immediately after the affair between the Indians and soldiers started up the road to warn the traders and emigrants above, having Mr. Charles Guerre [Gereau] and three men at the establishment. The Brules charged and took possession of the annuity goods, when the Ogallalas interfered in order to get their own share and forced the Brules to make a fair distribution, which was done under the direction of Mr. Charles Guerre, whom they compelled to act in place of Col. Whitfield, who had not arrived. They also took the goods belonging to the American Fur Company. No personal violence was offered to the people at Mr. Bourdou's or Gratiot's. After the last named assault some respectable traders residing on the road, above, who happened to be then below, brought word to Messrs. Ward and Guerre [Guerrier] that the Indians had robbed and destroyed all the trading establishments, as here, killing all the whites, and were coming up in strong force to attack the post and plunder and destroy all the traders and emigrants on the road as far as to the bridge [Richard's Bridge at present Casper, Wyoming], 130 miles above the fort. Messrs. W. & G., with over twenty hands belonging to their establishment, fearing an instant attack on their houses, fled for safety to the mountains without their property. The traders rode ahead, warning the emigrants they overtook on the road, and reached this place late at night, warning Mr. Jos. [Joseph] Bissonette, who keeps a trading establishment here. Mr. B., having only his clerk and a few hired men on the premises, made preparations to remove and at daybreak was off with his people and a wagon load of provisions, &c., driving up his herd of cattle, horses, and mules, and overtook and passed several Mormon trains. All reached La Prele creek, about twenty miles distant, and camped together. Soon after sundown, however, Mr. Charles Guerre, of the Fur Company, arrived, bringing information that no further mischief was meditated by the Indians, confirming all the previous intelligence, except the killing of any whites but the soldiers. The writer of this, sojourning a while at Mr. Bissonette's, accompanied the party on the removal and return, and we are now back again in possession, anxiously looking for some friends who are expected from below.

These troubles make traders feel uneasy. We trust, however, quiet is fully restored, and there is an end for a while of trouble. We learn that Lt. Fleming immediately sent off an express and made a requisition for reinforcements. The garrison is reduced to about fifty men. As the Indians are well provided with horses, guns, pistols, and ammunition, the force at the fort should consist of five hundred men, mainly dragoons, well mounted and equipped. The government agent, instead of making only an annual short visit, should reside at or near the fort. The great responsibility devolves upon the interpreter in interviews with Indians, and it is highly important he should be well qualified and entirely competent. He should be acceptable to the Indians and possess the confidence of the traders and whites, as well as of the government. No man in the country is so well qualified in every respect at Mr. Jos. Bissonette of this place, but, as he is settled at a good point for trading, the salary should be increased to more than double the sum heretofore paid to induce him to relinquish his business. In this case, I believe, Mr. B. would accept the appointment, although he will not solicit it. I am confident the mass of traders would be gratified at his appointment. He enjoys the respect and confidence of the Indians. It would not be amiss to say here that, if he had been the interpreter in the late affair, everything would have been quietly adjusted, and we would all have been spared the recital of the slaughter and pillage.—"S."

27th.—Since writing the foregoing we learn Mr. Bourdou's store was not pillaged, and he has removed his goods and cattle to the fort. All the other particulars are confirmed.

Since writing this letter a Mormon train came up with some later intelligence. The Captain states an effort was made to induce him to stop at the fort (having about 100 men in the train, well armed), it being represented to him that, as the force there was so much reduced, they needed aid, and it would be better for emigrants to stop. Capt. Carnes [Daniel Garn] replied he could fight his way along and could not maintain his oxen and horses there, and, if he could get along, he supposed an U.S. fort should be able to protect itself. He was then told, if emigrants would not aid, they could not expect any themselves in future. Capt. Carnes states the soldiers were buried near the spot where the bodies were found by soldiers sent from the fort. Thirty in all were killed, including Lt. Grattan and Mr. L., the interpreter. The opinion is universal that the expedition was very badly conducted, and the Indians are not blamed for defending themselves. It is also stated that the Brules have offered to make peace and to make reparation for the soldiers killed, after their fashion, in horses, and losing their share of future annuities, and that Lt. Fleming took or gave them forty days for consideration of the proposal.

Cap. Carnes believes no emigrants will be molested.

Ward and Guerre's houses were not disturbed, and several of the men had returned home just before the train arrived there.

He also reports that the Indian chief still survived, but we believe that is true what we heard that he died a few days afterwards of his wounds, having received four shots.

S., "Full Particulars of the Massacre at Fort Laramie, LaBonte Creek, 60 Miles below Fort Laramie, August 26, 1854," *Missouri Democrat*, Oct. 9, 1854. For more on Bissonette, see John D. McDermott, "Joseph Bissonette," in *The Mountain Men and the Fur Trade of the Far West*, vol. 4, edited by LeRoy R. Hafen and Ann W. Hafen (Glendale, Calif.: Arthur H. Clark, 1966), 49–69.

8. Lewis B. Dougherty, August 29, 1854
full particulars of a very lamentable occurrence

Lewis Dougherty, the young businessman stationed at Fort Laramie, followed his abbreviated account of August 20 with a longer, well-crafted version of the previous day's events. With this attempt Dougherty added considerable detail and corrected some of his earlier errors, such as the number of soldier fatalities, while offering a few strong opinions to fan the political flames. Again the venue was his father's local newspaper in Liberty, Missouri.

Born in 1828 and a University of Missouri graduate, Dougherty remained at Fort Laramie until 1856. He served as a Confederate officer for a Missouri regiment during the Civil War, survived, and thrived afterward as a successful Liberty banker.

Major John Dougherty, of this county, has furnished us with the following letter from his son, L. B. Dougherty, giving full particulars of the late massacre of U.S. troops near Fort Laramie by the Sioux Indians. The letter is dated Fort Laramie, Aug. 29, 1854.

Dear Father: I hasten to give you the full particulars of a very lamentable occurrence which happened between a detachment of U.S. soldiers of this fort and a band of the Sioux Indians on the 19th inst. A Sioux chief (named the Bear that scatters) came up from his village eight miles below this, where he with five or six hundred lodges were encamped, waiting for the division of their annuities, and informed the commanding officer, Lieut. Flemming [sic], that one of the Sioux warriors had killed a cow belonging to a Mormon train on its way to the Great Salt Lake City, and requested him to send down his soldiers and punish the offender. Lt. Flemming ordered Lt. Gratton [sic] (after his soliciting the favor) and twenty-nine men to be in readiness to start at 2 o'clock that day. Lt. G's command started down accordingly, with the interpreter, two pieces of artillery, and one mule wagon, in which the men were mounted. He arrived outside the village, ordered a halt, and sent the interpreter for the chief. He made his appearance in a few minutes and was told what was their business. The chief said he would go and see if the man would give himself up peaceably or not. He came back with this answer from the offender, "I am alone; last fall the soldiers killed my two brothers; this spring my only relation (an uncle) died. I have a gun with plenty of powder and balls, a bow and quiver full of arrows, and the soldiers will have to kill and then take me." Lieut. G. then marched his command into the centre of the Indian encampment and told the Indians he had come for the offender and would have him or all would die. After parleying a few moments, he ordered the men to fire. As soon as the muskets were leveled, the Indians rushed upon them. The two pieces of artillery were fired, wounding three Indians. The above mentioned chief received three wounds. Before the guns could be reloaded, Lt. G. and two men were shot down at the cannons, and then a retreat commenced, the Indians in pursuit. The whites were all killed, one, two and three in a place, none getting more than a mile from the village. The bodies were horribly mutilated. Some of them had their legs cut off at the knee, some their throats cut, and all except two or three had their heads mashed in and arrows shot through their noses close to the face. They were stripped of most their clothing. Lt. G. had a watch in his pocket, which they did not take, and was all by which he was identified. He was within three feet of the cannon; he was acting cannonier [cannoneer]. The bodies could not be buried for two days on account of the Indians.

The morning after the slaughter, the Sioux made a rush for the store of the American Fur Company, broke the doors open, and took all, both public and private. They compelled Mr. Bordeau to give them all they wanted out of his store and then threatened the lives of all on the river. I have never saw such a general stampede in any country. We have been kept in a terrible state of suspense by reports of their charging on the fort. They boasted of killing more than half the command. Several traders have come to the fort, "lock, stock and barrel." Others have gone with the Cheyennes for protection. The old American Fur Company fort is fixed up for the last resort. A small block house is being erected, which held by ten men will add greatly to the strength of the post, and protect the frame building from being fired. A government express started down the day after the massacre, and, should the authorities not send a large reinforcement, the troops could not be censured for leaving the post. There should be sufficient force to protect the post and the many licensed traders who are scattered over the country, to say nothing about the emigrating women and children to California and Oregon. All feeling of security is now destroyed, nor will it be restored until the Indians get a good drubbing from the government.

Nothing is doing in the store; all are well. No sick at present in the hospital. The agent, Gen. Whitfield, is here, taken all aback by the report of the massacre, not having heard of it until his arrival in the fort. I am of the opinion that not a less reinforcement than two or three companies of mounted troops will do any good here, as infantry cannot pursue the Indians when they come about on thieving expeditions. This massacre must be keenly felt by our government; the whole country must feel it sensibly. It being done in sight of the post almost is throwing defiance in the face of [the] government, which I think cannot be overlooked. The government lost twelve mules and one horse on the battle-field.

I had, on the night of the massacre, 26 head of horses and mules from the corell [corral], fourteen of which I recovered. Two or three days after, they also took two mules belonging to the mail contractor from the same corell. They are still in the possession of the Indians. All the whites on the river had more or less property stolen on the night of the bloody murder. We expect to hear frequently of bands of horses being stolen from this vicinity by war parties after these blood hounds and red devils procure meat enough for their families to subsist upon, and woe to the white man who may meet one of these parties, for his hair will be lifted. The Cheyennes, about one hundred lodges, are here waiting for their goods, which Gen. Whitfield brought over with him. They will receive them today. He goes direct to Washington to receive orders. He can do nothing here.

No more at present. Your son, Lewis B. Dougherty.

Lewis B. Dougherty, "The Massacre at Fort Laramie," *Liberty Weekly Tribune* (Mo.), Oct. 6, 1854. Agent Whitfield arrived at Fort Laramie on August 26, 1854, and departed on September 2. When his party returned to the States in early October, Dougherty's letter undoubtedly traveled with it. His later reminiscences of his frontier experiences were edited by Ethel Massie Withers, ed., "Experiences of Lewis Bissell Dougherty on the Oregon Trail," Parts 1–5, *Missouri Historical Review* 24 (April 1930): 359–78; 24 (July 1930): 550–67; 25 (October 1930): 102–15; 25 (January 1931): 306–21; 25 (April 1931): 474–89.

9. Hugh B. Fleming, August 30, 1854
I sent . . . Grattan.

Similar to Lewis Dougherty when given the opportunity to commit more thoughts to paper, post commander Hugh Fleming produced a longer, more thoughtful narrative. His official report, a basic building block of the Grattan story, contained additional points to his August 20 message worthy of emphasis here, one being a possible explanation for the irascible behavior of the drunken interpreter. Apparently Auguste Lucien had a long-standing grudge with certain members of the Sioux tribe. Another statement by Fleming accused the perpetrator of evil intent toward the Mormon emigrant himself and not just against his bovine property. Of more immediate importance to Fleming and his garrison was his written plea for more troops.

I have the honor to make a report of an engagement between a detachment of troops belonging to G company, 6th Infantry, and a band of Sioux Indians. The Indians have been committing depredations upon emigrants and traders in the country all summer, and those, too, of the most daring kind. A few days since they came within two miles of the fort and killed two head of cattle out of our interpreter's herd; pursuit was immediately made, but the troops were unable to overtake them. On the 18th of August, one of the Sioux went to an emigrant train passing along the road and tried to kill one of them, but, failing in this, shot down one of the cattle in the train, which left the poor emigrant in a very destitute condition. This occurred close to the fort, and I was compelled to take notice of it or give up entirely all protection to those travelling on this route. The head chief of the Sioux came and reported the fact to me and expressed a willingness to give up the offender.

Accordingly, I sent Brevet Second Lieutenant J. L. Grattan, 6th Infantry, with the interpreter, Sergeant Faver, Corporal McNulty, and 27 privates, to receive the offender; and the whole detachment were massacred with the exception of one man, who died at this place three days after this sad and bloody affair. How this occurred I am unable to state with any degree of accuracy. I have no reliable information as to the number of Indians killed and wounded; the "Bear," head chief, is reported among the killed. The

Indians are hostile, menacing the fort, but all my men are under arms, and I think we shall be able to keep possession of it. We stand much in need of more troops and hope they will be sent as soon as possible. Provisions must accompany the troops, as we have only sufficient for those now at the post. Lieutenant Grattan, it appears, was about the first one of the persons killed and died near a howitzer performing his duty. In a great measure I think the loss of men was attributable to his early loss, thus leaving them without a commander. We also lost twelve mules and harness, one horse, two howitzers, and one wagon, besides other ordnance stores; however, since, we have recovered the howitzers and wagon. What effect this success will have upon the Indians I am almost unwilling to conjecture; some, at least, it can make but little worse.

Should a sufficient force be sent out immediately by the government to punish the offenders in an effectual manner, no hostility from other surrounding tribes may be expected, but, should this not be done, then great sacrifice of life may be expected, as all the surrounding tribes, stimulated by neglect of this bloody massacre, will join hand in hand and rush on to the slaughter.

I have recommended that all traders in the country be prohibited from trading guns or ammunition on any pretence whatever, and the Indian agent, General Whitfield, has accordingly prohibited this kind of trade with the Indians till further orders. This I consider, with all who have any knowledge of the dangerous state of the country, as a commendable stroke of policy in General Whitfield. In fact, I might add, at present this is the only effectual means we have of protecting ourselves.

Lieutenant Fleming, headquarters, Fort Laramie, report to O. F. [Oscar F.] Winship, assistant adjutant general, "Inspecting the Department," Aug. 30, 1854, in *House of Representatives Reports*, No. 63. Portions of Fleming's August 20 and 30 reports are repetitive, and he—or another hand—took the opportunity to make a few minor editorial changes. The young officer used this later report primarily to reinforce the immediate needs of the besieged fort.

10. James Bordeaux, August 31, 1854

He acted very rashly and foolishly.

Trader James Bordeaux, who figured so prominently in the events of August 19 and their aftermath, pointed the finger of blame at the interpreter, not the army or the Indians, and had his employees attest to the same.

In answer to yours of this date I will inform you as far as I know of the cause of the recent difficulty between the U.S. troops under the command of Lieut. Grattan and the Sioux Indians; there was a Mormon train passed the village, and there was a man behind the train driving a lame cow, and the cow got frightened and ran towards the village; the Mormon left the cow, and the Indians then killed and eat [ate] it; the Mormon then reported to the commander of Fort Laramie, and accordingly Lieut. Grattan with a command of twenty-nine men and the interpreter went to the village to arrest the Indian that killed the cow, and he the Indian was not willing to give himself up. The Lieut. commanded his men to fire on the Indians, and a general battle ensued which ended in the defeat of the troops. I have been a resident of this country for twenty years and think that I am well acquainted with the manners, customs &c. of the Sioux Indians; also I think that the Indians were as peaceably disposed towards the whites as heretofore, and they have not committed any more depredations than they have heretofore; also I have not heard any threats from the Indians that they would go and take their presents, and they were waiting peaceably for your arrival to make the payment. The goods being stored in the American Fur Company's houses had no effect what ever in producing the difficulty, and I have heard many Indians say that they were glad that the goods would be given away from the fort, for the year previous they had nearly a difficulty with the soldiers and that they did not want it. The goods this year were stored I believe in as good houses as heretofore; also I think that there was rash means used that produced the difficulty. Also I think at the time that the Interpreter was under the influence of ardent spirits, and his manner of talking to the Indians was generally reckless and that at the time of this unfortunate affair he acted very rashly and foolishly. So no more at present.

Witnesses that the above Statement is correct, the undersigned being old residents and citizens. Rouville Bonnette, Eugene Guern [Guerin], Olivier Maurisitte [Oliver Morrisette], Joseph Jewette [Jouett], Samuel Smith, Antoniene Reynall [Antoine Raynall], Leo[n] F. Pallardy, John S. Smith.

James Bordeau[x] per Saml [Samuel] Smith to J. W. Whitefield [John W. Whitfield], Indian agent, Fort Laramie, Aug. 31, 1854, Letters Received, Upper Platte Agency, Records of the Bureau of Indian Affairs, Microfilm Publication No. 234, roll 889, NARA. The names of these frontiersmen of French ancestry and others appeared in a variety of anglicized ways in the historical record.

11. Obridge Allen, civilian traveler, late August 1854
They fell, to a man, on the last ground they had taken.

Obridge Allen may be the most important observer to the Grattan massacre because he alone seems not to have had a vested familial, political, or economic interest in the event—only that of staying alive after the mayhem erupted. Allen made the trip with Grattan from the fort and fortunately for him only so far as the Bordeaux (here consistently spelled throughout as "Bordeau") trading post. From his vantage point on its roof and from the trader's perspective as a go-between, he had an ideal view and knowledge of the proceedings. Allen's account is critical for understanding the sequence of events.

Although a literate writer, later a published author, and clearly considered then and now as a credible witness, Allen remains elusive in the historical record. His 1859 trail guide, *Allen's Guide Book and Map to the Gold Fields of Kansas & Nebraska and Great Salt Lake City*, hints at a continued presence in the American West. Notes by the historian LeRoy R. Hafen that accompanied a 1953 facsimile edition by Nolie Mumey added precious few mentions of Allen, the self-professed "Late Government Guide" of that publication.

On the 19th of August, 1854, Lieutenant Grattan, accompanied by an interpreter and twenty-nine enlisted men of the garrison of Fort Laramie, left that post between two and three o'clock P.M. for the purpose of visiting the encampment of the Sioux Indians, situated near Bordeau's trading-house, on the North Platte, about eight miles below the post, for the purpose of bringing away an Indian who had been charged with killing an ox belonging to an emigrant. On arriving at the trading-house of the American Fur Company, called Gratiot's Buildings, the parted halted and loaded its muskets, without capping. It then moved on about two miles further, when it was again halted, and told by Lieutenant Grattan the object of the expedition, who further assured his men that the Indian he was about to demand must be taken, if not freely given up, at all hazards, even if he (Lieut. G.) died in the effort; that he did not expect, however, to be compelled to fire a single gun; that, if obliged to fight, the party would obey no orders coming from any one but himself and the sergeant present; and that every order coming from the latter would be respected as coming from himself. He then detailed the men for the howitzers (one twelve-pounder and one mountain howitzer), and, finding a deficiency in the detail of one man, he gave his horse to one of the soldiers, saying that he would act as gunner himself. The party then proceeded to Bordeau's trading-house, about two miles further on and in the immediate neighborhood of the Indian camp, which lay stretched along the course of the Platte, having the road to the right and the river to the left and having a small patch of brushwood and a rather abrupt break in the ground between the camp and the river. Lieutenant Grattan halted near that part of the camp occupied by the Brules (among whom the Indian pursued had taken refuge) and had in that position another of the Sioux bands on his left flank and rear. He here ordered this infantry to cap and the gunners to load with grape and canister, inquired for Mr. Bordeau, and requested him to send for the head Sioux chief, the "Bear;" the chief came, with several other Indians, mostly unarmed. Lieutenant Grattan desired Bordeau to tell them that he had come for the Indian that had killed the emigrant's ox. The Bear seemed to be enraged and made some reply that I did not understand. I think they refused to give the man up, whereupon Lieutenant Grattan told them he would be obliged to fight them if they did not surrender the accused Indian. The Bear replied, "Go down to the lodge where the man is, and see what he will say." Lieutenant Grattan then ordered his men to mount (the wagon and gun-carriages), and the party moved into the village, the howitzers leading, and the wagon containing the infantry following in rear. I mounted my horse to proceed with them, after having asked Bordeau and another person if there was likely to be a conflict, and, receiving for a reply that they thought not, I waited on my horse about twenty minutes in conversation with Bordeau and a person named Raynall, when an Indian came up from the village for Mr. Bordeau to act as interpreter. He left with my mare, and I went on the house-top with Mr. Raynall to see what was going on. In a few moments after, Mr. B. returned, saying that he had not been where the troops were and that he was afraid there was going to be trouble in the camp. About fifteen minutes after this, another Indian came to ask the services of Mr. Bordeau as interpreter, as he was afraid there would be trouble in the camp, and the Indians would no longer listen to the government interpreter (Mr. Lucien Auguste [sic]). Mr. B. proceeded to within about twenty-five yards of the place where the Indians and Mr. Grattan were in council and then returned apparently much excited and ordered all the arms about the establishment to be loaded and a defensive attitude assumed, he himself running to his lodge for his gun. As he left, I saw the troops rise up and level their muskets, when the Indians instantly fired upon them, and the troops as promptly replied with musketry. I should have observed that while the council was being held, from three to five hundred warriors left the camp and prepared for fighting in the patch of brushwood and behind the little inequality of the ground before named. In less than a minute after the above exchange of shots between the Indians and the infantry, the field howitzer was discharged, followed immediately by the mountain howitzer. It was at this moment that Private Williams retreated with the limber of the field howitzer through the village directly towards the road, followed by the wagon which had brought the infantry, whereupon the Indians made a general rush upon the troops. The interpreter and the soldier in charge of the lieutenant's horse endeavored to escape on their animals but were followed about half a mile and killed. The remainder of the party endeavored to escape by means of the wagon, but, failing to overtake it, they halted and showed a determined front to the Indians, who had by this time come from every quarter of the camp and had completely surrounded them. They fell, to a man, on the last ground they had taken. I think that Lieutenant Grattan fell at the first fire; his body, as well as those of the two enlisted men, was found lying beside his gun.

The interpreter, Mr. Auguste, was evidently excited by liquor, and it was owing to his extravagant conduct towards the Indians, doubtless, that the collision took place. He had drunk nothing, apparently, when he left the garrison, but on arriving at Gratiot's House he left for a few minutes and re-appeared intoxicated. Lieutenant Grattan, seeing his condition and ascertaining that he had about half a gill of liquor about him, took it from him and destroyed it.

Upon seeing that the party had been destroyed, I mounted my horse with the intention of starting at once for the fort but was told by Messrs. Bordeau and Raynall that it would be rash in me to attempt to reach the garrison at that time. The Indians were already charging upon the houses. I tied my horse and went in, and upon my entrance into the house an Indian leaped in also and exclaimed, "Let us wipe out the whites here," and at the same instant he seized upon Mr. Raynall, when certain other Indians, relatives of Mr. Bordeau's, said to them, if they intended to kill the whites, to commence on themselves first, and one of these friendly Indians endeavored to shoot the man who struggled with Raynall. Mr. R. knocked up the gun, and the ball went into the ceiling, whilst he threw his adversary out of the door.

The village had commenced, in the mean time, to move off, crossing to the left bank of the Platte, leaving the Bear's lodge standing. In about an hour afterwards the warriors returned to Bordeau's, demanding various articles of goods in the store. Bordeau, thinking that these demands were made expecting he would refuse them and thus give a pretext for a quarrel, gave them all they asked. About 12 o'clock, midnight, they returned to the side [site?] of the old camp, to the Bear's lodge, and shortly after left Bordeau's place. An Indian [Swift Bear] then came into the house with a wounded soldier, about twenty other Indians being present, some friendly and some not. This Indian told those around him, "If you kill this soldier, you kill me, for I shall die with him." The hostiles then warned Bordeau that he had better not keep the soldier in the house, else they would "wipe out the whites," and they further told him to advise the soldier if he was able to walk to the fort, and, being told by him that he thought he was, Mr. B. directed the Indian who had brought him in to take him to the road and start him off in the direction of the fort. The Indian took him on the road about a mile and a half towards the garrison.

All was quiet from this time until day-break, when the Indians struck their camp and started their families towards the Raw Hide, about ten miles north of the Platte, and, when they had got their village in motion, they returned to remove the Bear and his lodge. Having got his lodge across the river, all the warriors returned to see how many soldiers they had killed and wounded the day before and reported twenty-nine men killed. They acknowledged at the same time that the Bear had been wounded, one of his arms being broken, besides receiving a shot through the body and one through the knee. Two other Indians were also slightly wounded. "Now," said they, "we have wiped out these soldiers, let us go to the fort and wipe them out there; the houses are of pine, and we can easily burn them." Mr. Bordeau said to them to take his counsel for once and not attempt to disturb the fort. The Indians then said they would go to Gratiot's (the American Fur Company's establishment) and take the goods belonging to the government, which were there awaiting the arrival of the Indian agent to be distributed amongst them, and at the same time I saw some thirty or forty of them going to Gratiot's. The remainder then left Bordeau's and went to overtake their village, and, fifteen minutes after, the wounded soldier before spoken of appeared again, and Mr. Bordeau was warned again that he had better advise him to conceal himself until the young men had left the vicinity. The soldier then went to the brushwood, near the river, and concealed himself.

About this time Mr. Bordeau and myself went down towards the river to see how many of the troops they had killed and what they had done with the guns. We found the larger howitzer on the ground where it had been dismounted. They had taken all the ammunition belonging to the guns, as well as the small howitzer, with them.

Mr. Grattan and two men were found near the large gun, and the remainder of the party were scattered along the road for a mile or mile and a half, all dead, and mostly killed by arrows. The Indians again made their appearance, and we returned to the house and watched their motions coming over the hills. Mr. B. said that they were either going to attack the fort or take the goods of the Indian agent at Gratiot's, and in about an hour afterwards an Indian appeared with a pack-mule loaded with these same goods.

The Indians stopping about the premises, seeing this, suggested that the goods belonged as much to them as to those who were appropriating them. It was better that they should go and take their share of the spoil, and, when they had departed for that object, the wounded soldier again made his appearance, and Mr. Raynall concealed him in the blacksmith shop. Finally we started him for the fort in a buggy, which broke down on the way, when I took him on my horse for the remainder of the way.—O. Allen.

I certify that the above is a true copy of the original statement in my possession, which original, being taken on paper by myself under the dictation of Mr. Allen, was written too hurriedly to be very legible, which is the reason for sending this copy instead. O. F. [Oscar F.] Winship, asst. adj. gen., Fort Kearny, Sept. 16, 1854. Respectfully forwarded to the commander of the Department of the West.

I regard this statement as the most reliable one I have yet heard, of the catastrophe of the 19th of August, near Fort Laramie. It is given by an individual who appears to be entirely disinterested, he having arrived at Fort Laramie from California but the day before the event transpired. He accompanied the expedition to Bordeau's house, from the top of which he witnessed all the movements of both parties. O. F. Winship, Fort Kearny, Sept. 16, 1854.

O. [Obridge] Allen, statement, late August 1854, in *House of Representatives Reports*, No. 63; O. Allen, *Allen's Guide Book and Map to the Gold Fields of Kansas & Nebraska and Great Salt Lake City* (Washington, D.C.: R. A. Waters, 1859; facsimile edition by Nolie Mumey, Denver: privately published, 1953). Allen and Bordeaux supported each other's statements regarding the interpreter's lack of sobriety. One error, though, that Allen introduced into the record was the interpreter's name, which he reversed to "Lucien Auguste" and which was repeated by Capt. Oscar F. Winship. To make matters worse, this error continued in Paul's *Blue Water Creek and the First Sioux War, 1854–1856* when the author, aware of the discrepancy in the various statements, flipped a coin and chose wrong. The research of John D. McDermott for this book now sets the record straight.

12. Oscar F. Winship, army officer, September 1, 1854

What transpired immediately after, there is much confusion,
contradiction, and uncertainty.

The appearance of Capt. Oscar Fingal Winship at Fort Laramie on August 26 changed everything. On his own initiative he commenced an investigation, the results of which served as the foundation for the documentary record of the event. Fortunately he possessed perfect credentials for the job. He came to the fort as part of a cross-country inspection trip that he had undertaken for the Department of the West, and he only coincidentally reached Laramie, one of many posts he examined that summer, a few days after the event. Casting a critical eye on the situation, he accumulated many of the accounts that follow in this compendium. Winship also offered authoritative, and to his discredit, overly dramatic appraisals of who was to blame (the Indians) and how the government should respond ("teaching these barbarians a lesson"). Although far from a dispassionate investigator, his role in preserving the history of the Grattan massacre cannot be minimized, nor can his role as a later instrument of the U.S. Army's vengeance.

An occurrence has come to my knowledge since my arrival at this post, which, in my judgment, demands from me a special report, although I am informed that the main facts in the matter have already been reported to the commander of the department.

A large body of Sioux Indians, composed of the bands of the Brules, Ogalalos, and Minicoujons, had been encamped six or eight miles below Fort Laramie for some time previous to the 19th ultimo, awaiting the arrival of the Indian agent, General Whitfield, to receive their annuities of presents. On the day previous to the date just named, an ox, belonging to a train of Mormon emigrants, was captured and killed by a Miniconjon Indian; in what manner and under what circumstances I must leave the general commanding the department to judge from the conflicting statements herewith transmitted.

On the same day that this depredation was committed, and the same that was complained of by the owner of the ox, a very influential man among the Sioux, called the Bear, chief of the band of Brules, came to the commanding officer of Fort Laramie, Second Lieut. H. B. [Hugh B.] Fleming, 6th Infantry, and reported the circumstances of the case. He said that the offender was a Minicoujon Indian, residing, for the time being, in the Brule camp, and suggested the propriety of sending a detachment of troops to demand him;

in which event, he had no doubt that the man would readily be given up or language to that effect.

Accordingly, on the 19th of August, 1854, a party of twenty-nine enlisted men, of company G, 6th Infantry, under the command of Brevet Second Lieut. John L. Grattan, of the same regiment, was ordered to bring in the Indian, if practicable, without unnecessary risks.

The Sioux encampment was situated on the north fork of the Platte, between Gratiot's trading-house of the American Fur Company and that of a Mr. Bordeau, which are distant five and eight miles, respectively, from Fort Laramie, following the Oregon route down the Platte. The Ogalalos and Minicoujons lay between Gratiot's house and the Brule camp and stretched along a mile and a half or two miles, parallel to and between the road and the river. They had to be passed, of course, in order to reach the camp of the Brules, which lay with one extremity resting on or near the lower extremity of the Minicoujon camp, and the other on the Oregon road in the vicinity of Bordeau's trading-house. The Brule camp was semi-circular in figure, having its convexity towards the river, and having in the rear of it a slight but abrupt depression in the ground, partially overgrown with bushes.

Lieutenant Grattan left the fort about 3 o'clock P.M., with his party and an interpreter, for the Brule camp. Arrived at Gratiot's, he halted and caused his small-arms to be loaded, without capping. He then proceeded about two miles further—that is to say, near the upper extremity of the Brule camp—and halted again to load two pieces of artillery (a 12-pounder howitzer and a mountain howitzer) with which he had been provided. He here explained to the party the nature of the service to be performed and how it was to conduct itself; then, resuming his march, he moved on to Bordeau's house, sent for Mr. Bordeau himself, and requested him to go for the chief above named, called the Bear, with the view to availing himself of the authority and influence of that Indian for the accomplishment of his mission. The Bear came but could not or would not deliver up the accused Minicoujon, and Lieutenant Grattan was, therefore, compelled to seek and take by force, if need be, the offender, or submit to the mortification of retiring without having accomplished the object of his mission, and, rather than do this, he resolved boldly to enter the Brule camp and take the Indian at all hazards, having previously informed himself of the precise locality of the offender. This was nearly in the centre of the camp and not far from the lodge of the Bear.

Up to this moment all the statements, verbal and written, which I have been able to obtain, substantially agree, but, as to what transpired immediately after, there is much confusion, contradiction, and uncertainty, owing, doubtless, to the conflicting interests, prejudices, and predilections of the spectators of the same and to the hurried and confused movement of events ever incident to crises of danger. That which appears certain is that, so soon as Lieutenant Grattan commenced his movement into the Brule camp, the younger warriors, not only of that band, but of the whole Sioux camp, commenced preparing to resist the capture of the Minicoujon depredator by assembling in brushwood and behind the bank, before alluded to as characterizing the ground in the rear of the Brule village. Not only this, but the old men, in council, clamored for delay, thereby indicating that they were unable to restrain their warriors or that they were playing into their hands by giving them time for preparation. Lieutenant Grattan doubtless imagined that these indications were all unfavorable to the object of his expedition and determined to bring the matter of an issue at once by submitting the alternative of an immediate surrender of the offending Minicoujon or instant hostilities against the Brules. The result proves what must have been the reply of the Indians, for, although it is impossible to ascertain which party struck the first blow, it is positively established beyond all contradiction that the troops had scarcely time to make a single discharge of their small-arms and the two pieces of artillery they carried with them before their commander and a large portion of their numbers were struck dead upon the ground they occupied. Those who escaped instant slaughter, after making a fruitless effort to disengage themselves from the network formed by a thousand or fifteen hundred warriors, fell fighting, individually or in small parties, until the whole detachment was, in the forcible Indian phraseology, completely "wiped out," but one man having escaped, with great difficulty, to the fort, and he died in two or three days afterwards of his wounds.

[Here is where the incomplete version in *House Executive Documents*, No. 63, ends. The Winship report continues:]

The above are all the reliable facts which I have been able to gather of this unfortunate affair, except that the interpreter, Mr. Lucien August [*sic*], who accompanied the expedition and who was also killed, was undoubtedly intoxicated and behaved in a very indecorous and offensive manner towards the Indians. His conduct unquestionably irritated the young men very much, but it is preposterous to assert, as many do here, that the insolence of a drunken interpreter, whose language the Indians well knew to be his own and not that of the officer for whom he came to interpret, was the only or even the principal cause of the massacre of the troops. He is well known to have been very obnoxious to the Brules, and his blood was doubtless sought for with more eagerness than that of any other individual of the party, but, if his death alone were desired, it is obvious that it could have been much more easily and safely accomplished than by an open and audacious act of hostility against the government of the United States, and this is further evident from the events which followed and which could have had no connexion whatever with the then butchered interpreter.

Immediately after the massacre of Lieutenant Grattan and his party, the Indians, intoxicated by their victory over the troops, whom they had hitherto regarded with respect and even fear, thought to crown their success by an assault upon the fort, which they knew to be in a very defenceless condition after the destruction of so large a portion of its feeble garrison, but it was not difficult to persuade them to reject an enterprise which offered them but few chances for success and no corresponding reward in case of victory, for they would have been compelled to burn up the buildings of the fort and all it contained in order to reach its garrison. They preferred the safer and better-rewarding exploit of plundering Gratiot's trading-house of the American Fur Company of the government goods there deposited, which only awaited the arrival of the Indian agent to be distributed among them. This insult to the government of the United States was perpetrated on the morning following the massacre of Lieutenant Grattan's party and may be regarded as the sequel to that barbarous outrage. There being no further mischief to do in this vicinity, which could be committed with impunity, they left for the north, probably for their accustomed haunts on White river, destroying on their way the houses, farming implements, &c., belonging to the government farm, which is located some twelve miles north of Fort Laramie, besides carrying off some ten or twelve animals, which they captured in the combat.

It is not for me to anticipate what action, if any, the government will take in this matter, although I cannot refrain from expressing it as my settled conviction, founded upon personal observation of not only the Sioux, but of the other principal tribes of the plains, that the time has now fully arrived for teaching these barbarians a lesson, which they are as yet very far from having learned, and that is how to appreciate and respect the power, the justice, the generosity, and magnanimity of the United States. It is a notorious fact—one which has been vouched for by every man I have met with who has resided or travelled upon the plains—that the Indians listen with contemptuous incredulity to the tales of their chiefs and great men who have visited the States, relative to the numbers and power of the whites. So true is this that those chiefs dare not tell the tithe of what they have seen in the States, lest they should be branded as liars, madmen, or fools and thus lose all influence and respect among their tribes. But I shall speak more fully upon this subject in the general report of the tour of inspection which I am now making [see account no. 27], where it can be more legitimately treated.

Should an expedition be sent against the Sioux, I cannot too strongly recommend that it be directed by way of the Missouri, upon which streams and its tributaries the Eau-qui-court or Running Water [Niobrara River], White river, Strayan [Cheyenne?], and Moro [Moreau], the Titons [Tetons] or Southern Sioux mostly live. Fort Pierre I should consider the most eligible point from which to operate against the Brules and Minicoujons, and Fort Laramie for operating against the Ogalalas. Troops could, and should, be sent to reinforce Fort Laramie at once, and a strong force might be despatched up the Missouri next spring, when the river opens—say early in April. The great advantages of sending troops up the Missouri are—first, that transportation by that route can be had which shall be cheaper, and much more speedy, than that by land; and, secondly, the appearance upon the Upper Missouri of a respectable body of troops would have all the effect of a surprise upon the Indians. Moreover, the distance of Fort Pierre from Fort Laramie is but little more than half of that from Fort Leavenworth to the latter, so that Fort Laramie might well be supplied from Fort Pierre, as there is already a tolerable wagon-road between the two points. There are other military considerations which indicate the propriety, if not the necessity, of establishing a post high up on the Missouri, and which I shall venture to urge in a project for the better occupation of the Indian country, to be set forth in my general report.

In conclusion, I would state that I have not deemed it necessary to repeat all the idle and inconsistent tales afloat here in regard to the incidents of the conflict of the 19th of August, such, for example, as relate to the initiative in the combat—whether Lieutenant Grattan shot the Bear, or the Bear Lieutenant Grattan, whether the Bear urged Lieutenant Grattan not to proceed to extremities, as some say, or whether he bantered him by saying, "You are a soldier—go and take the accused," as others assert. It would be impossible to reconcile all these conflicting statements—which are mainly the result of conflicting interests, prejudices, and predilections—as it would be immaterial to the true point at issue so to do. It should be borne in mind that the question is: had the government agent and commanding officer at Fort Laramie a right to demand the surrender of the offending Indian? If so—and I apprehend that no one will question this right—there can be no difficulty in pronouncing upon the character of the act by which a gallant officer and thirty men, in the service of the government, lost their lives in the effort to enforce said demand.

All collateral issues, got up by interested persons, to weaken the effect on the public mind of the stubborn fact that a detachment of United States troops were butchered to a man in endeavoring to perform a duty, recognised as perfectly legitimate by even the savages themselves, will, I trust, be treated as they deserve, and the government will doubtless know how to vindicate its own dignity and to protect the lives and property of its citizens.

Capt. Oscar F. Winship, assistant adjutant general, Fort Laramie, N. T. [Nebraska Territory], to Bvt. Maj. F. N. Paige [Capt. Francis Nelson Page], assistant adjutant general, headquarters, Department of the West, Jefferson Barracks, Mo., Sept. 1, 1854, in *House of Representatives Reports*, No. 63; the complete version appears in *Senate Executive Documents*, No. 91.

13. James Bordeaux, September 2, 1854

The Lieutenant came to me to learn the best way to get the offender.

This is yet another version by James Bordeaux, prompted by an August 31 request by agent Whitfield to document "what you know as to the cause of the recent difficulty." Given the choices posed by the agent—an environment of theft and violence, the temptation of the annuity goods, and a provocative interpreter—Bordeaux this time pointed the finger at Lieutenant Grattan for failing to heed the experienced frontiersman's sage advice and more controversially testified that the soldiers fired first. As evidenced in his subsequent reports, Captain Winship could hardly resist taking exception to the latter charge. Regardless of his perceived biases, the savvy trader demonstrated his skill in dealing with the Lakotas by saving his and many other lives after the Grattan killing when emotions flashed hot.

I have not the honor of your acquaintance, but from the situation of the country at the present time I take the liberty of writing to you to inform you of facts, as near as possible, concerning the fight between the United States

troops and the Sioux Indians on the 19th of last month, I having been an
eye-witness to the battle and having heard the true causes, I think, of its
having occurred. On the 17th of last month there was a train of Mormon
emigrants passed the village of the Brules, Wazzazies, and Ogalalla bands
of Sioux Indians, which were camped on the Platte river, six miles, more
or less, below Fort Laramie, and after the train had got pretty well past the
village, there was a man behind the train driving a lame cow, and by some
means or other the cow got frightened and ran towards the village. The man
in turn having some fears, and not knowing that the Indians would not
harm him, he left the cow, and an Indian, a stranger, from another band of
Sioux called the Minne-Cousha, killed the cow, and they ate it, and accordingly the emigrants, as they passed the fort, reported the affair, and on the
19th Lieutenant Grattan, with a command of twenty-nine soldiers, with the
interpreter, came to the village to make the arrest of the Indian who killed
the cow. The Lieutenant came to me to learn the best way to get the offender,
and I told him that it was better to get the chief to try and get the offender to
give himself up by his own good will, but he was not willing. The offender
requested of the Indians to let him do as he pleased, for he wanted to die
and that the balance of the Indians would not have anything to do with the
affair, and then the Lieutenant asked of me to go in the village with him,
and I started to go, when another express came and said that the offender
would not give himself up, and then the Lieutenant asked of me to go in the
village with him, and I started to go, and then the Lieutenant asked me to
show him the lodge that the offender was in, and I did so. He then marched
with his men into the village within about sixty yards of said lodge and then
fired upon the Indians. The first fire was made by the soldiers, and there was
one Indian wounded, and then the chiefs harangued to the young men not to
charge on the soldiers, that, being that they, the soldiers, had wounded one
Indian, they possibly would be satisfied, but the Lieutenant ordered his men
to fire their cannon and muskets, and accordingly the chiefs that had went
with the soldiers to help make the arrest ran, and in the fire they wounded
the Bear, chief of the Wazzazies, and as soon as the soldiers' fire was over,
the Indians in turn rushed and killed the Lieutenant and five men by their
cannon, and the balance of the soldiers took to flight and were all killed in
one mile or so from the cannon, and, when the Indians returned, they rushed
on my houses and tried to massacre us all, but, for some friends among the
Indians, we were able to stop them in their career and succeeded in pacifying

them. They also talked of coming to the fort and killing all of the soldiers, but, by my begging of the chiefs, they succeeded in stopping them. I told them that, if they did not do any more harm, possibly their Father would look over [overlook] the matter. The Indians then rushed into my store and helped themselves to what goods they wanted; also outside of the houses they helped themselves to cattle and horses. They kept us up and on guard all night, and I kept them, by talking, not to use any further means of destruction towards the whites and soldiers. The next morning they went to the American Fur Company's houses and took by force their goods that had been sent up by the government for their annual payment and were stored at that place; also they broke open the store of the American Fur Company and helped themselves to what they wanted. So no more at present.

Witness that the above is correct, the undersigned being present: Antoine Raynall, Peter Pew [Pugh], Zofiel Graph [Tofiel Groph], Antonio Le Whone [also spelled Lahonn], Samuel Smith, Paul [Pedro] Vial, Joseph Jewett [Jouett].

Respectfully forwarded to the commander of the Department of the West. In transmitting this statement I feel it incumbent on me to inform the department commander that Mr. Bordeau is an Indian trader and has a Brule wife and several Sioux connexions. His interests, of course, are opposed to the rupture between the government and the Sioux. The endorsers of his statement I am not acquainted with, except by repute. They are all mountain men, who, if we may credit the character they give each other, and the character they bear among disinterested persons, cannot be regarded as very reliable. At all events some of them stand charged here with making two different statements of the massacre of Lieutenant Grattan's party, from which imputation Mr. Bordeau himself has not escaped, although I am inclined to think he meant to be candid. He was not on the ground when the conflict commenced but was occupied in putting his houses in a defensive state. When, therefore, he speaks so positively as to which party fired first, he evidently betrays a strong bias in the premises. This feeling would commend a careful perusal. O. F. [Oscar F.] Winship, Fort Laramie, Sept. 2, 1854.

James Bordeau[x], statement, "Per Samuel Smith," Fort Laramie, Sept. 2, 1854, in *House of Representatives Reports*, No. 63; J. W. [John W.] Whitfield, Fort Laramie, to James Bordeau[x] et al., Aug. 31, 1854, Upper Platte Agency, Microfilm Publication No. 234, roll 889, NARA. See also James Bordeaux to John W. Whitfield, Fort Laramie, Aug. 29, 1854, in *Annual Report of the Commissioner of Indian Affairs, 1854*, 93–94.

14. Edward Claudey et al., traders, September 1, 1854

The Indians were all perfectly quiet.

The employees of the rival American Fur Company establishment, a few miles from Bordeaux's and the site of the heaviest fighting, weighed in. Collectively they gave no evidence to support the theory of a premeditated massacre.

We the undersigned personally appeared before John W. Whitfield, U.S. Indian Agent for the Upper Platte Agency, and after being duly sworn deposeth and saith that they were present at the trading houses of Messrs. P. [Pierre] Chouteau, Jr. & Co., near Fort Laramie, at the time the Indians came to take the goods belonging to their nation (the Sioux annuity goods for 1854); that when they came to the house, they demanded the key of the room where said goods were stored; that the clerk who had the key left the house to avoid giving up the key; the Indians then proceeded to break the lock and went in and took all of said goods and also a portion of the goods belonging to Messrs. P. Chouteau, Jr. & Co. That previous to the fight with the U.S. troops the Indians were all perfectly quiet and patiently awaiting the arrival of their agent; that they made no threats of taking the goods by force previous to the difficulty aforesaid that we ever heard of. That the Indians stated, when they came to take the goods, that they took them because they knew that, since they had killed the soldiers, that the agent would not give them their goods; that therefore they would have to take them. That the Goods were taken on the 20th Aug., the day after the fight with the U.S. troops. And further these deponents saith not.

Edward Claudey, John Savard, J. B. [John B.] Didier, and Joseph Turgeon, affidavit, Sept. 1, 1854, LR, Upper Platte Agency, RG 75, NARA. From information found in the Fort Laramie Collections, Turgeon's resume mirrored those of many of his French-American colleagues: trader to the Lakota since the 1840s, married into the tribe and raised several children, worked in the North Platte area through the 1860s, and probably moved away after the establishment of the Dakota Territory reservations in the 1870s.

15. Jean Baptiste Moncravie et al., traders, September 1, 1854

Interpreter and Officer were much excited.

But the American Fur Trade employees were not finished giving an account, or maybe agent Whitfield was not finished with them. A letter of the same date reiterated their sworn statement.

Although not necessarily eyewitnesses to Grattan's demise, they would have seen his command pass by. Their collective description of both Grattan and Lucien as being "much excited" was potentially devastating to the officer's reputation and the army's moral position since the term had an alternate meaning in that day—drunkenness. Of course, the concern of these men was to shift any potential blame from the company to others. The loss of the annuities—considered inviolate U.S. property before their issuance—became more and more important in the government's deliberations and growing anger.

In answer to your letter commanding a statement from us in the late affray between the U.S. troops under the command of Lieut. Grattan and the Sioux Indians, we believe that, if the Interpreter had spoken well to said Indians without abusing them, the affair would not have happened, for when they passed here both Interpreter and Officer were much excited.

They were very anxious for your arrival to see you and get the presents, for they were out of meat and were going to surround buffalo the following day after the affair took place so unexpectedly. They always have treated the whites with good will as heretofore; they have not committed more depredations this year than before; they never threatened of taking their goods by force; they only thought about that till after the defeat of the troops.

The goods being stored in the A. F. Co. store had nothing to do with the difficulty; in lieu of that we think that, if the goods had been in the Fort [Laramie], would have been the occasion of the destruction of said garrison, knowing that the force was small, the troops being separated.

J. B. [Jean Baptiste] Moncravie, Jean [John] Savard, J. B. [John B.] Didier, Joseph Turgeon, [——] Pratte, and [——] Robvin [?] to Col. [John W.] Whitfield, Fort John, Sept. 1, 1854, LR, Upper Platte Agency, RG 75, NARA. In the years to follow, the property losses sustained by the traders and their claims for damages continued as a source of contention—and documentation. These claims will be explored more fully in the subsequent volume of compiled Grattan-related accounts.

16. Orville A. Nixon, civilian traveler, September 2–3, 1854

We . . . stopped to walk over the battle ground.

Orville A. Nixon accompanied Whitfield, a fellow Tennessean and young lawyer-to-be, on the long road to Fort Laramie. Surviving portions of his day-to-day account commenced on their return to the States and past the recent killing field, which made a deep impression on the on-site observer.

[Sept. 2, 1854] We left Laramie Fort about 3 o'clock. Traveled 6 miles and encamped at the store of the fur trading company. These traders were robbed of nearly all they had. This is the place where the goods were deposited.

[Sept. 3] We broke our carill [corral] later than usual. We traveled down the North Plat[te]. Saw several Indian graves. All of them bury all their dead upon forks high off the ground. We traveled 4 miles and stopped to walk over the battle ground, the place of the late massacre. It was a level spot where part of the lodges was placed; the other was under a small hill or beach [bench?]. The Cason [caisson?] was in the heart of the village. I saw the lodge poles that was cut by the [cannon]balls. It was ten feet from the ground. The Lieutenant Gratten [sic] and five soldiers sank down by the Cason, and their carcasses still their, the flesh eaten off by the wolves. The battle ground was strewn with soldiers clothes, broken arrows, knives, &c.

We traveled 20 m[ile]s and camped on the North Platte. Our company was increased. We have 3 women with us.

"Orville A. Nixon Journal, Fort Laramie to Westport, Kansas [sic], 29 August to 28 September 1854," HM 17012, Huntington Library, San Marino, Calif.; "Orville A. Nixon," Biographies of Hickman County, Tennessee, Genealogy Trails History Group, http://genealogytrails.com/tenn/hickman/biographies_n.html. A typescript of the Nixon journal, "Book Second of My Trip to the Rocky Mountains, up the South Platte and North Platte Rivers," by James W. Dappert, Taylorville, Ill., can be found in Miscellaneous Manuscripts Collection, Kansas State Archives, Kansas Historical Society, Topeka. The transcriber added a note at the end of the September 3 entry regarding the three women: "Presumably widows of the dead men." If it referred to recent widows of the enlisted men, this observation may be correct, although Nixon makes no other mention of them in his journal.

17. John Jamison, civilian mail carrier, September 3, 1854
You will therefore excuse me for not giving all the particulars.

Correspondent and mail employee John Jamison knew a scoop when he heard it, and he made sure his hometown newspaper received the news first. He provided lurid details, for example, the number of arrows found in Grattan's corpse. Undoubtedly he was the "Jameson" who would lose his life on November 13, 1854, when Indians attacked the U.S. Mail party near Fort Laramie.

The following letter from Jamison, formerly of this city and now in the employ of the Salt Lake Mail Company, was received just before going to press. We sincerely hope that our correspondent has been imposed upon and that the details are not true in fact. Mr. J. is a printer and while in Independence was at work in this office. We rely upon what he writes us as being true, if he has not been imposed upon by someone assuming to be an express:

Big Blue, Sept. 3rd, 1854. Editors *Dispatch:* An express has just arrived from Fort Laramie bearing the news of a great fight between a body of Sioux Indians and twenty-five United States soldiers under command of Lieut. Graten [*sic*].

The facts as given by the express are about as follows: A lame cow belonging to the Mormons was driven into the Sioux village, consisting of about six hundred lodges of Brullus [Brulés] and Ogalolies [Oglalas]. Report was made to Lieut. Graton, who demanded of the Chief the surrender for punishment the Indian who had committed the theft. The Chief (Wa-toe Iowa) promised that he would, if possible, give up the animal. He returned without the Indian and stated that he could not bring him alive, but that, if the Lieut. still demanded him, he would kill him (the Indian) and drag him to them. Lieut. G. replied that, if there was any killing to be done, he would do it and immediately ordered his soldiers (they being in the centre of the village) to right and left. This order was obeyed by first firing two rounds with their cannon, and to no effect, and then with small guns, which had little or no effect.

The Indians then made a charge upon the soldiers, killing all but one, he being badly wounded. Lieut. G. had 16 arrows in his body. The interpreter had a dozen or more.

The Indians then went to the station of the American Fur Company [and] destroyed all their goods which could not be carried off. From each different station they carried off about 10 to 15 thousand dollars worth of goods.

The soldiers only wounded two Indians, one the Chief above mentioned. The soldiers ran, after [firing?] their small guns.

Just think of it! Our soldiers, only 25 in number, marching to a village of six hundred lodges and commencing an attack upon them. Each lodge will average three warriors, making 1,800 men against a force of only 25 men, they completely surrounded by their own act.

The mail must start immediately; you will therefore excuse me for not giving all the particulars. Truly yours, John Jamison.

John Jamison, "From the Plains," *Liberty Weekly Tribune* (Mo.), Sept. 15, 1854, from the *Independence Dispatch.* The author's frontier knowledge was reflected in an almost casually mentioned fact: one Indian lodge contained an estimated three men of fighting age. This ratio, give or take, appears throughout nineteenth-century literature when estimating the strength of Plains Indian congregations. R. Eli Paul, "Counting Indians," *Wild West* 18 (Dec. 2005): 27. The news of Jamison's later death appeared as "Letter from Salt Lake" in the *New York Times*, Dec. 7, 1854.

18. Anonymous correspondent, September 5, 1854

An express has arrived . . . bringing the most appalling intelligence.

On September 5, 1854, an anonymous correspondent fleshed out the report from Fort Laramie that arrived that day by horseback at Fort Leavenworth. As the site of the western extension of the nation's telegraph network, the Kansas fort served its purpose well because, for all practical purposes, the Grattan massacre had now become national news.

It seems unlikely that a Vermonter would have been the original intended recipient of this account, although the writer generously provided considerable context for a novice Eastern reader. The letter has yet to be found earlier in another newspaper.

A correspondent at Fort Le[a]venworth has sent the following account of the massacre near Fort Laramie.

Fort Leavenworth, Kansas, Tuesday, Sept. 5, 1854.

An express has arrived this afternoon from Fort Laramie, Nebraska territory, bringing the most appalling intelligence.

It appears that the Sioux Indians who occupy a large tract of country surrounding that fort have repeatedly taken advantage of the weakness of the forces stationed there by trespassing on the property of overland emigrants and otherwise annoying them.

A few days previous to the 19th of August, one of the tribe deliberately shot an ox belonging to a Mormon emigrant. This outrage the commanding officer of the garrison, Lieut. Flemming [*sic*], in the absence of Capt. [William S.] Ketchum, felt bound to notice, as such acts had before occurred. The chief of the tribe, Bear, said he would give up the offender if he was sent for. Accordingly on the 18th, a detachment under command of Lieut. Grattan, consisting of an interpreter, a sergeant, a corporal, and twenty privates, went in pursuit of him. On arriving at the camp of the Indians the offender said he would die rather than be given up and stepping forward fired an arrow at the soldiers. The soldiers returned the fire, when the other Indians commenced a fearful attack. There were about twelve hundred present, and in less than five minutes they had slaughtered the entire detachment, including the fearless lieutenant in command. Only one Indian, the chief, was killed. The messenger who brings the report started from Laramie on the 23rd ult.

Fort Laramie is very near the Rocky Mountains and is about 630 miles northwest from here. Only one small company of infantry was stationed there—a force which military men tell me is altogether inadequate. The Sioux is a large and warlike tribe, capable of bringing into the field 18,000 warriors. They have for a long time defied the power of the garrison and have not unfrequently sent in reports that they were going to exterminate all the troops stationed there. The country on the route to California and Oregon is poorly protected. The only fort between here and Laramie is that of Kearny on the Platt[e] river, about half way, so that the nearest assistance, if any, is three hundred miles distant.

The able secretary of war, Gen. [Jefferson] Davis, saw the necessity of more extensive forces in the Indian territory and in his last report recommended that congress should provide two additional regiments.

A few small companies of soldiers ought not thus to be placed at the mercy of savages. The helpless emigrants should be protected, and the cheapest way to afford this protection and keep down the Indians is to furnish our forts with sufficient troops.

These suggestions are not dictated by the excitement of the moment but are the results of some little observations in the Indian country.

Anonymous, "Frightful Encounter with the Indians at Fort Laramie—A Whole Detachment Massacred," Fort Leavenworth, Kans., Sept. 5, 1854, in *Vermont Patriot & State Gazette* (Montpelier), Oct. 6, 1854.

19. Newman S. Clarke, army officer, September 7, 1854
Fleming . . . needs more troops as soon as possible.

The startling report from Fort Laramie passed through normal channels when it was relayed to St. Louis, Missouri, the headquarters of the Department of the West. Brigadier General Newman S. Clarke, department commander, then forwarded it on, along with his immediate plans to reinforce the fort, to his superiors in Washington. Officials made little effort to shield the public from news of such magnitude, and military correspondence was routinely shared with major American newspapers, which rapidly disseminated stories throughout the country.

I communicate the following despatch just received from Fort Leavenworth: By express just arrived from Fort Laramie, Lieutenant Fleming wishes me to telegraph that on the 18th of August an Indian (Sioux) killed an ox belonging to an emigrant train, close to Fort Laramie. The head chief reported the fact to Lieutenant Fleming and offered to give up the offender. Brevet Second Lieutenant Grattan, with the interpreter, Sergeant Favor [Faver], Corporal McNulty, and twenty privates, were sent to receive him. The whole detachment were massacred without exception. How it occurred, Lieutenant Fleming is unable to state. No reliable information as to the number of Indians killed and wounded. The Bear, head chief, is reported killed. The Indians are hostile, menacing the fort. All the men are on duty, and Lieutenant Fleming thinks he can hold the fort but needs more troops as soon as possible. I shall order one or two companies from Fort Riley to proceed to Fort Laramie immediately.

Col. N. S. [Newman S.] Clarke, Sixth Infantry, headquarters, Department of the West, Jefferson Barracks, telegram to Col. Samuel Cooper, adjutant general, Washington, D.C., Sept. 7, 1854, Reports from the Department of the West, "Report of the Secretary of War," *House Executive Documents*, No. 1. The *Missouri Republican*, one of the great newspapers of St. Louis and the West, published its own "special dispatch" on September 10, 1854. Its article, "By Western Telegraph, the Battle at Fort Laramie," gave an ever-expanding readership the further boiled-down news of the Grattan disaster, herewith reproduced: "On the 18th ult., near Fort Laramie, a fight occurred between Lieut. Grattan, in command of twenty-three soldiers, and eight hundred Sioux Indians. All the soldiers were killed except one, and he was wounded. After the battle, the Indians went to the American Fur Company's station and destroyed all the goods which they could not carry off, amounting to ten or fifteen thousand dollars worth (It is understood that two companies of troops have been ordered from Fort Riley, to the relief of the garrison at Fort Laramie.)."

20. John Taylor, Utah official, September 12, 1854

The chief before he died told his people ... not to interfere with the emigrants.

News traveled almost as quickly to the West as it did to the East, and the primary recipient was Brigham Young, the leader of the Utah colony. In September 1854, John Taylor, like his Mormon peer Ezra Benson, a member of the Quorum of the Twelve Apostles, sent back to Young what facts he could gather on the trail before reaching Fort Laramie himself. The mention of the Indians shooting *three* Mormon cows, along with other inaccuracies in his letter, may reflect the expected mixture of fact with rumor. Of more importance than such details, though, was whether the emigrant road remained open and safe for the Latter-day Saints.

You have heard no doubt of the Indian difficulties at Laramie. The nearest account we can get of it is as follows. Three cows were shot belonging to Horace Eldre[d]ge's camp. They made complaints to the officers of the fort upon which a detachment of 25 men besides officers and interpreters were sent to demand the offenders. The head chief of the Sioux, Old Bear, deserved a parley before he gave them up. It is supposed that the interpreter misconstrued his words and said that they wanted to fight, upon which the captain [lieutenant] ordered his men to fire on the chief who fell mortally wounded. The Indians immediately massacreed [sic] the whole party which amounted to thirty-one. They proceeded immediately to the American Fur Companies [Company's] fort and took their annuities and all the goods belonging to the company amounting over their receipts to $20,000. The chief before he died told his people to Kile [kill] the soldiers but not to interfere with the emigrants who have hitherto passed in safety.

There was at that time about the fort about 8,000 of the Arapahoes, Choannes [Cheyennes], and Sioux. We apprehend no danger and hear the last of our camps had passed in safety.

John Taylor, Green River, to Brigham Young, Salt Lake City, Sept. 12, 1854, General Correspondence, Incoming, Letters from Church Leaders and Others, 1840–1877, Church History Library, Church of Jesus Christ of Latter-day Saints, Salt Lake City. Taylor succeeded Young to the church presidency after the latter's death in 1877. Hosea Stout, another church leader, recorded on September 28, 1854: "Eastern mail came in to day. The report of some 25 or 30 officers and soldiers being killed by Indians at Larimie [sic] is confirmed." Juanita Brooks, ed., *On the Mormon Frontier: The Diary of Hosea Stout*, vol. 2 (Salt Lake City: University of Utah Press, 1964), 528.

21. Thomas Sutherland, Utah emigrant, September 12, 1854
I have visited the grave.

According to Thomas Sutherland, the clerk for the Robert Campbell–led company, this party of Utah emigrants learned of the Grattan "affray" on August 27, 1854, while on the trail west of Fort Kearny. "We met two mountaineers going . . . to Fort Leavenworth with a dispatch from the commanding officer at Fort Laramie." As the train continued undeterred, between Ash Hollow and Courthouse Rock on September 6 it encountered the Whitfield party, and the agent cautioned them "to be on the look out as all the Indians had left Fort Laram[i]e and had gone, no one knew where." A little over a week later Sutherland reached the Bordeaux trading post and in his other assigned duty as company historian recorded a grisly scene.

[Sept. 14] Thursday. We did not roll untill late in the forenoon in consequence of some of the Brethern, being obliged to trade for cattle. We rolled 8 miles to Bordea[u]x Station. There is mountainears settled here and do blacksmithing and trade oxen and horses. It was at this place that the Indians killed the 29 soldiers with their officers [only one officer was killed]. They are buried close by the road. I have visited the grave, and some of the men's heads are not even covered. It was the settlers that buried them as the remainder of the soldiers could not leave the fort being few in number. There was also a man's face lying on the bank with the teeth firm in the jaw bone, and the flesh appeared recently taken off. Several military gloves were lying on the grass close by. We traveled on 4 miles and met 2 settlers houses where biscuit and beans are sold; indeed one of the houses has a sign board with "Bakery & Refreshments" written on it. We continued on and camped at sun set on the bank of the river after a drive of 14 miles.

Thomas Sutherland, "Robert Campbell Company Report, 1854 August 22," Robert L. Campbell Company, Mormon Pioneer Overland Travel, 1847–1868 (database), Church of Jesus Christ of Latter-day Saints, Salt Lake City. https://history.lds.org/overlandtravel/sources/4931/.

22. Sefroy Iott, trader, September 13, 1854
The first discharge killed Grattan.

B. Gratz Brown, the free-soil Democrat editor of the *Missouri Democrat*, had attended the 1851 treaty council near Fort Laramie as a correspondent for the proslavery Whig newspaper, the *Missouri Republican*. Brown probably crafted this account, which provides details of the interpreter's attempted escape and his last moments and unsurprisingly runs counter to his competitor's narrative. These are the kindest words one will read of Lucien, who Brown must have met in 1851, when he met Conquering Bear.

As was Lucien, Sefroy Iott was employed as an interpreter at Fort Laramie. Safely in the Oglala camp at the time of the massacre, he might be the "express messenger" who carried the first news to the East.

We have received through the medium of Mr. Lefroy [Sefroy] Iott, one of the Sioux interpreters, who came as an express messenger from the scene of the disaster, the full particulars of the late massacre of United States troops at Fort Laramie, which present the outrage in even more glaring colors than could have been anticipated from the brief notice we have already published. They are briefly as follows:

A Mormon emigrant who was traveling the road left, it seems, a lame cow which was unable to travel, and an old Sioux Indian, belonging to the band of Minnecongous found it upon the roadside and killed it. The Mormon stopped with his wagons at Fort Laramie and so soon as he learned that it had been killed, he made complaint to the officer at the fort and demanded redress. The officer in command, Lieutenant Fleming, when the story was told him, at once sent for the head chief of the Sioux—Matteiowan (the Bear)—and demanded that the Minnecongou Indian should be delivered up. Matteiowan informed him that if he would send a file of soldiers he would endeavor to have the Indian surrendered. Lieutenant Fleming then ordered out Lieutenant Grattan, with twenty-two men, and the U.S. Interpreter, Auguste Lucien, to accompany the Sioux chief to the Minnecongou village, which was situated some nine miles below the fort, near "Bordeau's House." The lieutenant with his command marched down, taking with him two six pounders and planted them in the Wa-zah-zie camp where the Indian in question was lodged. Matte-i-o-wan [Conquering Bear] then went into the village and demanded the Indian, but the chief would not listen to him. They told him that they would pay for the cow, or they would replace it or would leave the matter to be settled by the Agent when he came but that they would rather be killed themselves than give up the Indian. Matte-i-o-wan returned, made his statement to Lieut. Grattan, told him if he wanted the Indian, he would have to go and kill him, as he was unable to get him, and then returned to the Sioux camp.

Lieut. Grattan had replied that if there was any killing to be done he would attend to that matter, and accordingly immediately ranged his pieces of artillery and commenced firing upon the village. Three or four muskets were also fired at the same time, but the only result was to knock the top off of one of the lodges and to wound Matte-i-o-wan and his brother, who were standing in front, the former with three balls, the latter but one. So soon as the troops fired, the Indians returned it and pouring upon them a shower of arrows. The first discharge killed Grattan, who was standing by the side of the cannon. As soon as he fell, his command at once lost heart and attempted to fly, leaving their cannon, arms, and everything else. The Sioux then charged upon the flying soldiers and shot and tomahawked every man of them save one, who made his escape by taking down a ravine, and thus getting out of sight. The interpreter who was with the party, Augustine [sic] Lucien, who married a Sioux squaw, jumped on his horse and attempted to make his escape. He succeeded in getting rid of his immediate pursuers and in making a circle around the camp, but instead of striking for the prairie, he very foolishly attempted to run through the Brulie camp, which was directly between him and the fort, and which was already alarmed by the firing. The result was that an Indian ran out and shot his horse with his rifle and then came upon him with his tomahawk. Lucien cried out to him not to kill him as he was a Sioux by marriage, but the only reply the Indian made was to bury his hatchet in his head. The soldier who escaped down the ravine was found by a Sioux, named "Black Heart," and owed his life to his assistance in getting him back to the fort during the night.

The tragedy occurred on the afternoon of the 19th of August, and it was not until the next morning that news of it reached the fort. The Sioux then sent word to the Commandant to send out some of his men to bury his dead, and they would serve them in the same way. They also went to the depot of the American Fur Company, which is near their camp and where the annuity goods ($50,000 worth) were in store, and turned them upon the plain and divided them out.

Lieut. Fleming, upon consultation, sent some five or six of the traders down to see the Sioux and to bury the dead, but they told the traders very explicitly that the quarrel was not one in which they were concerned, and they had better keep out of it, and they drove them back to the fort. The consequence was that when the messenger left, the dead bodies were still lying exposed on the plains, only two, those of Lucien, and another having been buried by two returning Californians, who ventured to execute the hazardous task for $25 apiece.

Nothing further has been heard from the fort at the present time, and it would seem that the report that the Sioux had surrounded Laramie is not confirmed.

At the last accounts Mattie-i-o-wan, who was shot in three places, at the first discharge from the soldiers was on the point of death. In even this brief notice of him, we cannot forbear speaking a word in his praise. We knew him well, and a better friend the white man never had. He was brave and gentle and kind, a wise ruler, a skillful warrior, and respected chieftain. Even in accepting his position, assigned to him four years ago [three years ago in 1851] at the treaty of Laramie, he only consented after much persuasion and then remarked, when he did so, that he "gave his life to the Great Spirit." So far from any charge of treachery attaching to his conduct, his own fate is sufficient proof of his fidelity, and in recording it we feel like inscribing a worthy memorial of one of the most high-toned and chivalric of all the Indians whom we have known.

Auguste Lucien also was one whom all who knew him will deeply lament. A Frenchman by birth and in feeling, yet an American in his latter sympathies, he was one of the most social, true-hearted, and generous of all the voyageurs upon the plains.

His light and joyous humor was always the life of the camp; his skill as a hunter supplied the choicest of game, and his piquant and glowing gossip made the hours pass like a dream beneath the shadow of the mountains. But he has passed to the land of dreams and to the "happy hunting grounds" of which he delighted so to speak, imbued as he was with the fullness of an Indian's faith. May it be his lot to drink of the fresh waters of the new life, and may his spirit find a pleasant resting place.

Missouri Democrat, Sept. 13, 1854, which is a damaged issue; for the complete article, see *North American and United States Gazette* (Philadelphia, Pa.), Sept. 18, 1854; Charles E. Hanson Jr., "Sefroy Iott," *Museum of the Fur Trade Quarterly* 7 (Winter 1971): 4. In 1851 Brown favorably described Conquering Bear as having "an unspotted reputation for honesty, courage, and good behavior. His face indicates intelligence, firmness, and kindness, and his eyes are clear and piercing." *Missouri Republican*, Nov. 23, 1851.

23. Hugh B. Fleming, September 14, 1854

Inventory & final Statement of Serget. William P. Faver

Military regulations mandated that the personal effects of deceased soldiers be accounted for. These were the names—with some variations from other sources—of the enlisted dead. The inventory of their property has not been found.

Enclosed you will receive the Inventory & final Statement of Serget. William P. Faver, Corporal Charles McNulty, Musicians Henry A. Crabbe [Henry August Krappe], Henry E. Lewis, Privates Anthony Boyle, Charles Burke [Burkle],

William Cameron, Michael Collins, John Courtenay, John Cuddy, John Donahoe, James Fitzpatrick, John Flinn, David Hammill, John Mayer, John McNulty, John Meldron, Patrick Murley, Walter Murray, Patrick O'Rourke [O'Rourk], Charles Platenius, Adolphus Plumhoff, Stokely H. Rushing, Stanislaus Saniewski, Thomas Smith, Edward Stevens, John Sweetman, William Whitford, and John Williams, Late of Company "G" 6th Regt. of Infantry who was killed in a Engagement with the Sioux Indians near Fort Laramie, O. R., the 19th of August 1854.

Second Lt. Hugh B. Fleming, Sixth Infantry, commanding Fort Laramie, O. R. [Oregon Route], to Col. Samuel Cooper, adjutant general, Washington, D.C., Sept. 14, 1854, McDermott Collection. A St. Louis newspaper described the late Sergeant Faver as "a young man of fine personal appearance and most correct deportment. . . . We are informed he leaves a wife and one or two children to regret his loss." *Missouri Democrat*, Sept. 11, 1854.

24. William Kenceleur, trader, before September 16, 1854

I did not learn how many Indians were killed.

William Kenceleur, the informant for a western Iowa newspaper, had business interests in the Fort Laramie area, specifically in the engineering and operation of John Richard's toll bridge over the North Platte River, which catered to emigrants. Kenceleur's accurate conveyance of the facts may be questioned, considering his confusion of officer names and responsibilities (Grattan versus Garnett), and compounded by another hand's obvious, added editorial comment.

We are called upon to record another wholesale murder, perpetrated by the Sioux Indians, the latter part of August. Our informant, W. Kensler [William Kenceleur], a citizen of this country, returned from Fort Laramie yesterday [Sept. 15]. From him we obtained the following particulars: A band of six hundred Sioux Indians had been prowling around Choteau's Fort for some time, and on the day prior to the butchery of the soldiers, stole a cow from a Mormon emigrant, four or five miles this side of Fort Laramie. Notice of the theft was immediately conveyed to Lt. Garnet[t], commanding officer at the fort, who with a company of 28 men, immediately started in pursuit of the thieves and soon overtook them. They refused to give up the cow or make any reparation for the theft, and the commanding officer therefore ordered the cannon to be planted in front of the principal thief's tent and after a little further parleying was pointed upward and discharged. The top of the tent was torn off by the discharge; then the infuriated savages rushed the Americans and killed and scalped every one of them. I did not learn how many Indians were killed. After this murderous onslaught, the same braves attacked the American Fur Company's buildings, which they plundered of everything. They also attacked old Bordeaux's trading post and stripped it of everything. They then took up their line of march for Fort Laramie but concluded not to attack it. The force at the fort was too small to attempt to avenge the death of their comrades, and all that could be done was to forward the news of the outrage to Washington. It remains to be seen what action the U.S. authorities will now take. Murder after murder has been committed this season by blood thirsty savages, and as yet no retaliation. If volunteers are wanted, call on the West. Thousands are ready and willing to go and avenge the murder of their friends and neighbors.

William Kenceleur, "Horrible Outrage: Twenty Soldiers Murdered by the Sioux Indians," *Fremont County Journal* (Sidney, Iowa), Sept. 16, 1854. See also Jefferson Glass, *Reshaw: The Life and Times of John Baptiste Richard, Extraordinary Entrepreneur and Scoundrel of the Western Frontier* (Glendo, Wyo.: High Plains Press, 2014), 80–81.

25. Fort Laramie Orders, September 18, 1854
the loss of certain ordnance

Again, the proper military routine, rules, and procedures must be followed, in this instance a committee to investigate the loss by Grattan of his two pieces of artillery. Other accounts mentioned their later recovery from the field of battle. The board's report of its findings has not turned up.

Orders No. 21. Headquarters, Fort Laramie, O.R., Sept. 18, 1854. A Board of Survey to consist of Asst. Surgeon Charles Page, U.S.A., will convene this day for the purpose of examining and reporting upon the loss of certain ordnance and ordnance stores pertaining to the Post of Fort Laramie, O.R., and to Company G, 6th Infy., which were lost in an affair with the Sioux Indians near Fort Laramie, O.R., August 19th, 1854. Also certain ordnance stores reported as unserviceable. Hugh B. Fleming, 2d Lieut., 6th Infy., Comdg.

Fort Laramie Orders, 1854–55, Records of the War Department, U.S. Army Commands, RG 393, NARA; typescript in the Fort Laramie Collections.

26. Ezra T. Benson, Utah official, September 20, 1854
I was on the ground the third day after it was done.

Mormon church official Ezra T. Benson provided a sense of the initial shock of the tragedy and a hint of its impact on the residents of Utah Territory. A "general war" meant the massive involvement of the U.S. Army, a mixed blessing for many who had moved to Zion to avoid such government interactions.

There has been trouble between the soldiers and the Sioux at Laramie, thirty one soldiers being killed. I was on the ground the third day after it was done. The whole country is quite in an excitement, the traders fleeing in all directions and expecting a general war.

All this happened through an unwise move of Lieutenant Gratten [*sic*] and the interpreter. The chief offered to settle the question on fair terms, but the officer would not and commenced firing on the Indians. The cannon was elevated too high and only clipped the tops of the lodge poles; the old chief and his brother were wounded and have since died. Before the troops had time to reload, they were all shot down.

Ezra T. Benson, Pacific Creek, Sept. 20, 1854, "Latest News from Our Immigration," in *Deseret News* (Salt Lake City), Sept. 28, 1854, in Mormon Pioneer Overland Travel (database), https://history.lds.org/overlandtravel/sources/7283/latest-news-from-our-immigration-deseret-news-28-sept-1854-3. Benson's train arrived at Salt Lake on October 3.

Interlude

Recording the Story

Oscar F. Winship, captain of the Second Dragoons, U.S. Army, significantly shaped the events that marked the beginnings of the First Sioux War, as well as the work of subsequent historians, through his selective recording of the facts of the Grattan fight. A native of New York, Winship entered the U.S. Military Academy in 1836, graduated in 1840 twenty-second in his class, and began his service as a second lieutenant in the Second Dragoons, a regiment in which he served his entire life. He participated in the Second Seminole War and received a promotion to first lieutenant in 1844. He saw considerable action in the Mexican-American War, notably in the battles of Palo Alto, Resaca de la Palma, Churubusco, and Molino del Rey, as well as the final assault and capture of Mexico City in September 1847. He distinguished himself, but nothing that rated exceptional mention in a later regimental history. In 1851 he reached captain, his highest rank before his death in late 1855 at age thirty-eight while on leave from the First Sioux War.[1]

Although Captain Winship hardly made an imprint on the historiography of the Grattan fight until only recently, he did leave a lasting legacy.[2] Much of the surviving Indian testimony came as a result of his individual efforts.[3] He also left—or, at least, largely shaped—important historical documents critical to this compendium.

On August 26, 1854, Captain Winship, accompanied by John Whitfield, the Indian agent for the Upper Platte Agency, reached Fort Laramie after a two-month overland trip from Fort Riley, Kansas Territory. Whitfield's job was to dispense annuity goods to the gathered tribes, Winship's to conduct a routine inspection of the post. He had already visited six forts in the Department of the West in carrying out this administrative task. Fortunately for history, his timing could not have been much better. Having been earlier alerted on the trail by persons fleeing the Fort Laramie area, upon arrival at the post he quickly switched hats from inspector to investigator, specifically addressing the questions, How did Lieutenant Grattan get himself killed? By whom? And why?[4]

Winship collected several eyewitness accounts, such as those of trader James Bordeaux and civilian traveler Obridge Allen, along with supporting statements by Second Lt. Hugh Fleming, the post's temporary commander and Grattan's immediate superior, other officers, some civilians, distant bystanders, assorted latecomers, and secondary characters who became farther and farther removed from the events of August 19. Winship then prepared a report on the engagement itself, a compendium of selected primary documents that comprised the official field inquiry into the Grattan fight. The government soon published Winship's document, and its individual accounts are presented in this book. The report also can be found in its entirety in the U.S. Serial Set, where its accessibility as a source has ensured its use by historians ever since—with one caveat.

What one will not find are the written statements of an Oglala and two Brulé Lakota leaders—Man Afraid of His Horses, Little Thunder, and Big Partisan, all of whom had front row seats as the entire saga played out. Winship knew of all three statements; in fact, he copied them at departmental headquarters in St. Louis before forwarding them on to Washington. But they did not make the government publication, where they are conspicuous by their absence. They are presented here in their entirety and raise the question, Why were they ignored?

Simply put, this Indian eyewitness testimony put to the lie the government charge that the Indians planned to kill Grattan. Their imagined conspiracy to lure Grattan to his doom, their apparent savagery with respect to the mutilation of his corpse, and their plunder of government and civilian property after the fact created the justification for a stern response. No less a figure than Jefferson Davis, the nation's secretary of war, immediately drew this same conclusion. The trickling in of new evidence came too late in the timeline of unfolding events. The in-the-field military reprisal of 1855 overtook any substantive bureaucratic and legislative debate.

Winship made another contribution to the historical record. Before his September 2, 1854, departure from Fort Laramie for St. Louis and departmental headquarters, he carried out yet another post inspection. Winship's inspection report, of more immediate importance to military authorities, was far less known and distributed than his other work. One can stumble across the 130-page, handwritten report today in the record group for the Office of the Adjutant General. It long resided buried in a National Archives microfilm publication whose contents before digitization run into the hundreds of rolls and thousands of pages, where many such field reports went to die.[5]

To be fair, a few enterprising Western historians have unearthed several gems from the records of the adjutant general and the inspector general, and collectively they have produced an overlooked and unnamed subgenre in frontier military literature.[6] On the whole these reports, although jammed with description, are not scintillating reading. They offer, however, an excellent snapshot of the aims, aspirations, and motivations of the frontier military for a given time and place. And such is the case with the Winship report, which did not have to wait undiscovered for a century to make an impact.

Obviously the killing of Grattan colored Winship's observations and report. When he later submitted his written narrative in person to his superiors, his observations now carried the additional weight of an eyewitness to war, testimony to the deeds of a fallen comrade and those of an unpunished foe. Moreover, he wrote, "I have neither seen nor heard anything since making that report which could mitigate the atrocity of the affair."[7] Colonel Harney would respond with a Sioux expeditionary force that would number over twelve hundred better-armed, well-deployed infantrymen and cavalrymen.

Also, to no surprise, Winship's report provided no shades of gray and no suggestions for a negotiated solution to this conflict. He urged, "The murderers . . . should be held to a fearful account by the government."[8] Nothing in these documents dissuaded the governmental powers-that-be from having their war.

The Harney punitive expedition formed up and marched forth the next season, found a Sioux Indian village conveniently camped near the overland trail in western Nebraska, and destroyed it. Grattan's avengers marched on to Fort Laramie, later continuing on through the Dakota Badlands to join up with another force at Fort Pierre on the Missouri River, where Harney, his vengeance far from satiated, would hold a peace council where he held all the power. The First Sioux War formally concluded in the spring of 1856, but Captain Winship was not there to witness the war's end. Although he continued to play a role—that of Harney's assistant adjutant general in the field—he did not especially distinguish himself during the 1855 season. He took leave and left Fort Pierre before winter set, an apparently prudent decision, yet died of illness while at his home in Troy, New York, in December 1855. Winship left little in the way of a legacy, other than almost anonymously contributing to setting two nations on the road to war, an example, it would seem, of the pen being in truth mightier than the sword.

Notes

1. Theophilus F. Rodenbough, *From Everglade to Canyon with the Second United States Cavalry: An Authentic Account of Service in Florida, Mexico, Virginia, and the Indian Country, 1836–1875* (Norman: University of Oklahoma Press, 2000), 454; Paul, *Blue Water Creek*, 10, 142.
2. Paul, *Blue Water Creek*, 8.
3. The accounts of Little Thunder and Big Partisan were first brought before the public by R. Eli Paul in *Blue Water Creek*, 20–25, 169, 173, and in R. Eli Paul, "First Shots in the First Sioux War," *Wild West* 18 (Dec. 2005): 22–26, 28.
4. *House of Representatives Reports*, No. 63.
5. "Report of an Inspection of Forts Ripley, Ridgely, Snelling, Laramie, Kearney, Riley, Leavenworth, and Atkinson; Made by Brevet Major O. F. Winship, Asst. Adjutant General, U.S. Army, in the Months of May, June, July, August and September, 1854," Letters Received, Office of the Adjutant General, 1822–1860, Main Series, RG 94, Microfilm Publication No. 567, roll 508, NARA.
6. Notable examples of published inspection reports are George Croghan, *Army Life on the Western Frontier: Selections from the Official Reports Made between 1826 and 1845 by Colonel George Croghan*, ed. Francis Paul Prucha (Norman: University of Oklahoma Press, 1958); Robert W. Frazer, ed., *Mansfield on the Condition of the Western Forts, 1853–54* (Norman: University of Oklahoma Press, 1963); Robert W. Frazer, ed., *New Mexico in 1850: A Military View by Colonel George Archibald McCall* (Norman: University of Oklahoma Press, 1968); and Jerry Thompson, ed., *Texas and New Mexico on the Eve of the Civil War: The Mansfield and Johnstown Inspections, 1859–1861* (Albuquerque: University of New Mexico Press, 2001).
7. "Report of an Inspection."
8. Ibid.

Fort Laramie in 1853, one year before the Grattan fight. From James Linforth, ed., *Route from Liverpool to Great Salt Lake Valley Illustrated with Steel Engravings and Wood Cuts from Sketches Made by Frederick Piercy* (London: Franklin D. Richards, 1855). *Author's collection.*

James Bordeaux, whose trading post was within sight of Indian-soldier negotiations, played a central role in the events of August 19, 1854. *Courtesy Museum of the Fur Trade, Chadron, Neb.*

Man Afraid of His Horses (fourth from right), an Oglala Lakota leader, and James Bordeaux (far right) survived the violence of the Grattan fight to leave historically important eyewitness accounts. Photograph by Alexander Gardner at Fort Laramie, 1868. *Courtesy Newberry Library, Chicago.*

Spotted Tail, Brulé Lakota warrior and later head of his tribe, left no account of his participation in the Grattan fight or the attack on the U.S. Mail party. His 1855 surrender to the U.S. Army for his role in the latter, an act of great bravery, helped end the First Sioux War. *Courtesy Library of Congress, Washington, D.C.*

Opposite, bottom left. According to Fort Laramie trader Sefroy Iott, after Lieutenant Grattan fell, his command immediately lost heart and attempted to flee but to no avail. *Courtesy Museum of the Fur Trade, Chadron, Neb.*

Opposite, bottom right. Indian agent John Whitfield arrived at Fort Laramie a few days after the debacle, too late to issue the annuities that the Lakotas had gathered en masse to receive from the government. Whitfield later wrote, "The idea that one company of infantry can furnish aid and protection to emigrants who pass through this agency is worse than nonsense." Courtesy Library of Congress, Washington, D.C.

a

b

c

d

In 1854–55 Maj. William Hoffman, Sixth Infantry, provided constant and convincing criticism of Grattan's rash actions and withstood the resultant disapproval by army superiors. The old soldier (right) went on to serve the Union army in the thankless but important role of commissary general of prisoners. *Courtesy Library of Congress, Washington, D.C.*

Opposite. Four Mormon pioneers provided critical perspectives of the Grattan fight. Hezekiah Mitchell (a) safely passed by the large Indian encampment on August 15. Christian J. Larsen (b) owned the lame cow that High Forehead killed for food. The wagon train of William Athol MacMaster (c) reached the scene of the fight only two days after its occurrence. In spite of the prospective danger, high-ranking church official Ezra Benson (d) accurately reported to Salt Lake that the overland trail was safe for emigrant travel. From Frank Esshom, *Pioneers and Prominent Men of Utah: The Early History of the Church of Jesus Christ of Latter-Day Saints* (Salt Lake City: Utah Pioneers Book Publishing, 1913). *Courtesy Missouri Valley Special Collections, Kansas City Public Library, Kansas City, Mo.*

effect that they must all be drunk, and had better go
back to the fort. If the white chief there wished to
talk to him he had better send sober men whom he
could understand.

The result of this was that firing instantly commenced from the artillery ; the shots were directed
through the tépee

poles. The first cut down several, and the second passed
through the chiefs' lodge, killing an old bed-ridden chief
and wounding several of the women.

These two shots were all they fired. The blood of
the Sioux was up. They made one charge upon the
party and killed every one of them.

The interpreter started off on his horse towards the
fort, but was overtaken by one of the Indians—his own
brother-in-law. Wyuse threw up his hands. But the

No contemporary renderings exist of the Grattan fight or its immediate aftermath. Fanciful engravings, such as this one from a later memoir that stated "firing instantly commenced from the artillery," helped readers to visualize the event, however incorrectly. Illustration by Paul Frenzeny in Harrington O'Reilly, *Fifty Years on the Trail: A True Story of Western Life* (New York: Frederick Warne, 1889).

September 27, 1854–October 10, 1855

27. Oscar F. Winship, September 27, 1854

I . . . am ready and anxious to have any part . . . in avenging them.

A career soldier, a veteran of the battlefield, and an individual in a position of great responsibility, Capt. Oscar Winship could feed his superiors with the facts they needed to make a measured military response. Particularly with the details of the killing of Grattan's command and the deed's perpetrators, Winship did not disappoint. His inspection report transformed itself into a professional field intelligence document and gave the identities, the numbers, the strengths, and the locations of the army's prospective Indian foes. His observations, obviously informed by the frontiersmen of Fort Laramie, created a blueprint for commander William S. Harney of the U.S. Army and his subsequent plans for a punitive expedition. For example: "The Ogalalas occupy the North Platte and number about 300 lodges. The proportion of warriors to the lodge is . . . three warriors to the lodge. . . . They are deeply implicated in the last massacre near Fort Laramie. . . . The Brules inhabit the country bordering the White Earth River [White River in South Dakota]. They number 350 lodges and 1,050 warriors." And so it continues in a previously unpublished excerpt from the larger report that pertains to Fort Laramie.

Fort Laramie is situated on the left bank of the Laramie River about a mile and a half above its confluence with the North Fork of the Platte. Its Latitude is 42o 12'10" N. and its Longitude 104o 47'45" W. Its altitude above the Gulf of Mexico is 4,470 feet. Its distance from Fort Leavenworth, its present source of supply, is about 634 miles; from Fort Kearny, 337; from Fort Riley, 497; from Fort Pierre, on the Missouri, 360 by the present wagon route; so say the traders of Laramie, although Colonel [Aeneas] Mackay, late Quartermaster, makes it 240—a distance much less than the air line between the two points, if the maps be correct; for that line is the diagonal of two degrees of Latitude, and four of Longitude.

From Fort Atkinson is 539 miles; from the Arkansas crossing, 514; from Bent's New Fort, 386; from the Old Fort, 255; from Fort Massachusetts in New Mexico, 285; from St. Vrain's Fort on the South Platte, 140; and 509 from Salt Lake City.

The advantages of the position of Fort Laramie as a military one cannot be contested. It is situated on one of the only routes which are practicable through the first barrier of the Rocky Mountains, besides being in the centre of many of the most powerful and hostile tribes of the plains, such as the various bands of the southern Sioux, Blackfeet and Cheyennes; all of whom are capable, and many of whom have, within the last few months shown a disposition to do mischief to the Whites. But should a war be opened up, the Republican Fork, and across to the South Platte, which seems from all accounts to be perfectly practicable, the great bulk of the travel and emigration West would then, of necessity, take the direction of Bridger's pass, leaving Fort Laramie to the right, and would therefore diminish measurably its importance as a military post; for to determine the true position of these posts in an Indian country, reference must be had not only to the points where they are found most numerous, but where they can do the most mischief. Fort Laramie is one of these now, but the emigrant crossing at the mouth of Cherry Creek would become still more so, in the event of two great thoroughfares intersecting at that point.

For an idea of the immediate vicinity of Fort Laramie, see the rough sketch opposite, where it will be perceived that the fort is nearly surrounded by hills, which afford it a good shelter from the cold mountain blasts.

I wish I could speak as favorably of the buildings, &c., &c., which make up, in this instance, as in many others, what is misnamed a fort. These at Fort Laramie are almost anything but what they should be at such a post. With the exception of the Old Adobe Fort of the American Fur company found here at the establishment of the post, there is not one which could not be easily fired by night, by arrows armed with some inflammable substance, and thrown across the Laramie River into the hay ricks, stables, and store-houses standing on the opposite bank. The Indians know this well and would have availed themselves of it in the late Grattan affair had they not been dissuaded therefrom by a class of men who, whether for good or evil, have more influence over them than the government does or can, unless it chooses to see itself properly represented by a strong military force. The American Fur Company has controlled the tribes West of the Mississippi for many years past, but its influence is no longer one founded on the mutual interests of both parties, as formerly, but rather one of prestige, which much soon decline, now that the company can find but little more to pay expense of reimbursing that influence.

In the mean time Fort Laramie could easily be built up in a permanent manner, should the interests of the service require its longer continuance, which seems very likely. Bricks can be and already are made in the immediate vicinity of the post, with which it could be rebuilt on a plan more suited to the objects it is intended to subserve than the one now in use. . . .

I inspected the garrison of Fort Laramie on the morning of the 27th of August, having arrived at the post the day previous. I found it in command of 2nd Lieut. Hugh B. Fleming, 6th Infantry, and composed of an Assistant Surgeon, Ordnance Sergeant and Company "G," 6th Infantry, making a "Total" present and absent of 46, and an Aggregate of 30.

Company "G," 6th Infantry, had present on parade—2nd Lieutenant Hugh B. Fleming and 40 enlisted men.

Present at the post but absent from parade, 5 enlisted men, four of whom were herding cattle and one waiting on an officer.

Absent from the post on "Detached Service"—Captain William S. Ketchum, relieved from Regimental Recruiting service and ordered to join his company July 31, 1854. Permission granted him from Head Quarters of the Army to remain at his station until the 15th September, 1854. 1st Lieut. Richard B. Garnett—on General Recruiting service since the 18th of May, 1854.

In personal appearance, soldierly bearing, discipline, and tactical instruction the members of this company exceeded any that I had yet visited in this Department, notwithstanding the loss it has sustained eight days before. The Company gardens also, kitchens, and mess rooms were in excellent order, and the mess table was the best furnished of any I have yet seen in the service.

I next examined the company and Post Books and records, all of which I found neatly and regularly kept.

Quarter Master's Department. This Department was under the charge of 2nd Lieut. Hugh B. Fleming, the Commanding Officer of the post, who had been performing both the duties of Quarter and Commissary since the death of Lieut. Grattan, which occurred in an engagement with the Sioux Indians on the 19th of August last.

Employés. Only one citizen is employed in the Quarter Master's Department at this post, who is an interpreter hired at a monthly compensation of $50.00 by the authority of the Secretary of War. Soldiers are employés on extra duty, such as clerks, mechanics, teamsters, and laborers. The number so employed varies from ten to twenty men, according to the season of the year. A large detail is required in the summer months to procure hay for the use of the post.

The Means of Transportation. Consist of 30 mules, 5 horses, 18 oxen, and a proportionate quantity of wagons, harness, yokes &c., which are all much worn and in great measure unserviceable. There are but 18 animals (three teams) fit for working. The oxen are old and are seldom worked, on account of sore feet [Winship apparently missed the irony of this last statement, that of oxen with sore feet.—the Editors] The horses (with the exception of one) are those turned over by Captain [Rufus] Ingalls, Assistant Quarter Master, during his last sojourn at the post, as broken down and unfit for travel.

The Amount of Disbursements. On account of the Quarter Master's Department in the fiscal year ending in June, 1854, are as follows:

The amount of purchases			$ 1.20
"	"	paid hired citizens	1,116.00
"	"	paid Soldiers on Extra Duty	505.50
"	"	paid for public postage	10.41
"	"	paid for apprehension of deserter	30.00
Total			$1,663.11

The resources of the Country for supplying the Department are very limited. Fuel and hay only can be supplied in the vicinity of the post; the former consists of pine, cedar, and cottonwood, and the latter is very scarce and has to be transported for a considerable distance.

Subsistence Department. 2nd Lieut. H. B. Fleming is in charge of this Department, assisted by an issuing Sergeant, and having five other enlisted men employed under his direction as herders &c. This post is, I believe, supplied by contract, but I neglected to ascertain the cost of the ration, which however, cannot be far from 28 cents, as the cost of transportation alone from Fort Leavenworth to this place is $7.91 per 100 pounds, and everything but Fresh Beef has to be furnished from the States.

Issues to Indians. The following are the issues to Indians in the year ending in June 1854:

339 lbs. pork
2,123 " Bacon sides
153 lbs. of Coffee
143 " of Sugar
693 lbs. Bacon hams
2,852 " Flour
613 " Hard Bread
384 Quarts of Beans
11 Gills of Salt
48 Bushels & 20-1/2 pounds of dried Apples, and 9 lbs. jerked Beef

The amount of Disbursements on account of the Department is as follows: $602.01 paid to Men on Extra duty in the Department, and for commutation of whiskey rations, $23.12 amount of purchases. Total $625.13.

Sales to Citizens and Officers. Sales to Citizens in the year ending June 1854: $5,136.38-1/4. Sales to Officers: 588.87-3/4. Total, $5,725.26.

The books and papers of this Department as well as those of the Quarter Master's Department were examined and found to be regularly kept.

The Medical Department was under the direction of Asst. Surgeon Charles Page, assisted by a Steward, Matron &c. There were no sick at the post when I visited it. Indeed, there is comparably no sickness at Fort Laramie. The following Meteorological tables extracted from the Hospital Register may serve to show in part the reason of this. [Tables of barometer and thermometer readings are not included here.]

I beg leave to state here before dismissing the subject of Fort Laramie that I have not deemed it necessary to go into a detailed account of the massacre of an Officer and 29 men of its garrison by the Sioux Indians, on the 19th of August last, a special report of which affairs has already been forwarded to the Commander of the Department. I would merely say here that I have neither seen nor heard anything since making that report which could mitigate the atrocity of the affair referred to therein, nor that could induce me to withdraw the recommendations I then made. The murderers of [John Williams] Gunnison, Grattan, [Joseph Edward] Maxwell, [Michael E.] Van Buren, and other gallant and meritorious officers should be held to a fearful account by the government which they have so faithfully served. I, for one, am ready and anxious to have any part, no matter how humble, in avenging them.

I left Fort Laramie on the 2nd of September, still in company with the Indian agent General Whitfield, whose movements (being encumbered with an ox train) somewhat delayed my own, but I did not feel justified in separating from him at a time when such unmistakeable signs of hostility were manifested on the part of the Sioux Indians. I therefore continued with him until within three days journey of Fort Kearny, when I left him. . . .

Sioux. This great tribe of Indians is divided into a vast number of bands, covering a greater extent of country than any other, perhaps, except the Comanches. I shall confine myself to those bands habitually residing south of the Missouri, as it is with them that the government must, for the present, come in more immediate contact.

The Ogalalas occupy the North Platte and number about 300 lodges. The proportion of warriors to the lodge is strongly insisted upon by the Sioux traders about Fort Laramie to be stronger than that fixed for the Southern tribes. I will therefore allow them what they ask, three warriors to the lodge, for the Sioux bands, mostly giving it as my opinion that this is an over estimate. The Ogalalas, then, must be set down as mustering 900 warriors. They are deeply implicated in the last massacre near Fort Laramie, although they disavow any general participation in the act. One of the best evidences, however, of their guilt is that on my way from Fort Laramie east, I passed in the vicinity of an Ogala[la] camp, numbering some 30 lodges, near the crossing of the South Platte, and although my party did not number ten men, and presented anything but a hostile appearance, not an Indian visited us even to ask for sugar and coffee, a circumstance which was then not less agreeable than surprising to us. Big Head is the chief of the Ogalalas and is a very influential man.

The Brules inhabit the country bordering the White Earth River. They number 350 lodges and 1,050 warriors. Their chief, if he be yet living, is the Bear, the man who figured so conspicuously in the Laramie massacre. He is a man of great influence among the Sioux but of doubtful disposition toward the whites. I have heard that the American Fur Company have been obliged to purchase his friendship at no considerable cost, and I cannot but entertain a suspicion that his professed friendship for Lieut. Grattan cost that young officer his life and those of his party. Certain it is that after having suggested the sending of a detachment of troops to capture a depredator residing in his own camp, he failed through inability, or want of disposition, to deliver him up and thus brought about a catastrophe more appalling than any one of the numerous and bloody affairs which have transpired in the Indian country within the last twelve month[s].

The Minicoujous occupy the country between the two forks of the Sheyen [Cheyenne] and number 400 lodges and 1,200 warriors. Red Fish is their chief. They were hostile to the government before the difficulty at Sarpy's Point, and they can scarcely have become more peaceably disposed since that event.

The Black Feet live on the Missouri, near the mouth of the Moro [Moreau], not far above Fort Pierre. They number 250 lodges and 750 warriors. Flat Foot is their chief. The agents and employees of the American Fur Company can give much more valuable information concerning this and indeed every other Sioux band than I can. It is sufficient here to say that the Black Feet are very hostile to the people of the United States.

The Oncpapas [Hunkpapas] occupy the same country as the Black Feet and are not more favorable towards the whites. They muster 350 lodges and 1,050 warriors. Little Bear is their chief.

The Sans Arc live on the head waters of the Moro, number 180 lodges, and Crow Feather is their chief. I have been able to gather little other information concerning them.

"Report of an Inspection of Forts Ripley, Ridgely, Snelling, Laramie, Kearney, Riley, Leavenworth, and Atkinson; Made by Brevet Major O. F. Winship, Asst. Adjutant General, U.S. Army, in the Months of May, June, July, August and September, 1854," Letters Received, Office of the Adjutant General, 1822–1860, Main Series, RG 94, Microfilm Publication No. 567, roll 508, NARA.

28. John Wilkins Whitfield, Indian agent, September 27, 1854
I left for Fort Laramie.

Travel companions John Wilkins Whitfield, Indian agent, and Captain Winship arrived at the Missouri frontier settlement of Westport (since swallowed by present Kansas City) on September 26, 1854. This is a portion of Whitfield's annual report on the "condition of the Indians within the Upper Platte agency," which served as a prelude to his full report on "the unfortunate affair," as he repeatedly described the Grattan fight in this and other accounts.

Elsewhere in this report and not included here, Whitfield recommended, "this agency is too large for any one man" and that it be broken into more manageable administrative pieces. In another belated, ironic understatement he wrote, "Each agency should be supplied with interpreters under the control of the government; at present it is very difficult to procure reliable interpreters."

After distributing the goods at St. Vrain to the Cheyennes and Arrapahoes, I left for Fort Laramie, taking with me fifteen thousand pounds of goods. When within about fifty miles of Fort Laramie I met about twenty-five lodges of Sioux retreating from there, and from them I first learned of the unfortunate affair that had taken place. They stated that a fight had taken place between the Sioux and the soldiers, in which every soldier had been killed, and perhaps the fort had been taken before that time, as the Sioux were talking about it when they left. On my arrival at Laramie, I learned the facts of the unfortunate affair, and, as I have made a special report on that subject, I will not extend this report. . . .

As I had the pleasure of travelling from Fort Atkinson, by Fort Laramie, to Fort Leavenworth, with Major O. F. [Oscar F.] Winship, U.S. Army, who visited that country for the purpose of inspecting the military posts, I beg leave to refer the department to his report; and if his suggestions are carried out, I have no doubt that in a few years the Indians of the plains will be brought under the control of the government.

Jno. W. [John Wilkins] Whitfield, Indian agent, Platte Agency, Westport, Mo., to A. [Alfred] Cumming, superintendent, Indian affairs, St. Louis, Sept. 27, 1854, in *Annual Report of the Commissioner of Indian Affairs, 1854*, 92–93, 95.

29. Thomas Lorenzo Obray, Utah emigrant, September 28, 1854
no Mormons in the fight

More than half the accounts presented in this section are from army personnel and government officials and employees. Many were published by the government at the time, although without annotation or context, and they have provided fodder for historians ever since. It is always refreshing, though, to hear another voice, in this case, one of the Mormon emigrant accounts, brief as it may be, that has survived in the historical record.

The train that included Thomas Lorenzo Obray, a thirty-two-year-old Welshman who lost his wife of three weeks, Louisa, on the journey, reached its Utah destination on October 1, 1854, the arrival duly noted in a later issue of the Salt Lake's *Deseret News*. Brother "Shepherd" may refer to Charles Shelton, Obray's brother-in-law, also a member of the same train.

The Bros. Shepherd and Obray arrived on the 26th inst. express from the church train on the 21st, from whom we learn that the Danish company were on Black's Fork on the 21st. . . .

In addition to the news of the fight between U.S. troops and the Sioux, contained in the letter from Elder [Ezra T.] Benson to the Presidency and published in connection, we learn from Bro. Obray that a lame cow strayed from the loose herd of the Danish company into a Sioux camp, where they were merry making, and they killed and ate her. Upon requisition of Lieutenant Gratten [sic], the chief proffered to pay for the cow, but the person who killed her was demanded and being sent for by the chief said he did not want to be given up but would relinquish his and his family's share of the annuity money, then due, in payment for the cow, which being refused firing began on the part of the troops. The Sioux have not interfered with the emigration and have shown no disposition to do so, and there were no Mormons in the fight.

Thomas Lorenzo Obray, "Latest News from Our Immigration," *Deseret News* (Salt Lake City), Sept. 28, 1854, Mormon Pioneer Overland Travel, 1847–1868 (database), Church of Jesus Christ of Latter-day Saints, Salt Lake City, https://history.lds.org/overlandtravel/sources/7283/latest-news-from-our-immigration-deseret-news-28-sept-1854-3. See also "Immigration," *Deseret News*, Oct. 3, 1854; Edith Parker Haddock and Dorothy Hardy Matthews, *History of Bear Lake Pioneers* (Paris, Idaho: Daughters of Utah Pioneers, 1968), 53.

30. Edward J. Steptoe, army officer, from J. H. Reid [Reed], a "gentleman," September 29, 1854

expecting to get the Indian without any trouble

Capt. Edward Jenner Steptoe, whose army command had passed through Fort Laramie earlier in the season, relayed from Salt Lake City to Secretary of War Jefferson Davis the information he deemed critical in understanding the "difficulty" at Fort Laramie. His source was J. H. Reed, a young gentlemen and Grattan confidante, who claimed the Indian who had killed the cow had fired first on the soldiers.

During the past week very contradictory rumors of some difficulty between the Indians and the troops at Fort Laramie were rife here, but it was only upon the arrival of the mail yesterday [Sept. 28] that the facts could be ascertained. These rumors kept me in most painful suspense, which was only removed by the cheering assurance of a gentleman there that the surviving garrison is prepared and able to defend itself in any further emergency.

Hearing it whispered about that the difficulty was occasioned entirely by the rashness of Lieut. Grattan, I think it due to the memory of that young officer that you shall be thoroughly informed as to the facts, and therefore take the liberty of extracting from a private letter just received.

Mr. J. H. Reid [sic], a gentleman who accompanied my command as far as Fort Laramie, where he remained sick, writes: "The best authenticated account seems to be that Mr. Grattan, expecting to get the Indian without any trouble, went into the midst of the Indian village with his men and pieces. He could not well have avoided this, as the lodges covered a space of three miles. The Chief of the Brules, among whom the offender was staying, went with Mr. Grattan to the man, and he refused to go, saying 'he had two guns, plenty of arrows, and could fight.' About the time that Grattan regained his command, this Indian fired. G. then ordered his musketry to fire. The Indians, who had gathered about him to the number of fifteen hundred, perhaps, fell flat on their faces, and the balls passed over, as did also the whole charge of the pieces which were fired immediately afterwards. The whole party was then destroyed before either the cannonor [cannoneer] [or] the muskets could be re-loaded. They were all killed with knives and arrows. Lieut. G. had dismounted and given his horse to one of the men while he worked as gunner and was found where he fell by the side of his piece."

This statement shows that Lieut. Grattan did not take the initiative, and it goes to confirm my opinion that the attack upon the troops was part of a deliberate plan. Why the attack was not followed by one upon the fort, I do not know.

Mr. Reid inveighs sever[e]ly against the traders, a number of whom were in the vicinity. He asserts that they behaved in a dastardly manner, fleeing from their stone and adobe houses, which could have been easily defended, and not even stopping at the fort to give information that a fight had taken place.

My only purpose in troubling and intruding upon you with this letter is to throw a little light on the matter in justice to Mr. Grattan.

Bvt. Lt. Col. [Capt. Edward Jenner] Steptoe, Salt Lake City, report to Jefferson Davis, secretary of war, Washington, D.C., Sept. 29, 1854, which includes excerpts of letter from J. H. Reid [Reed], Fort Laramie, in *House of Representatives Reports*, No. 63.

31. William Vaux, army chaplain, October 1, 1854
We all huddled together.

After the alarm sounded among the Fort Laramie garrison, Chaplain William Vaux and his dependents sought refuge in old Fort John on the post grounds. Written more than a month after the massacre, no other surviving account reflects the terror felt by those huddling within the walls of the decrepit adobe structure.

We are favored with the following letter from Bishop [Jackson?] Kemper, being the report to him, of Rev. William Vaux, Chaplain, U.S.A.:

Fort Laramie, Oct. 1st, 1854. My report for the current year includes one Baptism, three Marriages, and three Funerals. The fort during this period has been garrisoned but by one company of infantry, and none of the officers having families there has been little society, either for church or social privileges and enjoyment. The past summer, however, will be ever memorable for the most unprecedented massacre of a young officer and his entire command of 29 soldiers by different bands of Indians who were assembled near here to receive their annual presents. Several depredations had been committed by them during the season of emigration, and on this occasion a detachment was sent to the Indian village to claim, as a prisoner, a recent offender, and a hostile demonstration, on the part of the detachment to enforce their object, was the signal upon which upwards of 1,500 warriors rushed upon them and in the most brutal manner assassinated the whole command, mutilating their bodies in the most savage and barbarous way. They then helped themselves to the stores of neighboring traders and of the American Fur Company and further designed to attack and burn the fort, putting to death every white person, and actually marched on this fiendish mission but were providentially dissuaded from their purpose. The shocking spectacle of the martyred and gory bodies lying over the place of slaughter was exposed for two days, none daring to remove or attempt to inter them. Alarms for the safety of the fort and its remnant of inmates were frequent by day and night messengers, and we all huddled together, for mutual defence, in the ruins of the old adobe walls, fortifying our position as well as we could. To describe our situation for many days demands a more graphic pen than mine—suffice it to say, that had the attack been at first made upon us, we must all have perished! An Indian was heard to utter this significant expression, "The blood of one

Indian is the blood of the nation!" All, however, has been quiet since this awful catastrophe—the bodies of the murdered men lie buried in one vast grave, and the murderers have gone in different directions, where, doubtless, they are expecting that pursuit and chastisement which a vigorous government will not fail to administer. Two more companies of soldiers are on the way to our relief, and the threatened danger has passed away. But what shall Christians say to such facts?

William Vaux, "Report from Fort Laramie, Oct. 1, 1854," in *The Spirit of Missions*, vol. 20 (New York: Board of Missions of the Protestant Episcopal Church, 1855): 40–41.

32. John W. Whitfield, October 2, 1854
I could have settled the whole affair.

A few days after writing his annual report, Agent Whitfield offered his take on the Grattan fight. One can almost see this civilian government official and his military counterpart (Winship) independently gathering and sorting through the many variations on the story to which they had been exposed. When compared to Captain Winship's report, that of Whitfield sounded less strident and more measured, dependent on the statements of others to shape his conclusions rather than on personal or political prejudices.

I have the honor to report to you that I returned to this place on the 26th ultimo [Sept.], after an absence of nearly four months.

As difficulties have recently taken place between the Sioux Indians and a detachment of United States troops near Fort Laramie, I have thought best to make a special report on that unfortunate affair and place all the facts before the department that I have been enabled to gather. I was on the South Platte at the time of the fight, and consequently I have to rely on the statements of those who were present and others who have resided in the country for a long time and who are well acquainted with the Indians. Their statements I have no doubt are correct.

On my way from Fort St. Vrain to Laramie, I met about twenty-five lodges of Sioux Indians, who informed me that a few days previous a Mormon train had passed their encampment and that a lame cow had strayed into the village and that a Minnecowzue Sioux from the upper Missouri agency had killed and eat[en] her.

Two days afterwards Brevet Lieutenant [John] Grattan, with twenty-nine soldiers and his interpreter [Auguste Lucien], came down to demand the Indian who had committed the depredation by killing the Mormons' cow. The Indian refused to surrender, and a fight ensued in which the lieutenant, interpreter, and every man were killed. On my arrival to Fort Laramie I immediately commenced investigating the affair to ascertain all the facts connected with the fight. I sent for a number of the traders and others who were likely to know anything about it, and I addressed them a letter, which they answered.

I preferred that they should write their own statements and give their own version of the affair. I beg leave herewith to enclose the correspondence. [No statements or other attachments accompanied this published source.]

Agreeable to the intercourse law, a different policy should have been pursued by the commanding officers. No regulations that I have yet seen give officers the right to arrest and confine any Indian for an offence of no more magnitude than stealing a cow. Different orders may have been given at Washington; if so, troops sufficient to carry out such orders should be placed in the Indian country. I regret that the demand for the offender had not been postponed until my arrival. If it had been, I could have settled the whole affair without the least trouble. To have prevented a collision, I have no doubt but that the Sioux would have paid any number of horses, for I was told by several reliable gentlemen that they offered to pay for the cow, and, if the intercourse law is to be obeyed, nothing more could be required. Indians consider themselves disgraced for life if arrested and confined. This feeling is general among all Indians but more especially the wild tribes; consequently they prefer to die to being taken and confined. In this case it is evident that that was the feeling of the Indian who committed the depredation, and, if the lieutenant had understood the character of Indians, I doubt whether he would have done as he did. Why Lieutenant Grattan took the position he did, in the midst of the village surrounded by at least fifteen hundred warriors, perhaps never will be known, for it is evident that he must have known before he went into the village that a fight would be the result if he fired a gun.

If Lieutenant Grattan had left the interpreter he had, who was drunk and swearing he would take their hearts, and procured the service of some prudent sober man, no such difficulty in my opinion would have taken place, for it is evident that the Sioux Indians desired no trouble, and, even after one gun had been fired and one Indian wounded, the chief begged the young men not to fire—that perhaps the soldiers would go away.

I do not consider a whole nation bound for an offence committed by an individual until they make it a national matter, which was not done in this case, for, from all the evidence I could get, the head chief and others went into the village to try and persuade the offender to surrender, and, after he had refused, he stated that he did not wish any of the rest to have anything to do with the affair.

The head chief begged the lieutenant to go back, and he would bring the man, dead or alive. No doubt Lieutenant Grattan's want of knowledge of the Indian character and the rash language used by a drunken interpreter was the cause of the unfortunate affair. The Sioux, or the bands in the Platte agency, have heretofore been regarded as the most peaceable and friendly Indians on the prairies to the whites. This is the only case I have ever heard of their disturbing the stock of any train during this season, and, if the Mormon had gone into the village, he could have got his cow without any trouble, but he took fright and left the cow. The Indians killed and ate it. This is the history, in a few words, of the commencement of the whole affair.

The forts at present located in the Indian country are most emphatically poor affairs. They can give no protection to any person beyond the reach of their own guns. Infantry in the Indian country, so far as protecting the roads is concerned, are about the same use as so many stumps would be. Emigrants are compelled to protect themselves and buy their way with sugar and coffee.

The Sioux after the fight took possession of all the goods that had been sent by government to them. By the terms of the contract, Messrs. [Arthur Ingraham] Baker and [Alexander] Street were to hold the goods in their own possession until my arrival. Their train arrived early in August. The question with them was whether they should keep them in their own wagons or store them in a good warehouse. Believing the goods would be safer in a warehouse, they there placed them. The goods would have been taken from the wagons, and, even if they could have got them stored at the fort, they would have been no safer, for at the time of the defeat of Lieutenant Grattan's party but ten soldiers remained in the fort; the balance were some distance off on duty. I regard it fortunate that the goods were not at the fort, for, if they had been, the fort and all its inmates would have been destroyed. As to whether they could have taken the fort or not, I presume none will say they could not have done it. It was with the greatest difficulty that Mr. Bordeaux and others could, by hard begging, persuade the Sioux from going up to the fort the night after Lieutenant Grattan's party were killed. The Indians knew I would not give them their goods after the fight and that in all probability the government might send troops after them. Believing this, it is reasonable to suppose they would take the goods.

J. W. [John Wilkins] Whitfield, Indian agent, Platte Agency, Westport, Mo., to A. [Alfred] Cumming, superintendent, Indian affairs, St. Louis, Oct. 2, 1854, in *Annual Report of the Commissioner of Indian Affairs, 1854*, 96–98. The probable identities of freighters Baker and Street come from Louise Barry, *The Beginning of the West: Annals of the Kansas Gateway to the American West, 1540–1854* (Topeka: Kansas State Historical Society, 1972), 1138, 1191.

33. Paul Carrey, civilian traveler, from "ten Canadians," October 2, 1854

He would eat their hearts raw.

The Huerfano settlement mentioned below was located at the confluence of the Arkansas and Huerfano Rivers in present southern Colorado. It turned out to be a poor refuge for those fleeing Fort Laramie because Ute Indians attacked the settlement on Christmas Day, 1854.

Details on Paul Carrey, "a French gentleman" from St. Louis, are meager, but he apparently had traveled extensively on the Great Plains. That and his social rank might have made him a more credible witness to his peers. His accusation that Conquering Bear was guilty of premeditation in the killing of Grattan is, of course, nonsense. As a gatherer of bits and pieces about the Grattan fight, though, his greatest value may be that of a Frenchman talking to fellow francophones, especially about the drunken interpreter, here referred to by his first name (Auguste).

August 14. Met, 150 miles south of Fort Laramie, eight or ten men on their way to the Huerfano settlement. One of these had been my guide from the upper Missouri. I felt astonished at seeing them leaving the country of the Sioux, where they had been trading for many years. They answered to my questions on this subject, "that the Sioux were too bad; that there was no longer any security among them for their stock or families; that, since the day some Sioux had been killed by the troops, they were speaking of nothing else but revenge and were determined to kill all the soldiers residing on their lands. Their impression was that all this would end in war; that the trade would be ruined—so they preferred leaving the country."

On my arrival at Laramie a few days after, I found there some ten Canadians, who took me for Major [Capt. Oscar F.] Winship's guide. I asked them for some details of the fight which had taken place on the 19th. They all agreed in saying that, since several days, the Sioux were speaking of nothing else but their intention of avenging themselves—boasting they were strong enough to destroy all the soldiers if they could only find them out of the fort.

They told me that on the 18th, I think, a Sioux killed a cow belonging to an emigrant. Immediately the "Bear," chief of all the Sioux nation and particularly of the "Brules," came to the fort and reported the fact to Messrs. Fleming and Grattan. He added that the culprit ought to be punished; that he would have given him up himself, but that he was not a "Brule;" he was a Minicoujon, though he had his tent among the "Brules." He was afraid, he said, that in case he should give him up himself, the warriors of his nation would accuse him of being too partial to the whites. It was better, he thought, for Mr. Fleming to send a detachment of twenty or thirty men; the culprit would then surrender.

Lieutenant Grattan started with twenty-nine men and "Auguste," the interpreter. Auguste [Lucien], when he started, was in a state of intoxication, and crossing the village extending alongside of the road for a distance of about three miles he dared them to accomplish their threats—adding that he was coming with thirty men and a cannon and that this time he would eat their hearts raw.

As Lieutenant Grattan proceeded through the camp to reach the lodge of the culprit, which was situated at the further extremity of the camp, every warrior, taking his arms and mounting his horse, came and took his position behind the lodge of the culprit and that of the "Bear." They were protected by an accident of ground and shielded by bushes.

Lieutenant Grattan proceeded first to the house of Bordeau, situated at the extremity of the village.

He then called for the "Bear" and summoned him to surrender the culprit. To this summons the "Bear" answered he could not surrender him; that his warriors were opposed to it, but perhaps the culprit might surrender himself. The latter, however, refused to do it, saying he would sooner die. The "Bear" then told Lieutenant Grattan that the best plan would be for him to retire to the fort; that perhaps in a few days the man might be talked into surrendering himself.

Lieutenant Grattan answered; he had come there to seize the man and would not retire until he had him. Then, said the "Bear" impatiently pointing to the man's lodge, "if you will have him, go and take him yourself."

Lieutenant Grattan with his party entered the camp and proceeded towards the lodge of the culprit. Before reaching the lodge he halted and conversed again with the "Bear."

Auguste, as I have previously said, being in a state of intoxication, Lieutenant Grattan sent twice for Bordeau, that he might take him as an interpreter.

On receiving his first message, Bordeau started but turned back immediately, saying, "those whites are going to be murdered."

To Lieutenant Grattan's second message, he refused coming. "I acted so," he told me afterwards, "because I had my family and property to watch over, and I had to put my house in a state of defence."

In the meanwhile the Indians had nearly surrounded Lieutenant Grattan and his party at the distance of 20 or 25 paces, armed and ready for a fight.

Lieutenant Grattan then commanded "fire." The Indians instantaneously rushing on the troops, in less than a second himself and nearly all his men were killed. Some tried to escape but were soon joined by the Indians and experienced the same fate, with the exception of one who was spared but only to die the next day from his wounds.

Not a single Indian was killed; the "Bear" received three wounds, and two other men slightly wounded.

A few days after, Bordeau requested me to give him some information about the Huerfano settlement, saying, as war between the United States government and the Indians was inevitable, and there was no longer any security for himself and family, he was going to leave the country, hard as it was for him to leave his trade and houses. He would wait, however, until the arrival of the Indian agent.

A few days after, the Indian agent having arrived, Bordeau and the other traders returned to their houses.

I afterwards was told, it was said among the Indians that this had been prepared beforehand by the Bear, who had told them to be ready for the fight, the Bear having himself killed Lieutenant Grattan as he ordered "fire."

I learned, also, that at the fort the Bear was constantly to be seen with Lieutenant Grattan, who had a great confidence in him.

Having been asked by several persons in this city, whether at the time Lieutenant Grattan was not in a state of intoxication, I will state that Mr. Reed, a gentleman from this city, who lived for nearly two months in Lieutenant Grattan's own quarters, told me he had never seen him intoxicated, and, at the moment he started, he was perfectly sober.—Paul Carrey.

Winf'd [Winfield Scott] Hancock, adj. Sixth Infantry, Jefferson Barracks, Mo., to Assistant Adjutant General, Headquarters, Department of the West, Oct. 2, 1854. I have transmitted this paper, thinking it might throw some light upon one or two disputed points in connexion with the subject of the late massacre at Fort Laramie, O.R. The writer, Mr. Carrey, is a French gentleman of credit and standing in St. Louis, Mo.

Paul Carrey, "Extract from My Journal of a Trip from Fort Leavenworth, Missouri, via Forts Atkinson and Laramie, to Fort Kearney, O. R. [Oregon Route], Furnished at Request of First Lieutenant W. S. [Winfield Scott] Hancock, Adjutant Sixth Regiment of Infantry, Oct. 2, 1854," in *House of Representatives Reports*, No. 63. At this time Hancock was a first lieutenant in the Sixth Infantry, stationed at Jefferson Barracks, near St. Louis, Missouri, a far cry from the heights he later reached—war hero at Gettysburg in 1863, the rank of major general in 1866, and presidential candidate in 1880. Hancock incorporated the Carrey journal extracts in his own opinion piece, signed "A West Pointer," which took to task those who opposed the army's punitive expedition that was taking the field. "As for Mr. Bordeau's testimony," continued the diatribe, "I do not deem it worthy of the space it would cover in your columns, for he has made no less than three or four distinct written statements, differing from each other, and all totally differing from his first verbal statements, made to the officers at Fort Laramie but a day or two after the massacre at Sarpy's Point. . . . Mr. Bordeau's Brule connections and Brule interests preclude him from giving a perfectly fair statement of this matter, however honestly he might strive to do so. He sees objects through Brule spectacles." "Mr. [Thomas Hart] Benton versus Hostilities against the Indians," *Missouri Republican*, May 13, 1855. For details of the El Pueblo massacre of 1854, see Janet Lecompte, *Pueblo, Hardscrabble, Greenhorn: The Upper Arkansas, 1832–1856* (Norman: University of Oklahoma Press, 1978), 246–53.

34. A. J. Smith, F. E. Welch, and J. H. Steinberger, civilian travelers, October 3, 1854

the Indian version of the fatal occurrence

This hearsay evidence came via three merchants who had returned to the Iowa settlements in the company of Captain Winship. Smith, Steinberger, and Welch offered up fascinating details of the massacre, "the Indian version" as they termed it, although an extended time with the Winship-Whitfield party probably influenced their collective narrative. A few details even ring true because of their uniqueness, particularly the boots and manure stuffed in the cannon! More seriously, this account mentions the hard feelings from the 1853 skirmish between soldiers and Indians that lingered into the following year.

Through the politeness of A. J. Smith, F. E. Welch, and J. H. Steinberger, Esqrs., who arrived last week from the Plains, we have obtained the following additional intelligence. They left Salt Lake City on the 10th of August. . . .

. . . Met the troops sent to Utah [Captain Steptoe's command], on account of the Indian difficulties back on Green River—arrived at Fort Laramie a few days after the fatal massacre—found about 600 lodges the Menwecosia [Miniconjou] band of Sioux (who had perpetrated the murder), about 12 miles below the fort at the American Fur Company's station, and also a large number of Cheyennes, awaiting the arrival of Maj. Whitfield (successor to Maj. [Thomas] Fitzpatrick, Indian Agent, deceased) to arrive with and distribute their presents and annuities. The Sioux had, immediately after the perpetration of the murders, seized upon the presents intended for them, which were lying at the station but done no further mischief. They alleged that the murder was not committed on account of the attempted arrest of the man who shot the cow but in revenge for the death of a number of the Indians by the soldiers last season, for some murder of whites by the Indians.

The mangled bodies lay for three days unburied in sight of the inhuman traders, excusing themselves through fear of the Indians, but, when two hundred dollars was offered for performing this last sad service, there was no trouble in its accomplishment. The Indian version of the fatal occurrence is: That the two pieces of ordnance were brought within their encampment. Lieut. Grattan commenced a parley regarding the killing of a cow when Big Bear, the chief, came up with a sort of lance and struck at and wounded him, calling him a squaw and a coward, and charged him with being afraid to fight. Grattan drew his revolver, fired a number of times, wounding the chief and then elevated the cannon and fired, intending to intimidate the Indians from further violence without taking their lives. The whole band of Indians then made a rush at and killed upon the spot all but one, who finally escaped and lived to get to the fort but could make no explanation of the occurrence. He stated that he had been repulsed by one of the French traders and driven away; although he had seven holes shot through him, he lived to crawl 20 miles to the fort. Lieut. Grattan was found under the cannon, pierced with twenty arrows and a number of balls. He had fallen across the cannon where his life's blood still adhered. They then filled the cannon with manure and pulled off and thrust in the Lieutenant's boots.

Major Whitfield arrived soon with the goods for the Cheyennes, via [the] Arkansas [River], and commenced the distribution. Two bands refused to receive their portion upon the required condition that they should cease committing thefts and depredations upon emigrants to New Mexico, and their portions of goods returned to the States. The other chiefs informed the Major that next year they wanted a few shirts, 1,000 white squaws, and the remainder of their annuities in cash, and nothing else would be received. The Major took from this tribe a young man, a captive (formerly from Iowa) who was made a prisoner last spring whilst out hunting, also two Mexican boys of the age of about eight or ten years respectively. The Indians were very loth [loathe] to give them up and only did so by the payment of presents and positive threats and afterwards tried to rescue them at South Fork.

General [Capt. Oscar F.] Winship, Military Inspector, with a small force, accompanied Maj. Whitfield to Laramie—made the necessary examinations and returned with the Major, with whom our informants also came through.

They found an abundance of buffalo after crossing the South Fork of the Platte, which continued until they reached the new settlements in Kansas, about one hundred miles from the Missouri River. In some places they were forced to tie up all their cattle and loose stock to keep them from running off with the buffalo that were passing around them. The company had an abundance of the finest meat in the world and lived fat. Our informants returned on the south side of the Platte on account of the company for safety. They went out on the north side and report that to be much the best route. They took out a train of goods which they readily sold.

A. J. Smith, F. E. Welch, and J. H. Steinberger, "More Particulars of the Massacre at Fort Laramie," *Council Bluffs Bugle* (Iowa), Oct. 3, 1854, reprinted in *New York Daily Tribune*, Oct. 20, 1854, *New York Herald*, Oct. 21, 1854, and *New York Times*, Oct. 24, 1854.

35. Newman S. Clarke, October 5, 1854

I commend his suggestions as to future operations.

This commentary by Newman S. Clarke, the commander of the Department of the West, is included primarily because of his endorsement of Captain Winship's recommendations, as well as the information that he, Clarke, was the source of the Paul Carrey journal extract. This must have added considerable weight to Carrey's words. Interestingly Carrey did, indeed, return to Sioux country the next year as a "topographer."

I enclose herewith a special report of Major Winship and the papers accompanying it.

I commend his suggestions as to future operations as worthy of consideration and add that it would be desirable that mounted troops, dragoons, and light artillery, in conjunction, be used in operations against the hostile Indians.

In addition to the Major's report and the accompanying statements, I forward an extract of a journal kept by Mr. Carrey, a respectable French gentleman, kindly offered by him. Mr. Carrey is intelligent and adventurous, fond of and addicted to expeditions upon the plains. He would, I have reason to believe, return to the region of the Sioux, if furnished, at the expense of the government, with a guide, animals, and servant, offering to collect there information as to the numbers, condition, locale, and haunts of the Sioux and the features of the country. He would go if it be thought proper to send him under the auspices of a Mr. Sarpey [Peter A. Sarpy?], a St. Louis Creole having trading establishments in the region of country the usual roam of that people. I believe Mr. Carrey can be relied upon and would procure useful information. Moreover, he is a good topographer.

I suggest that in all cases of wrong committed by an Indian, his tribe should be deprived of annuities and presents until reparation be made, even though war should not become flagrant, and especially that the practice of giving arms and ammunition to Indians and allowing traders to sell them be discontinued, and that the prohibition to sell be rigidly enforced.

P.S. As an additional precaution, I suggest that, whenever and wherever it can be done without a violation of treaty stipulations, blacksmiths or armorers in the Indian country be withdrawn in order that Indians may not have the means or opportunity to obtain repairs to their firelocks.

Bvt. Brig. Gen. [Col. Newman S.] Clarke, Sixth Infantry, commanding, Jefferson Barracks, Mo., report to Col. Lorenzo Thomas, assistant adjutant general, Headquarters of the Army, New York, N.Y., Oct. 5, 1854, in *House of Representatives Reports*, No. 63. For another instance of Carrey's service on the frontier, see James A. Hanson, *Little Chief's Gatherings: The Smithsonian Institution's G. K. Warren 1855–1856 Plains Indian Collection and The New York State Library's 1855–1857 Warren Expeditions Journals* (Chadron, Neb.: Fur Press, 1996).

36. Christian J. Larsen, Utah emigrant, October 5, 1854

They shot one of our cows.

Christian John Larsen, a Danish eyewitness to the killing of the Mormon cow, had his journal entries recorded a couple of months later in official church records. His brief, benign account made no connection between the killing of the cow—described almost as an act of charity—and the next day's disaster. Maybe his mind was elsewhere; supposedly his daughter Martha was born on the trail on August 14.

Thursday, Aug. 17. We passed a large encampment of Indians before we reached Ft. Laramie. They shot one of our cows which was lame, and we let them have the meat. They also shot another animal belonging to Hans Monsen [Monson]; it came into our camp wounded, and we had it butchered. We camped for noon half a mile from Ft. Laramie, crossed the river, and passed the fort about 4 o'clock P.M.

Monday, Aug. 21. Bros. Hans Peter Jensen and J. Bentsen joined our company again. They reported that the Indians had killed forty soldiers in Ft. Laramie. In the afternoon we crossed the Platte River and camped, joining Darwin Richardson's company of emigrants. All with whom we came in contact had something to tell us about the Indian fight in Ft. Laramie. From that day and for several days afterwards we traveled closer together and made large camps at night.

Christian J. Larsen journal, excerpts in Journal History of the Church of Jesus Christ of Latter-day Saints, October 5, 1854, Hans Peter Olsen Company, in Mormon Pioneer Overland Travel, (database), https://history.lds.org/overlandtravel/sources/10254605260248933418-eng/; Obituary of Martha L. Larson Colemen, Fort Laramie Collections.

37. John Taylor and Nathaniel Henry Felt, Utah officials, October 6, 1854

A man from the Danish company came up to the fort and complained.

Nathaniel Henry Felt, John Taylor's assistant, may have had at least an equal hand in crafting this account, hence the use of the first person plural ("we" and "us"). They had made good time on the trail since Taylor's last letter from Green River, writing this letter near present Lexington, Nebraska. Maybe their urgency mirrored their journey's purpose—to inaugurate a Mormon newspaper in New York City.

On the 18th [Sept.] we arrived at Devil[']s gate where we learned that the mail from the valley had been waiting a sufficient force to venture on to Laramie and had left two days before.

19th met the mail from the States. They informed us that all was quiet on the road.

On the 20th met Bro. Aaron Farr and train some 10 miles this side of the crossing of the N. Platte, in good spirits and progressing well.

21st met Bro. [William Adam] Empy [Empey] and co. near Deer Creek where we campd. for the night, and Bro. Wm. Taylor went back with us and spent the night with his Bros.

22nd Just after leaving the [text missing], we met Bro. R. Campbell & Co. in good spirits, though I presume they will need assistance before they get to the valley. On the evening of the 25th within 10 miles of Fort Laramie we met a party of [Thomas S.] Williams & [William Henry] Hoopers [Hooper] train in rather a poor condition for want of more team[s?] and the Captn. seemed to be somewhat discouraged. Bro. Jas. Needham and several families were with them and liable to feel the severity of a mountain winter.

On the morning of the 26th we went up to the fort where we learned the particulars of the Indian difficulty.

They informed us that a man from the Danish company came up to the fort and complained that the Indians had killed his cow that was lame and lag[ge]d. behind the Co., upon which orders were given for a company of 29 men and two pieces of cannon, under the command of Lieut. Gratton [*sic*] with an interpreter to go to the camp of 10 or 12 hundred Sioux warriors who were 8 miles below, and demand of them the man that shot the cow. When the company arrived at the encampment of the Indians, they drew up in the centre of their lodges and made the demand. And from some misunderstanding with the interpreter (who it is said was drunk) orders were given to fire, "the guns being elevated, so as to shoot over their heads (intending no doubt to intimidate them), wounding the principle Chief severely," and before the piece could be reloaded, the Indians poured upon them a shower of shot and arrows, killing 26 of the soldiers upon the spot and the rest in detail; the Interpreter was pursued some distance and killed—and one man got into the brush, was found, bro[ugh]t to the fort speechless and died next day.—Immediately after the men were kill[e]d., one of the bands of Indians went back to the Am[erica]n. fur company's post (5 miles from Laramie) in which was stored the government amenities [annuities?], and took away $15,000 that belonged to them as amenities and some $10,000 belonging to the Fur Co. which the Co. expected [the] Govt. would of course make good to them. It is said the Indians have crossed the river and gone North. Yesterday we met a man who said that the Sioux's had stole some 27 horses at Ft. Kearny.

John Taylor to Brigham Young, "75 Miles to Fort Kearny," Oct. 6, 1854, Church of Jesus Christ of Latter-day Saints. See also "Washington L. Jolley Company, 1854," Mormon Pioneer Overland Travel (database), Church of Jesus Christ of Latter-day Saints, Salt Lake City, https://history.lds.org/overlandtravel/companies/173/washington-l-jolley-company-1854; Fred E. Woods, "A Gifted Gentleman in Perpetual Motion: John Taylor as an Emigration Agent," in *Champion of Liberty: John Taylor*, ed. Mary Jane Woodger (Provo, Utah: Brigham Young University Religious Studies Center, 2009), 177–92.

38. Mr. McConnell, civilian traveler, October 13, 1854
He saw the graves of the murdered soldiers.

The identity of McConnell, the source of this story, has not been determined, nor has his credibility as a witness. Of primary interest, though, to the Missouri River settlements, whose economies depended on a safe and open overland trail, was the threat from Indian raiders, and McConnell's garbled account did nothing to ease fears.

As noted in the Sutherland account recorded a few days earlier, McConnell mentioned the common grave of Grattan's command. This feature became a point of interest for passersby for the next few years.

Through the kindness of Mr. [initials illegible] McConnell who reached Council Bluff City, Iowa, a few days since from Salt Lake Valley, we glean the following news from the plains.

He left Salt Lake on the 4th of Sept. Mr. [Almon Whiting] Babbitt's train had arrived and were all well.

Passed Ft. Laramie on the 22nd ult. [Sept.] Old Bear [Conquering Bear], the head chief of the Sioux, had died of his wounds received at the massacre, and, his influence no longer controlling the tribe, it was supposed the Sioux would become still more troublesome. The soldiers were fortifying the fort, and Lieut. [Hugh] Fleming was satisfied he could withstand any attack the Indians might make. Some 200 U.S. dragoons were on their way thither and were daily expected at old Ft. Kearny [on the Missouri River] on the 3rd inst. [Oct.]

He met several war parties of Shians [Cheyennes] before arriving at new Ft. Kearney [Fort Kearny on the Platte River]. Two days previous to meeting them they had stolen 22 mules belonging to the U.S. which had been grazing in the vicinity of the fort. The traders in the vicinity of Ft. Laramie had nearly all left the place on account of the danger apprehended from the Indians. The war party of Shian Indians whom he met were returning from burning the Pawnee village and had a large number of their horses. The Pawnees were making great haste away and will perhaps winter with the Pottawattamie Indians. He saw the graves of the murdered soldiers. A young man by the name of [Jesse A.] Jones—clerk in the store house at Ft. Laramie—went down to see the fight with the Indians and finding the wounded soldier took him on his horse and galloped away for the Ft., followed by the Indians, nearly escaping with his own life. He, however, we presume, was not among the soldiers when the fight commenced. Mr. McConnell came through in company with some St. Joseph merchant trains, health of the train good, and found no trouble with the Indians during the journey. Near new Ft. Kearney he heard the report that a war party of Sioux Indians were intending to make a descent ere long on the Omahas [members of the Omaha tribe], but little credence however was paid to the report.

Mr. McConnell, "Late from the Plains," *Omaha Arrow*, Oct. 13, 1854.

39. Alfred J. Vaughan, Indian agent, October 19, 1854

I have taken particular pains to obtain a true statement of the affair.

From 1852 to 1857 Alfred J. Vaughan served as the United States agent for the Upper Missouri Indian tribes and annually reported on the "conditions of the Indians within this agency," a vast expanse of territory and an immense responsibility. To this document, or "the foregoing" as he termed it, Vaughan attached an additional message that related specifically to the troubles along the North Platte River, an area outside his jurisdiction but not of his interest or concern. The Lakota tribes paid scant attention to agency boundaries, and so did Vaughan.

A marginal note: when Vaughan referred to the "proper kind" of soldiers, he meant mounted troops, not infantry of the sort killed so easily at Fort Laramie.

The foregoing was written at Fort Union, at which time it was my intention to have dispatched it to the department from that place, after which I concluded to come on myself to this post and arrived here last evening and regretted much to learn of the unfortunate massacre of Lieut. Grattan and party near

Fort Laramie. I have taken particular pains to obtain a true statement of the affair and think the following can be relied upon.

The Wahza-zhe, Brulee, and a part of the Ogal-al-lah bands of Sioux Indians were all encamped about six miles below Fort Laramie. An emigrant train in passing had one of their cows killed by them. Complaint was made to the commanding officer at Fort Laramie [Lt. Hugh Fleming]. Some Indians visiting the fort told the commandant that the offender would be surrendered by the head chief if sent for. He immediately dispatched Lieut. Grattan with a command of 25 or 30 men; they arrived at the lodge of the head chief [Conquering Bear], where the lieutenant demanded the surrender of the Indian who had killed the cow [High Forehead]. This was refused, and they defied the officer to take him, and, from the number of armed Indians crowding around him, Lieut. Grattan saw that their intentions were hostile. He ordered his men to fire upon them, which they did, wounding the head chief mortally (since dead) and another Indian. They then discharged the two cannon without effect, having been too much elevated, and before they could reload, the Indians, who awaited ready, closed upon them and massacred the whole party. As soon as this was accomplished, they proceeded to the trading-house of James Bordeaux and robbed him of everything, and it was with difficulty that the whites escaped with their lives. From thence they proceeded to the trading establishment of Messrs. P. [Pierre] Chouteau, Jr. & Co., where the goods intended to be distributed to them from the government were stored. They broke open the house and took the whole of them, then broke the store of Messrs. Chouteau & Co. open, robbed it of a large stock of goods left from last year's trade and an entire new stock just arrived from the Missouri, amounting to about twelve or fifteen hundred dollars.

The commander of Fort Laramie was unable to render any assistance or protection to the whites on the Platte, not having men enough to protect his fort had the Indians attacked it as they at one time stated they would do.

On the following day the whole of these Indians moved off. They are now scattered in small bands within 60 to 150 miles of this place and are trying to enlist the Indians in this section of the country to join them in a general war on all whites. They keep war parties continually on the road between this and the Platte, and any white man found on the road will certainly be killed by them. They state openly that next spring they will keep parties constantly on the emigrant route and kill all they find.

I assure you that my situation here, as well as that of all the traders and their men, at present is perilous in the extreme. There is but one course for the government to adopt and that must be done promptly—to send a sufficient number of troops of the proper kind and pursue the bands of Indians who have been concerned in this affair and chastise them in such a manner that they will not only respect but fear the government in future. Without a salutary lesson there is no knowing to what extent they will commit murder and depredations on the whites.

On my way to this place a few days since I arrived at the Yanctonnais village of Sioux Indians, encamped on the river about 100 miles above this place. They generally belonged to a band who have always been more or less averse to carrying out the provisions of the "Laramie treaty" [Fort Laramie Treaty of 1851, negotiated at Horse Creek]. I immediately called a council with the chiefs and braves, and, after talking over all matters with them and giving them good and proper advice, which I thought they received in the spirit I intended they should, I made them a present of some tobacco, provisions, &c., when, to my surprise, the principal chief, called "Red Leaf," arose with the knife in his hand, cut all the bags containing the provisions to pieces, scattering their contents on the prairie, then threw the gunpowder in the river, and about fifty of them discharged their guns at it. This band of Indians have been very refractory for a number of years; the different agents who have seen them have all told them that troops would be sent to chastise them if they did not alter their conduct. They regard this now as only a threat, and, until the presence of troops intimidates them, they will always be dangerous and troublesome.

At Fort Clark I found one hundred lodges of Aukpapas [Hunkpapas], Blackfeet [Lakota], and Sioux Indians, who had been waiting there a month to see me. In the council I held with them, the principal chiefs told me that they would not receive any presents from the government and to do what I pleased with their portion of goods for they did not want them, that they preferred the liberty to take scalps and commit whatever depredations they pleased in preference to goods from their Great Father. They talked very hostile, and I replied to them that, just as certain as the sun rose and set, their Great Father would not only chastise them for their bad conduct but for the indignity offered to him in not receiving their presents.

Alfred J. Vaughan, Indian agent, Fort Pierre, to Alfred Cumming, superintendent, Indian affairs, St. Louis, Oct. 19, 1854, in *Annual Report of the Commissioner of Indian Affairs, 1854*, 87–89.

40. "W," anonymous correspondent, October 25, 1854

If he erred at all, it was in placing too much confidence in an Indian.

The following detailed, lengthy, and opinionated summary of the events of August 19, penned by the anonymous correspondent "W," obviously came from the pen of Capt. Oscar Winship. His motivations for having this appear in the *National Intelligencer*, a Washington newspaper of extensive reach and influence, are equally obvious—first, to respond to published criticism of Grattan, and second and more important, to place the blame of the outcome on the Indians and not the army, and more specifically, to libel the victim, Conquering Bear, who "betrayed Grattan and his command." The accusations against the Lakota leaders (for premeditation) and their warriors (for firing their bows and arrows first) prompted Winship's stern call for retribution, an appeal that also appeared prominently in the official report he submitted elsewhere to his superiors.

To the Editors of the *National Intelligencer:* I beg a space in your columns for a statement relative to the massacre of Lieut. Grattan's party of United States troops at Sarpy's Point, near Fort Laramie, on the 19th of August last. I am induced to ask this favor in consequence of the number of newspaper and other reports of the affair which have reached me since my return from a tour of the plains, and which, I am convinced, are calculated, if not intended, to shield the guilty parties at the expense of the dead.

I was not present at this massacre, and cannot, therefore, speak as an eye-witness; but I have been at great pains to collect the facts in the matter from those who were, written or verbal statements from nearly all of whom I succeeded in obtaining on the ground and from the witnesses themselves, in a week or two after the affair occurred. Many of these statements are incoherent and inconsistent with each other, but they all agree enough in certain material points at least to fix the character of the transaction, which is all that could be expected. I shall endeavor to enumerate these material points as briefly as possible.

For some time previous to the 18th of August last a large body of Sioux Indians, say four thousand souls, comprising the better part of the Ogalala and Brule bands of the same, together with fragments of other bands, had been

encamped on the North Platte between the trading house of the American
Fur Company and that of a Mr. Bordeau, situated, respectively, some five and
eight miles below Fort Laramie.

On the day above named, a Mormon emigrant train passed this camp, and
an ox or cow belonging to one of the emigrants was captured and killed by
one or more Indians from the camp. The owner of the bullock complained
of the depredation to the commanding officer of Fort Laramie, Lieut. [Hugh]
Fleming and invoked his authority for remuneration. Soon after this report
came the chief of the Brules to Lieut. Fleming and confirmed it in all essential
particulars. This chief, known by the name of the "Bear," was a man of great
influence among the Sioux and had the confidence of the whites generally and
especially of the officers at Fort Laramie. Lieut. Fleming had no hesitation,
therefore, in acting upon the suggestion made to him by the chief to send
a detachment of troops to demand the offending Indian, who the Bear said
was a Minicoujou, residing in the Brule camp, adding, in substance, that he
would be given up on such demand without any difficulty.

Accordingly, on the day following, the 19th of August, Lieut. [John] Grattan, twenty-nine enlisted men (who volunteered for the duty), and the post
interpreter (Mr. Auguste [Auguste Lucien]) were dispatched to the Sioux
camp for the offending Minicoujou. They left the fort at 3 o'clock P.M. with
two pieces of artillery (a 12-pounder field and a mountain howitzer) and a
wagon to carry such as could not be transported on the gun-carriages.

Arrived at Gratiot's trading-house of the American Fur Company, a halt
was ordered and the small arms of the party loaded without capping. The
march was then resumed and continued until within reach of the Indians,
when a second halt was ordered, the howitzers loaded with grape or canister
and the small arms capped. In this state of preparation for an emergency the
party moved on the road opposite to and some six hundred yards from the
centre of the Brule camp, which, in form of a semi-circle, lay between the
road and the river, having the Ogalala camp above and Mr. Bordeau's trading
establishment below and partially embraced within it.

Here Lieut. Grattan sent for Mr. Bordeau, who was a trader of thirty years'
standing in the country, to consult with him as to the best means of accomplishing the object of his mission, and it was agreed that it was best to send
for the Bear and prevail upon him to deliver up the offending Minicoujou,
without going into the Brule camp with the troops. Mr. B. went for the
chief, who returned with him, followed by several other Indians, then mostly

unarmed. Lieut. Grattan demanded of the Bear the delivery of the offender, according to his implied promise made at the fort the day before. The Chief evaded the demand and, in fact, positively refused to comply with it at this time. His language is variously represented. Some say that he asked for more time; others, that he would leave it for the offender himself to decide whether he would be taken of his own accord, and others, still, say that the Chief replied to Lieut. Grattan's remark that he must have the Indian if he had to take him for force, "Well, if you cannot wait, go and take him yourself." At all events some such reply left the officer no other recourse than to attempt the accomplishment of the object of his expedition by taking the offender by force if need be. Accordingly he ascertained precisely the locality of the Minicoujou, which was nearly in the centre of the Brule camp, and proceeded at once, with his whole party, in that direction, supposing, doubtless, that unless resistance to the capture had already been determined upon by the Indians (which could not be without treachery on the part of the Bear), so bold a step would secure the offender and thus overcome the greatest apparent scruples of the Chief, namely, the putting himself in opposition to the manifest sentiments and intentions of his own band. But in this he showed that he still relied too much upon the influence and integrity of the Bear (for whom it is well known that he had the greatest esteem, believing him to be incapable of cowardice or treachery). He gained the locality of the Minicoujou depredator, whom he found haranguing the populace like Mark Anthony, although in his own instead of Caesar's name, saying that he wanted to die and that this quarrel was one of his own raising, and he wished to fight it out himself with his own bow and arrows, and he desired no one else to be involved in it, &c., when he well knew that not less than five hundred warriors were within arrow shot of him and of the troops, waiting only for the favorable opportunity to arrive to slake their thirst for the blood of the latter. This is no fancy portrait of the copper-skinned orator, for I have it from a reliable spectator [Obridge Allen?] who witnessed the progress of affairs from a point which overlooked the whole field of operations, that as soon as Lieut. Grattan left the road for the Brule camp, hundreds of warriors took up their position behind the latter where the ground favored their movements and their concealment until the moment for action should arrive, thus showing that it was the object of the expedition of Lieut. Grattan, which was well known from the first, and not his own or his interpreter's conduct, as has been preposterously asserted, that brought about the collision which followed.

Lieut. G. had now made his final disposition for the issue, whatever it might be, surrounded all the time by men desiring, or pretending to desire, a delay in the demands he had made. At last he was compelled to cut short this parley and demand the instant surrender of the man he came for, under penalty of immediate hostilities against the camp. The mask was then dropped by the Indians and their true designs rendered apparent, which were to gain as much time as possible before responding definitely to a requisition which required no time at all to consider upon (if they intended to do justice), in order to render resistance to it more effective.

Lieut Grattan gave the preliminary orders for a file or battle fire, but, before they had been executed, or at any rate before the fire itself had fairly commenced, his devoted little band was assailed by such a storm of Indian projectiles as to throw confusion into its ranks. The Lieutenant himself had previously dismounted and given his horse in charge to one of his men and was superintending the fire of the two howitzers, which made a single discharge each, when the man in charge of the limber, the interpreter, and wagoner took to flight, not, however, before Lieut. Grattan and a large number of the detachment had fallen in their tracks. Of the remainder some endeavored to overtake the wagon, and some two or three succeeded but were soon overwhelmed by the pursuing savages, who by this time came pouring in from all sides and from every quarter of the Sioux camp. The interpreter and the men in charge of the animals were all killed before they had gone half a mile, and the remnant of the party, which had made a stand near the road, were struck down to a man in their last position. In short, but a single individual of the whole party finally escaped from the bloody massacre, and he died two or three days after of his wounds.

Lieut. G.'s body was found the next morning lying beside the gun he had superintended and served, and, together with those of two of his men also found near the howitzer, was interred almost literally under the soil their blood had moistened. The rest were buried in a common grave at no great distance from the position they had occupied on the day of the massacre. Peace to their ashes! May neither the tongue nor the pen of the interested, hypocritical, and carping critic ever disturb their repose or succeed in averting one jot or tittle of the just retribution which an outraged government and an indignant people owe to their savage and treacherous murderers! This detachment was composed of the elite of the best infantry company in the department of the West and was commanded by an officer who, whatever errors of judgment he may have committed in this affair, was at least every inch a soldier and has won a soldier's grave, which is more than any of his detractors will ever accomplish if they can help it. If he erred at all, it was in placing too much confidence in an Indian, and that is an error that older and more experienced soldiers than he was had committed before and with results, too, not less fatal to themselves and to all concerned. Such mistakes, however, are common to great and generous minds and are, after all, less dangerous than those committed by men who distrust all mankind and whose manners lead them to impute conduct and motives to the unfortunate dead which have not a shadow of foundation in fact or in probability. Precisely such conduct and motives have been charged upon poor Grattan. One person writes to the [St. Louis] *Missouri Democrat* the "full particulars of the massacre at Fort Laramie," where he says that Lieut. G., after having shot the Bear and ordered his men to fire, left the field; whereas his body was found precisely on the spot where he stood when the engagement commenced, transfixed by a score of arrows! Again, this veracious chronicler of "full particulars" &c. says that "Lieut. Grattan might have been prompted throughout by vindictive feelings which illy qualified him for the duty assigned him." Yes, and he might not, but, as we have nothing to do with what he might have been, we will content ourselves with what he was—a known and staunch friend of the Bear, by whom he would have sworn until the moment when he shot him (if he did shoot him), and that was the moment when he became convinced that the Bear had betrayed him and his whole command. There are other precious historical facts recorded in this Democratic document which can scarcely be reviewed in an article already too long but which may serve to stimulate officers who are liable to be called upon to sacrifice themselves for the maintenance of the dignity of the government, the interests of the country, and the rights of its citizens.

After all, I do not know why I should have been betrayed so far into these side issues, got up by interested traders and traders' understrappers [underlings] with Indian wives, Indian habits, manners, and tastes, and many of them with Indian blood in their veins, if it were not that they seem to have got a hold upon the public at the expense of truth, justice, common honesty, and a wise policy. There is scarcely a school boy in this country of books and newspapers that does not know that the government has a right to demand offenders against its own laws and within its own territorial jurisdiction. The Indians, who neither read nor write, know it well. And, yet, if an officer or agent of the government endeavors to enforce such laws, though under the most stringent orders of his government, there will be found hundreds of interested interlopers who will monopolize the public ear, saying that Capt. So-and-so, or Lieut. So-and-so did not post his artillery in the right place, that he, or his interpreter, or both, were drunk and therefore the Indians were perfectly right in disregarding their treaty obligations.

To show that this illustration is no caricature, I could point out persons who contend that [the] government should take no notice of the massacre at Fort Laramie because Lieut. Grattan did not wait until the Indians were ready to deliver up the depredator for whom he was sent or because he did not take up a position where, in fact, he could have done them no harm, although his party would have been none the more secure in the end; for in view of twelve hundred men already determined and prepared to fight, twenty or thirty men stand but a small chance, even with a choice of position.

Finally, to come to that class of cavillers [cavaliers] who assert that the expedition was a Quixotic one, and that the commanding officer was reprehensible for dispatching it, I have merely to say that, in all human probability, had no soldier been sent out, none would have been killed, but this spirit of masterly inactivity would scarcely be in keeping with the spirit of this fast age, and if we were always to delay action until we were assured of success, no enterprise, either of a peaceful or warlike character, would ever be undertaken.—W.

W. [Winship, Oscar F.], "The Late Massacre near Fort Laramie," *National Intelligencer* (Washington, D.C.), Oct. 25, 1854, reprinted in *Missouri Republican*, Nov. 2, 1854.

41. Obridge Allen, November 19, 1854, or before
I'll have him or die.

A wild card arrived at Fort Laramie in the form of Maj. William Hoffman, the commander of the relief column and a man of his own mind. Apparently on orders, he investigated the Grattan massacre, took additional testimony including a second, invaluable account from civilian Obridge Allen, and forwarded it up the line. This version offered considerable more detail on the entire event and became, in retrospect, an indictment of the deportment of the late Lieutenant Grattan, damned by his own words. One doubts if Hoffman's military superiors appreciated his thoroughness and Allen's candor.

I arrived at the post the day before the massacre of Lieutenant Grattan and his command. On the day of the massacre I accompanied the party to Mr. Bordeau's trading house. We stopped a few minutes at Mr. Gratiot's, eight or nine miles below this post, where, fearing there might be some trouble with the Indians, I left my overcoat. While here, Lieutenant Grattan ordered his men to load, and just below the house he gave them orders, telling them to obey only his orders or those of the sergeant; said he, "When I give the order, you may fire as much as you d———d please." He told them he didn't believe a gun would be fired, but he "hoped to God they would have a fight."

As we passed the Oga-lar-lar [Oglala] village, which was on the river three-fourths of a mile from the road, and a mile and a half above that of the Brules, Lieutenant Grattan told some person—I don't know to whom he was speaking—to tell them not to leave their camp; if they did, he would "crack into them."

About half a mile from this point I looked back and saw that the Oga-lar-lars were driving up their horses, and I called Lieutenant Grattan's attention to the fact. On reaching Mr. Bordeau's, the Lieutenant asked for him, and when he came out, he told him what he had come for and requested him to send for the Bear, the chief of the Brules. The chief was somewhere near and came in a minute or two. The Lieutenant asked Mr. Bordeau to tell him that he had come for the man who had killed the cow, and he wanted to know if they would give him up. The Bear made some answer, and I asked the man with whom I was talking what he said. He replied, "They are not going to give him up." Then Mr. Grattan said to Mr. Bordeau in a very emphatic manner, "You tell the Bear that I have come down here for that man, and I'll have him or die." The Bear then spoke to the Indians who were standing about—there were a good many—and they all went into the village. He then asked the Lieutenant to go down to the lodge and see the man himself. Then Lieutenant Grattan marched his party into the village accompanied by the Bear, who was mounted behind the interpreter. I then went with a friend, a trader, to his lodge a few steps off and returned in a minute or two and mounted my horse to join the Lieutenant, and just then Mr. Bordeau asked me to let him have my mare to ride to the village, and I did so. I then got on top of the house to see what would happen.

The party was halted about thirty yards from two lodges which were pitched on the edge of a small slough which runs through the camp; in one of which the offender lived. The two cannon were placed near each other, the largest on the right, and the infantry were divided into two parts, half on the right of the cannon and half on the left. The cannon were loaded at Bordeau's house. The men all sat down on the ground.

The council lasted about three quarters of an hour, and during this time I saw many Indians collecting and mounting their horses near the river, and the women and children were leaving the village. At length I saw the soldiers stand up and bring their pieces down as if to fire, and at that moment I heard, I thought, the report of Indian guns, followed immediately by that of muskets. The two cannon were fired directly after. I then saw the limber of the gun turned and start to leave the camp, followed by the wagon. A man was trying to get into the wagon. At the same time the soldiers all commenced to retreat, pursued by the Indians. The limber was overtaken in a quarter of a mile, and the wagon reached the first point of the bluffs which crosses the road, near half a mile, before it was overtaken. The footmen, about eighteen in number—some who had been with the cannon, without arms—reached the road between the two bluffs which cross it, about a mile, where they were all killed by Indians who followed them and, as I supposed, by those who came from the Oga-lar-lar camp above. I saw a great many coming from there over the second point of bluffs. Three or four men were killed near the cannon. The interpreter, who was mounted, and a soldier, who was on the Lieutenant's horse, were overtaken by some Indians who came from near the river below Bordeau's house, passing close to it, near the wagon where they were killed. The soldiers were loading and firing as they retreated.

Mr. Bordeau's house was surrounded by some two or three hundred lodges in one group having a vacant space in the centre, and adjoining this group was another of about a hundred lodges, also having a space in the centre. It was in this village that the lodge of the offender was situated, about three hundred yards from the house.

When the firing took place, there were only about fifty Indians in front of the troops. The others were either concealed in the slough or were getting ready near the river, which was three or four hundred yards distant.

I have heard that it is said that Lieutenant Grattan was intoxicated at the time, but there is no truth in the charge. He did not drink a drop of liquor, that I saw, from the time he left the fort till I parted with him, and there was no appearance of his having drank anything. At Mr. Gratiot's he took a drink of water. On the way down, I noticed that the interpreter was drunk, and I told Mr. Grattan that he had a small flask of liquor. The Lieutenant asked him for it to take a drink, but instead of drinking he broke it on his saddle.

I remained at Mr. Bordeau's all night. The Indians came back there immediately after the affair and tried to break into his house, but some friendly Indians, and men with him, prevented their doing so. They came thus frequently during the night, and Mr. B. gave them what goods they demanded of him.

Mr. Obridge Allen, statement accompanying a report by Maj. William Hoffman, Fort Laramie, Nov. 19, 1854, in *House of Representatives Reports*, No. 63; also in *Senate Executive Documents*, No. 91, where he is listed as "Olbridge" Allen.

42. J. H. Reed, civilian traveler, November 19, 1854, or before
as much difficulty in determining who fired first as in any other details

Was it an "ox" or a "cow" that the Indian killed on August 17, 1854? Commonly an ox refers to a mature, castrated male; a cow is female. Both terms appear almost interchangeably throughout this volume, and the exact gender of the bovine in question may always remain unknown. A second account by J. H. Reed, made at the request of Major Hoffman, did nothing to settle that minor quibble, although he contributed a bit more substance about the demands by its Mormon owner for redress. Apparently civilian Reed, still recuperating at the fort in November from a summer mishap or illness, took the initiative to put together and expand from various sources his version of events. Among his more important contributions were his earlier conversations with Lieutenant Grattan, and ultimately Reed became his most passionate defender.

At the request of Colonel Hoffman, I make the following statement in regard to the massacre of the troops under the command of Lieut. Grattan on the 19th of August last.

I was on my way to Salt Lake City with Col. Steptoe's command, when I met with an accident which entirely disabled me, whereupon I was conveyed by my friends in the train to Fort Laramie. Arriving there on the 16th of July, I was taken to Mr. Grattan's room and remained there a recipient of his kindness until his death. During this time several instances of insubordination manifested themselves among the Indians. The most prominent was the killing of some cattle belonging to the post interpreter, even within the government reserve. At length the act was done which led to the massacre of Mr. Grattan and his men. I state nothing in this paper which I do not believe myself, and my belief is founded, not on the quantity of reports which I may have heard, but on the character of the men from whom they came. I am glad to say that every man in the country, who has not a direct interest in another direction, comes to the same conclusion that I do.

A few days before the slaughter of the troops, an emigrant informed Mr. Fleming, who was temporarily in command of the fort, that on the road below an Indian had shot at him and afterwards had killed a cow, or an ox, belonging to him. Nothing was said on the subject, and we set it down as another instance of the contempt felt by the Indians for the power and authority of the government. On the 18th of August, Martoh-Ioway (which literally means the "Bear that scatters") [Bear that Scatters His Enemies or Conquering Bear], who was appointed a chief of the tribe by Col. [David D.] Mitchell in his treaty of 1851, came to the fort to inform Mr. Fleming that a cow, belonging to an emigrant, had been killed by an Indian and to tell him that, if he would send down for the Indian, he would be delivered up to him.

Before proceeding I will state that, although it is now denied by some persons in this neighborhood that the Indian did shoot at the emigrant and asserted that the cow was deserted by its owner and wandered into the Indian village, yet I do not believe such to be the facts. The emigrant, as I am informed, stated that he had been shot at, and the Indians confirm it. The story derived from the Indians is that the man who did the deed had lost some relatives in a skirmish which took place in the summer or fall of 1853; that the offender said that his relatives were dead, and that he wanted to die, but not until he had avenged himself upon the whites. The Indians, in continuation, say that this offending Indian approached the owner of the cow, who was with the animal, with three arrows in his hand—one of which he shot at the emigrant but missed him. The Indian then said, "I have missed you; you are in the hands of God Almighty, but I will kill your cow," which he did. The emigrant was offered ten dollars for his cow when passing the trading-house of Mr. Bordeau, but declined accepting that amount, asking twenty-five dollars for her.

To return to the place from which I digressed. On the day following the one on which the "Bear" had informed Mr. Fleming of the matter, I asked Mr. Grattan if he would like to be sent against the Indians. He said he would like very well to go but would not go unless he had orders to bring the offender. He did not think that it would be necessary to fight in order to obtain him, but in the course of this conversation, as well as on several other occasions, he told me that, if it was ever necessary to fight Indians when they were in their village, he would place his artillery some three or four hundred yards from their village and run the risk of their driving him from his position. This assertion was made to me while Mr. Grattan was preparing to start on the expedition. I am not, therefore, prepared to believe that he marched straight into the midst of two or three villages for the purpose of attacking them. Mr. Grattan had, ever since I had known him, a great admiration for the "Bear" and implicit confidence in him. Whether the "Bear" was treacherous or not, no man can tell. I have it from the best authority that before Mr. Grattan had left Mr. Bordeau's houses for the purpose of marching into the village, and while he was still demanding the man, the "Bear" spoke to the young men in the Sioux language, and from that moment they commenced catching their horses, stripping off their robes, and preparing for battle. They certainly had taken their positions and were concealed when Mr. Grattan entered into their midst. Some who were in the vicinity say that the "Bear" told Mr. Grattan "that he was a soldier; to come in and take the man." Others say that promises were made that the man would be given to him. It was something that occurred after they were in the village which produced the fight, as all accounts agree that Mr. Grattan did not commence firing upon his entrance, but some time elapsed during which his men were lying about on the grass. His musketry was discharged before his cannon, and the "Bear" was wounded in three places. There is as much difficulty in determining who fired first as in any other details of the transaction. It is my belief that no Frenchman in this country can tell the same story twice the same way if the incidents come under their observation when they are cool, much less can they take notes accurately and report the details correctly when they know that the scene which they are witnessing involves life and property.

Every one whom I have heard speak on the subject coincides in saying that great blame is to be attached to the interpreter. He has been for a long time very odious to the Indians, and there is no doubt that, on this occasion, he inflamed them by rash speeches and threats. Mr. Grattan made several unsuccessful efforts to restrain him.

Some other reports prejudicial to Mr. Grattan's memory were circulated for a short time after his death. They bore the marks of untruth with them and failed to obtain credence. Such were the stories of his having run away during the fight, his being intoxicated at the time, and his boasting on the way down that "he was going down to give the d——d red skins hell." Some of these stories I believe to be untrue; the others are disproved by witnesses in whom I confide.

J. H. Reed, statement accompanying a report by Maj. William Hoffman, Fort Laramie, Nov. 19, 1854, in *House of Representatives Reports*, No. 63; also in *Senate Executive Documents,*

No. 91. When Reed retold the dialogue of Conquering Bear to Lieutenant Grattan to be a "soldier" and "take the man," he did not mean a soldier in the American army sense but a Lakota soldier or *akicita*. The Lakota akicita, members of a select male society, were young, respected men who kept peace and good order in the Indian camps. James R. Walker, *Oglala Society*, ed. Raymond J. DeMallie (Lincoln: University of Nebraska Press, 1982), 28–34. For more on oxen (or, as one author termed them, "educated cattle") see Diana L. Ahmad, "'I Fear the Consequences to Our Animals': Emigrants and Their Livestock on the Overland Trails," *Great Plains Quarterly* 32 (Summer 2012): 165–82; Dixon Ford and Lee Kreutzer, "Oxen: Engines of the Overland Migration," *Overland Journal* 33 (Spring 2015): 4–29; and Kyle D. Kauffman and Jonathan J. Liebowitz, "Draft Animals on the United States Frontier," *Overland Journal* 15 (Summer 1997): 13–26.

43. James Bordeaux, November 19, 1854, or before
I then told the chiefs that they had better be in a hurry.

The next account by trader James Bordeaux, who continued to defend his Indian kinsmen and customers, added more detail and polish to his previous efforts. He provided considerable context to the role of the chiefs. Especially moving were Conquering Bear's words, "I must go and put on my dress-coat." In 1851, as a symbol of his new authority of "chief of the Sioux," the Bear received an army officer's uniform, or "chief's coat," from government officials, and he felt compelled, almost duty-bound to wear it at the finale.

I was at home when Mr. Grattan came down with his party. He stopped at my house and told me he had come down to take prisoner an Indian who had killed a cow belonging to a Mormon, and he wished me to assist him. At his request I sent for the chief Martoh-Ioway [Conquering Bear], who is the chief of the band (the Brules) to which the offender belongs, and on his arrival from the camp, which was very near my house, I told him for Mr. Grattan that he had come down for the Indian who had killed the cow and that he (the Indian) must go with him to the fort to remain there till the agent arrived, when he would decide what should be done in the matter. The chief said, "Very well, but I must go and put on my dress-coat before I give an answer." He returned in a few minutes with three other chiefs, and they were immediately followed by a messenger from the camp, who said that the man refused to give himself up—he said he would die first. Lieutenant Grattan then asked where his lodge was, and the chief pointed it out to him. The lieutenant said he would take his command within sixty yards of it, and he'd have him, dead or alive. He then moved around the house and went a little way into the camp, when he halted. Then a second messenger came and said, as the former had said, that the man would not give himself up—he would rather die. The lieutenant said again that he would go within sixty yards of the lodge and that he must have him. He then told his men what he was going to do and how they must act; that when he gave the word, they must fire on every man that was not a white man. I then told the chiefs that they had better be in a hurry and get the man as quick as they could. The chief said it was their custom to make a demand four times, and, if it was not agreed to then, then they acted, and he wanted the lieutenant to observe this rule. He said that he was determined to go to the lodge. I told him that he was going into a very bad place and that he had better prepare himself well. He said he had two revolvers with twelve shots. I told him to take them out of his holsters and be ready. I then turned back and got upon a robe press, where I could see him till he halted. During this time his interpreter was in the camp, bantering the Indians and irritating them. I told him that he would make trouble and that, if he would put him in my house, I would settle the difficulty in thirty minutes. He said he would stop him. He had told him several times to stop, but he did not mind him.

As soon as he halted, he was immediately surrounded by Indians, and one of the chiefs came running to me and said, "My friend, come on; the interpreter is going to get us into a fight, and they are going to fight if you don't come." I got on a horse to go, but finding the stirrups too long I turned back, and the chief came to me a second time urging me to go. I started with him, but, when I got within 150 yards, I saw that it was too late—the excitement was too great. At this moment the first gun was fired by the soldier on the right, and I then heard an Indian call out not to fire; that they had killed one man and might be satisfied, but the words were hardly out of his mouth before the firing commenced on his left; then I turned back home, and, before I reached the house, I heard one cannon fired, and, when I got on the top of my house, I saw the second cannon fired by Lieutenant Grattan, and then he fell. As he was firing the cannon, I saw the soldiers putting three wounded men in the wagon, and, when he fell, the wagon moved off. Two other men fell about ten feet from him. One soldier who was holding on to the wagon was killed in about twenty yards, and the wagon was pursued by Indians on horseback to a little rise about half a mile distant, where they stopped it and killed the other soldiers. I then completed the arrangements I had been making to protect myself. A rush was made on the house by a number of

Indians, but our friends among them interfered and prevented them doing us any harm. Then a chief, Little Thunder, came and told me that, since the Indians had killed all the soldiers at the camp, they were going to kill all at the fort and burn it up. I told him to stop them; that if they did not do any more harm and did not disturb anybody on the river, I thought their grandfather would forgive them for what they had done. He went out immediately and with all the other chiefs harangued the Indians and did all they could to put down the excitement, but my opinion is that, if the sun had been two hours higher, they could not have stopped it.

They immediately broke up their camp and crossed the river—all except the old chief, who was wounded, who remained with a strong guard about him all night. Little Thunder was going backwards and forwards all night to keep down the excitement. Indians were coming to my house all night begging; they said they had been waiting on the agent two months, that their children were starving, and that they were bound to have what they wanted. The chiefs told me to give them what they wanted because they were just trying to pick a quarrel with us to kill us all, and I gave them whatever they demanded. During the night some of the friendly Indians brought in a wounded soldier and said, if his wounds did not kill him, nobody should hurt him. A few minutes after, a chief came in and advised me to hide him somewhere outside for fear some of the other Indians would find him there and make it an excuse for killing us. The man said, if I could send someone with him, he would prefer to go to the fort, and I sent a white man [Obridge Allen] and two Indians with him, who accompanied him about a mile, and he then said he could go himself. About 1 o'clock at night I sent an express up to Lieutenant Fleming to tell him what had occurred. The next morning, after they had taken the wounded chief over the river, about 500 of them came back and took from me what they wanted and then went up to the American Fur Company's house and took from there the presents which were stored there for them. In the evening they returned and took the goods belonging to the Fur Company. The massacre took place on Saturday evening, and on Monday morning I received a note from Lieutenant Fleming, requesting me to bury the dead, and I did so. It is not true that the Indians told me I should not bury the dead—that the soldiers must come and do it themselves.

After daylight in the morning the wounded soldier returned just as the Indians were leaving, and I kept him till next day, Monday, when I sent him to the fort.

There was no excitement before the soldiers arrived, and, when they came in sight, the Indians expressed their surprise and wondered who they were. No one at my house knew anything of the difficulty and had heard nothing of the soldiers coming.

Mr. [James] Bordeau[x], statement accompanying a report by Maj. William Hoffman, Fort Laramie, Nov. 19, 1854, in *House of Representatives Reports*, No. 63; also in *Senate Executive Documents*, No. 91, with minor changes.

44. William Hoffman, army officer, November 19, 1854
Lieutenant Grattan left his post with a desire to have a fight.

Latecomer Major Hoffman now weighed in with his conclusions, the first of several credible contributions to this compendium: Grattan fired first, there was no premeditation by the Indians, and the hapless Conquering Bear was shot down for no good reason. This failure to hew the party line produced an immediate rebuke from his Washington superiors (note the comment added at the end by Adjutant General Samuel Cooper). Grattan's bravery or judgment could not be publicly questioned. Hoffman responded later by soliciting more damning testimony to back up his case.

William Hoffman Jr., a New York native born in 1807 and the son of Lt. Col. William Hoffman, a veteran of the War of 1812, graduated from West Point in 1829 as a classmate of Robert E. Lee. He served in infantry regiments of the Regular Army up to 1860. To say this veteran, no-nonsense officer had seen long and hard service in the antebellum U.S. Army would be a laughable understatement. Hoffman served the Union army as its commissary general of prisoners and retired honorably from the service in 1870.

I have the honor to make the following report of the massacre of Lieutenant Grattan and his command, as requested by your instructions of [blank].

It appears that in August last, a cow belonging to a Mormon emigrant was killed by a Sioux Indian belonging to the Minicoujon [This is spelled *Minicongee* in another printed version of this account.] band, who was at the time living with the Brules. On the 18th the Bear, the head chief of the Sioux, reported the fact to Lieutenant Fleming and told him he would give up the offender. On the 19th Lieutenant Fleming sent Lieutenant Grattan, with the interpreter, a sergeant, corporal, and twenty-seven men, and two twelve-pounder howitzers, to receive the man, with discretionary orders in case of refusal to give him up.

There is no doubt that Lieutenant Grattan left his post with a desire to have a fight with the Indians and that he determined to take the man at all hazards. On reaching Mr. Bordeau's trading-house, which was just within the camp, he had an interview with the Bear, and, finding that he could not or would not give up the man, he moved his command into the camp and placed his cannon and his infantry in line fronting the lodge occupied by the offender. Here he held a council with the chiefs, which, resulting unsatisfactorily, he appears to have ordered his men to fire. After the first discharge of their muskets the soldiers were quite at the mercy of the Indians, and they were all massacred.

It does not seem that the affair was anticipated by the Indians, but they evidently prepared themselves for it as soon as they knew what the troops came for.

What occurred after the party entered the village is only known through the Indians.

One report says that just at the close of the interview Lieutenant Grattan took out his watch and said, "It is getting late, and I can't wait any longer," to which the Bear replied, "I have done all I could, and, since you will have him, now push on and take him," or something to that effect, and then turned to walk away. As he did so, he was shot by the soldiers and wounded in three places. I am inclined to think this report true.

It is not improbable that the Bear was sincere in his desire to give up the man, but he could not carry out his wishes.

I enclose the report of Lieutenant Fleming in relation to the affair, a statement made by a young gentleman, Mr. J. H. Reed, of St. Louis, who were here living with Lieutenant Grattan and who heard all the reports that were circulated at the time, and statements made by Mr. Bordeau, at whose house the first talk with the Bear took place, and by a young man named Allen, a man of character and veracity, I think, who accompanied Lieutenant Grattan from the post to Bordeau's house. It is Mr. Bordeau's interest to put the case in as favorable a light for the Indians as he can. These statements will enable the General to form a judgment on the merits of the case.

Endorsement by Samuel Cooper, adjutant general, Jan. 3, 1855. There is nothing in the accompanying papers to corroborate Lieutenant Colonel Hoffman's statement that "there is no doubt that Lieutenant Grattan left this post with a desire to have a fight with the Indians." While this remark adds nothing to the character of Lieutenant Grattan for bravery, it would seem to detract from his judgment as an officer.

Bvt. Lt. Col. [Maj. William] Hoffman, Sixth Infantry, commanding Fort Laramie, N. T. [Nebraska Territory], report to Capt. F. N. [Frank N.] Page, assistant adjutant general, Department of the West, Jefferson Barracks, Nov. 19, 1854, in *House of Representatives Reports*, No. 63; also in *Senate Executive Documents*, No. 91; E. D. T. [Edward D. Townsend], "Necrology—William Hoffman," in *Sixteenth Annual Reunion of the Association of Graduates of the United States Military Academy at West Point, New York, June 12th, 1885* (East Saginaw, Mich.: Evening News, 1885), 36–39.

45. Hugh B. Fleming, November 19, 1854
I gave Lieutenant Grattan orders . . .
not to hazard an engagement without certainty of success.

In yet another report, Lieutenant Fleming offered up more details on the massacre, possibly putting a fine line now on his controversial instructions to Grattan. Fleming assumed that his subordinate would be acting against only fifteen lodges of Minicon-jous. At the generally accepted ratio of the day of two to three warriors per lodge, the doomed detachment of roughly equal size would look more reasonable on paper. Of course, Fleming's notion was largely fanciful since there was no practical way to discriminate this Indian group from the larger conglomeration of Lakota villagers, many of them kinsmen and all of them interested parties in a potential conflict.

In compliance with your instructions I have the honor to make the following report concerning the massacre of a detachment of G company, 6th Infantry, by the Sioux Indians near Fort Laramie, and also the orders given Lieutenant Grattan by me.

On the 18th of August, 1854, an emigrant came to the fort, reported that the Sioux Indians had killed one of his cattle and that he had barely escaped with his life. The same day the head chief of the Sioux, the "Bear," came and reported that one of the Indians had killed a cow belonging to an emigrant, and he wished to state to me that the offender did not belong to his band, but was a Minicoujon [spelled *Miniconga* in another printed version of this report]. At the same time he spoke about the depredations of the Minicoujon band at the bridge, 130 miles above the fort, this summer and said their hearts were bad towards the whites and promised to give up the offender. On the 19th I sent Lieutenant Grattan, with the interpreter, one sergeant, one corporal, and twenty-seven men, with two twelve-pounder howitzers, to receive the offender. I learned that there were only about fifteen lodges of the Minicoujon band encamped with the other Indians, and I gave Lieutenant Grattan orders to go and receive the offender and, in case of refusal to give him up after ascertaining the disposition of the Indians, to act upon his own discretion and to be careful not to hazard an engagement without certainty of success. I also gave Lieutenant Grattan directions to tell the chief that the Indian would not be injured in any way whatever and that I would keep him at the fort till his father, the agent, arrived. It appears the chief tried, or at least made Lieutenant Grattan think he tried, to give up the Indian who committed the depredation. Last year we had a skirmish with the Minicoujon band but were on the best and most friendly terms with all the other, and the force sent was sent only to act, if necessary, against the few lodges of the above hostile band. It may be thought that the treacherous Indians were trusted too far, but at the same time we must remember that with so few troops as were stationed at Fort Laramie, so far in the Indian country, surrounded by thousands of Indians, it becomes absolutely necessary to rely on the good faith of some of them even for the safety of the garrison itself. Lieutenant Grattan, with his whole command, was massacred, and I have no doubt, from all I am able to learn, he was dealt with in a most treacherous manner.

"Report of Lieutenant Fleming" [Second Lt. Hugh B. Fleming], Sixth Infantry, Fort Laramie, to Maj. William Hoffman, commanding Fort Laramie, Nov. 19, 1854, in *House of Representatives Reports*, No. 63, also in *Senate Executive Documents*, No. 91. Hoffman not-so-diplomatically added: "Lieutenant Fleming does not say in his report, that having himself headed a successful expedition against a village of Miniconzhoes the previous year, in which three or four were killed, it was promised to Lieutenant Grattan that he should go out on the next occasion; nor that the expedition was only determined on at the dinner-table a short time before it marched; nor that the commanding officer was so little aware of what was going forward that he did not know how many men went with the party; nor that Lieutenant Grattan was a volunteer and earnestly sought the duty; yet these are all relevant facts." Hoffman to Cooper, Oct. 11, 1855, Fort Laramie Collections.

46. William Hoffman, November 19, 1854

The mail from Salt Lake was attacked by Indians.

The November 13 attack on the Salt Lake mail party was seen as another unacceptable affront to government authority. Maj. William Hoffman, now commanding Fort Laramie, was demonstrably outraged. Military authorities, though, did not see the act for what it really was—kinsmen's revenge for the killing of Conquering Bear.

Nevertheless, this incident, along with the fear of further Lakota measures, effectively brought the overland mail to a halt. This could not stand.

I have the honor to report that on the evening of the 13th [Nov.] the mail from Salt Lake was attacked by Indians about twelve miles this side of Horse Creek, three of the four persons with it killed, and the fourth, a passenger, severely wounded. Fortunately he was found soon after by a man from Mr. Dix's [Drips's] trading house and taken to the house.

On the evening of the 14th I received a note from Mr. Dix and a statement made by Mr. Kincaid [Kinkead], the wounded man, giving an account of the affair. It appears that the Indians were concealed by the road side, some ten to twenty in number, and at the first fire the conductor, who was riding a few yards in advance, and the mail drivers fell, and Mr. Kincaid on looking out of the carriage received a wound in the neck. For a little time he was senseless, but on recovering he jumped on a mule and tried to escape. The Indians followed him, and, after shooting him with arrows three or four times, they knocked him off his mule, which they took, and left him lying on the ground. They saw him get up, and one of them waved his hand as to tell him to go away. He was able to return nearly to the trading house, some five to six miles.

Immediately on receiving Mr. Dix's note I despatched Capt. [William Scott] Ketchum with a subaltern and forty men to the scene of the murder to collect what information he could by a careful examination of the ground and to pursue and destroy the murderers if it were practicable to do so. I directed him also to secure the mails and other property that might have been left by the Indians.

The report of Capt. Ketchum which accompanies this will show you the result of this expedition. To expedite the movement I placed his men in wagons.

This act of unqualified hostility on the part of the Sioux, following immediately on the arrival of a reinforcement to this garrison, shows very conclusively how far they are awed by the presence of the increased force and how far they are governed by their recent treaty of peace. A repetition of these outrages, I think, may be anticipated at every opportunity that presents itself to the Indians.

I need not trouble the General with my views in relation to the appropriate garrison for this post further than to respectfully refer him to my letter of the 18th Sept. written at St. Louis.

The strength of the rank and file of this command is now 153, whereas it should be 253.

It is perhaps proper for me to offer a suggestion or two, which I do with all deference, in relation to the mode of making war on these Indians. It is folly for Infantry, or mounted men, to go in pursuit of small parties of marauders who can always out travel us, and who can at a moment's notice scatter over miles of country, while the soldiers must move together, slowly following the trail if they can find it. But instead of a fruitless hunt after a small war party, let a pursuit of months, if necessary, be made up to their camps, where their old men and their women and children are. Their people must starve, or their villages must stop where the buffalo are, and there is where they will be overtaken. It is not a rapid and short pursuit that will accomplish this but a long and persevering one from spring to winter if necessary. The Sioux country should be entered from Fort Pierre on the Missouri, from Fort Kearney [Fort Kearny on the Platte], and from this post at the same time, and in one season they should be so punished that not only they, but all other Indians, should be deterred from ever again molesting a white man on the plains.

During this winter it will be extremely hazardous for the mail to attempt to get through to this post without a strong guard, and, in the expectation that the contractors will not be able to furnish such a guard, I respectfully suggest that the mails be sent up from Fort Leavenworth with an escort of fifteen mounted men.

Maj. William Hoffman, headquarters, Battalion Sixth Infantry, Fort Laramie, N. T. [Nebraska Territory], to Capt. F. N. [Frank N.] Page, assistant adjutant general, Department of the West, Jefferson Barracks, Mo., Nov. 19, 1854, received at department headquarters December 18, 1854, Letters Received, Department of the West, RG 393, NARA. For the names of the mail party fatalities, see "Massacre of the Salt Lake Mail Party by the S[i] oux Indians," *Weekly Brunswicker* (Brunswick, Mo.), Dec. 16, 1854.

47. William Scott Ketchum, army officer, November 19, 1854

I proceeded to the scene of depredation.

Capt. William Scott Ketchum, a member of a large cohort of experienced, battle-hardened officers of the Mexican War who saw frontier service in the 1850s, followed up his crime scene investigation of the mail party murders with this report of his findings. Although Ketchum provided considerable details, he reached no conclusions on a motive for the murders.

In obedience to the instructions of the Commanding Officer of the post, herewith, I have to report that I proceeded to the scene of depredation where I found property belonging to the mail contractors and employers and turned it over to the mail agent and took his receipt therefore. The three men killed were buried by direction of Mr. [Andrew] Drips, a trader, before I reached the ground. He had collected the mail, which I brought to this post and turned over to the post master.

I found, aided by the command, seven arrows, which were picked up in the immediate vicinity of the murder, and I received several from Mr. [James] McClosk[e]y who had aided in burying the dead. I found three places where a single person had squatted or kneeled down for concealment and two single tracks resembling a moccasin foot print near the place of attack. I also struck a trail made by five or six horses or ponies and three shod mules, which I followed until it crosses the Platte river and until I lost it below the Sand Hills in the gravelly soil and short grass. Mr. McClosky, a trader, was the only "volunteer" who accompanied me as far as we could follow the trail. As regards the "volunteers" mentioned in my instructions, I have to state that Mr. [Jean Pierre Bugnion "Bunyan"] Gratiot and one employé accompanied me from his trading house four miles from this place [Fort Laramie] to the trading point of Mr. Drips eighteen miles from the post, and there they left the command. Two men, Mr. McClosky and one other citizen, accompanied me to the place where the dead were buried, where one left and returned to his trading station five or six miles this side of the grave.

Finding it impracticable to follow the trail any farther, I recrossed the Platte river and proceeded by the mail station to within a mile or two of Mr. Boauvai's [Geminien P. Beauvais's] station about 65 or 67 miles from this post, and there I was told by Mr. B. that his hunters had just returned from a hunting excursion upon which occasion they had proceeded below Smith's Fork, some 14 or 15 miles, and had seen no signs of Indians or the mail party expected from the states. As this party had been over the road for at least two or three days travel below Mr. B.'s station, I concluded that, as I had but two days rations with the command, that I ought to return, which I did not do however until I offered to pursue the mail route to Ash Hollow on the upper crossing of the South Fork, provided the mail agent could let me have provisions for the command. The agent could not furnish provisions and stated he was entirely dependent on the mail wagon expected from the states that day. He also told me that he had only about 15 pounds of flour left from his former supply.

On my return I brought the mail agent, the mail, and the wounded man, Mr. Kinkead of Salt Lake City, to this post. Mr. Kinkead can give all the particulars, mode of attack, &c.

I would also state that the government or hired interpreter at this post [Lucien's successor?] was not directed to accompany the expedition or, if he was, that he failed to do so.

Capt. W. Scott Ketchum, Sixth Infantry, commanding party, Fort Laramie, O. R. [Oregon Route], to Lt. John T. Shaaf, Sixth Infantry, acting post adjutant, Fort Laramie, Nov. 19, 1854, received at department headquarters Dec. 18, 1854, Letters Received, Department of the West, RG 393, NARA.

48. Charles E. Galpin, trader, November 20, 1854
all the information . . . relative to your Platte Indians

Post-Grattan communication between the principals of the Indian trade naturally concentrated their attention on determining the dangers inherent in continued commercial ventures. Ominously, the finger of Charles E. Galpin pointed solely at the Brulé Lakotas who ranged along the Platte River and its tributaries as likely recipients of future punishment. For Captain Winship, who copied this letter, the question of more immediate military importance was, Where were the "Platte Indians?"

Galpin operated as a trader in the Fort William–John–Laramie area in the early 1840s until transferring to Fort Pierre on the Missouri River in 1845, where he still resided as a Pierre Chouteau and Company employee in the winter of 1854–55. His letter of November 20, 1854, provided some needed context to understanding the area's "state of affairs."

Your esteemed favor of the 26th October reached here safely, and I congratulate you much upon your very good luck; if your teams had been ten days sooner, they would have been taken and stocks all killed by your Platte Brulees, who have been watching the road since the difficulty at the Platte.

From the present existing state of affairs with the Indians I deem it most prudent and wise not to send anything from here belonging to your outfit. The Indians have repeatedly notified me and also the Agent not to suffer any more travelling upon this road [the Fort Laramie–Fort Pierre trail], at least until their present difficulties are settled with the government. And that in my opinion will not be until the troops will have killed at least one half of the Brule band.

They made several attempts to rob my traders but were prevented by our Missouri Indians. How long they will remain quiet and peaceful with us is very uncertain, and I fear much that it will not be long before they will completely destroy some of my outposts.

They are constantly soliciting the Missouri Indians to join with them, and really I am sorry to say they will succeed in persuading a large portion of our Indians to take sides with them in the spring, at which time they boldly say they intend commencing hostilities upon every white man they may meet with and particularly the Emigrants.

The Brulees will winter near the Missouri, and, as for their doing much in way of hunting and making robes this winter, I think is quite out of the question; therefore they are more of a nuisance than help in the way of trade. The Ogalalas, I understand, are somewhere back of the Black Hills and from what I can learn will winter near the place where Bernard Jeanis [Janis] wintered last winter high on the Platte, say Red But[t]es, or the Crossing, and perhaps may winter with a band of Crows that generally winter in that section of the country.

So this is all the information I am able to give you relative to your Platte Indians.

C. E. [Charles E.] Galpin, "For A.M.O. 1854" [or "U.M.O." as in Upper Missouri Outfit?], Fort Pierre, to G. B. P. [J. P. B.] Gratiot, North Platte River, Nov. 20, 1854, in "Extract, A True Copy: O. F. [Oscar F.] Winship, A. A. G.," Letters Received, Department of the West, RG 393, NARA. See also Frederick T. Wilson, "Old Fort Pierre and Its Neighbors," in *South Dakota Historical Collections*, vol. 1 (Aberdeen, S.Dak.: News Printing, 1902), 294–85, 364–65; John S. Gray, "The Story of Mrs. Picotte-Galpin, a Sioux Heroine: Eagle Woman Learns about White Ways and Racial Conflict, 1820–1868," *Montana: The Magazine of Western History* 36 (Spring 1986): 7. The scientist Ferdinand V. Hayden spent the winter of 1854–55 with Galpin at Fort Pierre. David A. White, ed., *News of the Plains and Rockies, 1803–1865*, vol. 4, *Scientists, Artists, 1835–1859: Original Narratives of Overland Travel and Adventure Selected from the Wagner-Camp and Becker Bibliography of Western Americana* (Spokane: Arthur H. Clark, 1998), 452–53.

49. Alfred J. Vaughan, Indian agent, November 21, 1854

All of the Indians who were present at the unfortunate massacre . . . are now in this vicinity.

Although his official duties lay with serving as a conduit between Native peoples and the federal government, unofficially Alfred J. Vaughan served as a source of military intelligence for the U.S. Army. His report helped fill in the blanks on the likely locations of potential Indian adversaries. In fact, those implicated in the Grattan affair, he reported, were now at Fort Pierre, his station. Three Fort Laramie–area traders had already lost their stores of goods to the Indians, and Vaughan had no wish for the government to be liable for another.

A Virginian and a Confederate sympathizer, Vaughan left government service in 1862. His namesake son became a general in the Confederate army, but in spite of that, the senior Vaughan possessed a sterling reputation, so much so that after the war he returned to Indian country to assist the government in negotiating a new set of treaties with the Upper Missouri tribes.

By an express received at this place from the Platte [overland via the Fort Laramie-Fort Pierre trail] I have received information that some of the traders from that place intend coming over here with a number of waggons loaded with goods to trade with the Indians. All of the Indians who were present at the unfortunate massacre of Lieut. Grattan and his party are now in this vicinity; they, as well as several bands of the Missouri Sioux with whom they are encamped, have notified me that should any traders come among them from that quarter, here, they will kill their oxen and horses and rob them of their merchandise. They have killed several cattle belonging to the traders here and shot arrows in several others, some of which I have seen cut out. I therefore must respectfully and earnestly request that you will prevent them from coming here as I am satisfied it will be attended with serious consequences.

I have by this conveyance notified Mr. [Seth] Ward, whom it is thought will be on the way, and, should he come after receiving this notice, I shall consider it my duty to apprise the government that he was warned of the consequences, thereby preventing him from being remunerated for any depredations that may be committed on him by Indians.

The Indians in this quarter since the arrival of the Brules are very refractory, and, if the government does not chastise them and that speedily, there is no telling the result. I do assure you that the lives of all the whites are in extreme jeopardy.

Mr. [J. P. B.] Gratiot sent his teams here for merchandise, among which are considerable guns and ammunition. I have refused to let it go, and, since the gentleman in charge of this Post [Charles Galpin?] has reflected upon the matter, he has come to the conclusion that it would be running too great a risk even to send his teams back, as the Indians are now said to be waylaying the road between this and the Platte.

A short time since a war party of the Brules came into the forks of White River with seventeen fine American horses, which was stolen from Fort Kearney [Fort Kearny on the Platte]. Another war party has started out to watch the movements of things at Fort Laramie and no doubt will steal every horse they can lay their hands upon.

Alfred J. Vaughan, Indian agent, Fort Pierre, to Fort Laramie commander, Nov. 21, 1854, Letters Received, Department of the West, RG 393, NARA. See also John C. Ewers, *The Blackfeet: Raiders on the Northwestern Plains* (Norman: University of Oklahoma Press, 1958), 229–35. Biographical information about the senior Vaughan can be found in the biography of his son. Lawrence K. Peterson, *Confederate Combat Commander: The Remarkable Life of Brigadier General Alfred Jefferson Vaughan Jr.* (Knoxville: University of Tennessee Press, 2013), 3–6, 193–99.

50. Anonymous correspondent (J. H. Reed?), November 22, 1854
a man of undaunted courage

The barely concealed identities of the anonymous letter writer ("a gentleman . . . left behind") and the army officer who forwarded the letter to an eastern newspaper ("T.") were J. H. Reed and Robert Ogden Tyler. The latter was one of two West Point cadets whose surnames started with the letter "T" who had graduated with John Grattan in 1853; although both cadets in question received appointments to the artillery, only Tyler accompanied Captain Steptoe to Utah in 1854.

Reed continued to cast Grattan as a brave and faultless participant. Ignoring that blind spot, he provided a few more details to the mix: Auguste Lucien had lost a couple head of livestock to the Indians shortly before August 19; the number of Indian warriors was estimated at 1,500; and Grattan's men were all finished off with arrows and knives, not by guns.

An officer of the Third Artillery, now at Salt Lake City with Col. Steptoe's Detachment United States troops, requests the publication of the following account of the late massacre at Fort Laramie. In writing to a relative of this city [Hartford, Connecticut] he says:

I send you an extract from a letter written at Fort Laramie by a gentleman of our party, who had been left behind seriously injured in a buffalo hunt. I wish to give it publicity, as we learn that stories to the discredit of my class-mate, poor Grattan, have been reported by traders, who desire to throw the blame upon him instead of the Indians in order to protect the loss of trade which they would suffer in case of an Indian war. I knew Grattan well as a man of undaunted courage, and at the first attack he jumped for a gun and fell in the act of working it. If he was rash, he paid the extreme penalty and died at his post like the gallant gentleman and soldier that he was.—"T."

On the 19th of August poor Grattan was ordered, with twenty-nine men and an interpreter, to go below the fort five miles, where the Indians were encamped, waiting for their annual presents, to bring up to the post an Indian who had killed an ox belonging to an emigrant. The Indians had also, two days before this, killed near the fort two oxen belonging to the interpreter. Grattan took two pieces of artillery, but no one expected a fight, as the head chief had been in the day before and told Mr. Fleming to send down, and the offender should be delivered up.

It is impossible even here on the spot to give anything like a correct version of the affair, as no one of the party survived with the exception of one man who had been kept alive by a trader and was brought in two days after the fight delirious. He died the next day without an interval of reason.

The best authenticated account seems to be this: that Grattan, expecting to get the Indian without any trouble, went into the midst of the Indian village with his men and pieces. He could not well have avoided this, as their lodges cover a space of three miles. The Chief of the Brules, among whom the thief was, went with Grattan to the man, but he refused to go, saying he had two guns and plenty of arrows and would fight. About the time that Grattan regained his command, the Indian fired. Grattan then ordered his musketry to fire—the Indians, who had gathered about him to the number of fifteen hundred warriors, fell flat on their faces, and the balls passed over them, as did also the charges of the artillery pieces which were discharged immediately after the musketry. The whole party were "rubbed out" before either musketry or artillery could have reloaded—they were all killed with arrows and knives. Grattan had dismounted and given his horse to one of the men, while he worked as gunner—he was found where he fell, close behind his piece, wounded in several places and one arrow sent directly through his heart. The man to whom he had given his horse jumped upon it and had cleared the lodges when it was shot from under him, and he was immediately filled with arrows.

The Indians next prepared to attack the fort, and they could easily have taken it, as there were only ten men left in it and no one expecting Indians. We received no news of the affair till late at night, before which time the Indians might easily have "raised our hair"—that was their only chance, however, as we immediately sent out a party to bring in the hay makers and other men from the farm—by Sunday morning we had received an addition to our numbers of about forty men and so fortified the old adobe fort that all the Indians of the plains could not take it. The Indian Agent arrived here the day after the affair, but he was unfortunately just too late, as the Indians had helped themselves to all goods which had been deposited at the house of the American Fur Company. He had, however, some presents with him for the Cheyennes and Areposas [Arapahos]. Those interesting bands gathered about him here, and received their presents. About 9 o'clock the same night we heard persons crossing the Laramie, and it was soon ascertained that the Agent's "red children" had stampeded his cattle and mules and were trying to run them off.

The traders of this country are the most notorious liars and cowards that ever trod the earth—their time is given up to drinking, gambling and fighting, and, when they fight, "they fight for a funeral"—but to show their cowardice many of them who had stone and adobe houses, which ten men could defend against all the Indians of the world, deserted their homes, left their goods, and broke for the South Fork of the Platte—one left his trading house below, while the fight was going on and rode past the fort without stopping to tell us a word, and the last we heard of him was at La Bontie [LaBonte's trading post], sixty miles above us, still flying.

Anonymous [J. H. Reed?], "The Recent Massacre at Fort Laramie," dateline Hartford, Conn., Nov. 22, 1854, in *New York Times*, Nov. 23, 1854.

51. William Hoffman, November 29, 1854
doubtless there is much fiction and exaggeration

How do the estimates of the number of Lakota warriors by Captain Winship and here by Major Hoffman compare? Winship listed 300 Oglala lodges and 900 warriors, 350 Brulé lodges and 1,050 warriors, and 1,000 lodges and 3,000 warriors for the combined numbers for the Miniconjou, Hunkpapa, and Blackfeet Lakota tribes. Hoffman countered with lower numbers: 230 Oglala lodges and 700 warriors, 275 Brulé/Wazhazha lodges and 800 warriors, and 815 lodges and 2,400 warriors for the combined Northern Sioux.

Another estimate from Lt. Gouverneur Kemble Warren, a participant of the Sioux Expedition and an astute scholar of the northern Plains, later came up independently with another set of figures: 460 Oglala lodges with 736 warriors and 380 Brulé lodges with 616 warriors. Warren also tweaked the ratios: "eight inmates to a lodge and one-fifth of them warriors, an ample allowance." No evidence exists to explain these differences, but, whatever the numbers, the U.S. Army would undoubtedly send an equal or greater punitive force to meet the anticipated foe.

Unfortunately the map mentioned by Hoffman has not surfaced, but as with the population estimates, it probably was trader influenced. The roads mentioned were fur trade trails, long used and rarely mapped by their itinerant travelers. That would wait until 1855 when Lieutenant Warren of the Topographical Engineers systematically undertook the mapping of this part of the country.

Pursuant to your instructions of 17th ult. [Oct.], I have the honor to make the following report in relation to the country occupied by the Sioux, their numbers, the best points for operating against them, &c. &c.

These Indians are divided into several bands, who live in different sections of the country and have separate interests.

The Oga-lal-lahs occupy the country from the head waters of Powder River, south to the South Fork of the Platte, and between the forks of the Platte. They generally winter on the Powder River or between it and the Platte. The northern part of their country is intersected by the Black Hills, but wagons can pass thro' it in various directions with little difficulty. It is abundantly supplied with wood and fine streams of water. They have two hundred and thirty lodges, and counting three warriors to a lodge, and twelve persons, they number about 700 warriors, and of all ages and sexes about 2,700.

The Brulees have 200 lodges, and the Wah-sah-zhes, a branch of the Brulees and generally associated with them, have 75 lodges, and in all they number 800 warriors and 3,300 men, women, and children. The Bear, who was made Chief of all the Sioux at the treaty held near this post in 1851, recently deceased of wounds received when Lieut. Grattan's party was massacred, was a Wah-sah-zhe and the chief of that band. It is made up of murderers and outlaws from other bands of Sioux. The country of the Brulees extends from the sources of the White River south across the L'eau-qui-court [Niobrara River] and the Platte, the country from the head of Loup Fork, west to a point opposite Horse Creek, is made up of sand hills, interspersed with small lakes. This country has no timber in it and very little other grass than the buffalo grass. It is almost unknown except to the Indians, with whom it is a favorite resort in winter. There are traders who have crossed it occasionally. Troops would have no difficulty in passing from one river to the other.

The Min-i-con-zhos have 275 lodges, and their kindred bands who live on the Missouri, the Onk-pa-pas, have 200 lodges, the Black Feet (a band of Sioux) 200, and the No bows 200, in all 815 lodges, and they number about 2,400 warriors and 9,780 men, women, and children. They occupy the country from the Missouri, west to the sources of the two forks of the Cheyenne in the Black Hills, and from the Moro [Moreau] river, south to White river. The whole of the country is well watered and timbered and is a favorite range of the buffalo.

From the forks of the Cheyenne west it is much broken by ranges of the Black Hills, but troops with wagons would find little difficulty in penetrating it by two or three different routes.

Accompanying this is a rough map, made up from a description of the country by those who are best acquainted with it, and though not accurate it will give a very good foundation on which to base a plan of operations. Two roads are laid down on the map from this place, over which heavily loaded wagons have passed, one to Fort Pierre on the Missouri, and one to the North Fork of the Cheyenne by White River, and returning by a more direct route thro' the Black Hills. Wagons have also crossed from Ash Hollow on the Platte north to L'eau-qui-court.

A movement against the Brulees may be made by a force from Fort Kearney, by marching up the Platte and crossing at Ash Hollow, and also from this post, and, to penetrate the Oga-lal-lah country or that of the Miniconzhos from the west, troops can move with great facility from this post.

Operations may also be conducted against the Miniconzhos and their allies from Fort Pierre or some other point lower down on the Missouri.

I would respectfully recommend that three commands, each consisting of two companies of Dragoons and three companies of Infantry, with one or two mountain howitzers, be sent into the field against the Sioux, one from Fort Pierre, one from Fort Kearney, and one from this post. A single command sent into so extensive a country might be eluded by the Indians during a whole season.

I deem it proper to state in this connection, that, a few days since, a messenger was sent in by the Chiefs of the Oga-lal-lahs to a trader who lives a few miles above on the Laramie with the following message which they desired should be delivered to me.

They say they took no part in the massacre of Lt. Grattan's command. One of the chiefs was shot at by the Brulees for interfering in behalf of the whites. As they were leaving the morning after the massacre, word was sent to them that the Brulees were going to take the presents which were stored at the American Fur Company's store, and, as they were entitled to a share of them, they returned and took their part. They then came up in this vicinity and sent word to Lieut. Fleming that they would establish their camp wherever he said and that they were ready to assist him if he desired it. This part of their statement is true, and the Interpreter who brought the message to Lieut. Fleming said that at the request of the chiefs he had been haranguing the young men all night to prevent their leaving the village. Afterwards they were at the Forks of the Cheyenne, when the Miniconzhos were receiving presents, including arms and ammunition, from the Indian Agent of that district. The Miniconzhos wished them to take presents also and to remain with them and take part in the war. This they declined, and they immediately moved their village over to Powder River, and, so far as stealing horses goes, they and the Crows are now at war with the Miniconzhas. 25 lodges of Miniconzhas, who would not join in the war against the whites, are with them. The chiefs express a great desire to be at peace with us and wish to have an interview with me.

The Oga-lal-lahs had nothing to do with originating the difficulty in the Brulee village, and as a body they did not join in the massacre, but it is possible that some of the young men did take part in killing the soldiers.

They say they will remain quiet where they are till they hear from me. Under your instructions I could only say that, until I heard from Washington, I had no word to send them.

The messenger brought word also that there was a camp of a thousand lodges of Brulees, Miniconzhas, Yanktons, Omahas, and Poncahs on the L'eau-qui-court, who say they will keep up the war on the road all winter, and in the spring they will meet the troops who are sent against them. It was from this camp that the party went who took the mules from Fort Kearney in September.

He says also that 40 lodges of Brulees are on the L'eau-qui-court where the Bear is buried, and they say they will kill all the whites they find on the road. The son-in-law of the Bear headed the party which stole the mail mules from Fort Kearney recently, and it was from this camp that the war party went that attacked the mail wagon on the 13th inst., killing three men and wounding the fourth and carrying off $10,000 in gold among the booty.

These are Indian tales, and with some truth doubtless there is much fiction and exaggeration.

The messenger says too that the traders on the Missouri sell the Indians as much ammunition as they want and tell them that they are their friends, while the traders on the Platte will sell them none and are not their friends.

I have prohibited all trade with the Sioux by the traders in this vicinity, and they are not permitted to sell ammunition to any Indian.

My command nominally consists of three companies, but in fact it is less than two companies.

I respectfully suggest that twelve to fifteen Delawares be sent out with each command to serve as guides and scouts. Without their existence troops would find it difficult, if not impossible, to overtake Indians who are flying from them. They may be engaged at Fort Leavenworth very readily.

Maj. William Hoffman, headquarters, Fort Laramie, to Col. Samuel Cooper, adjutant general, Washington, D.C., Nov. 29, 1854, Letters Received, Department of the West, RG 393, NARA. This report was received at the headquarters of the Department of the West, St. Louis, Missouri, on January 5, 1855. G. K. [Gouverneur Kemble] Warren, *Preliminary Report of Explorations in Nebraska and Dakota, in the Years 1855-'56-'57* (Washington, D.C.: Government Printing Office, 1875), 48. Only after the conclusion of the Great Sioux War in 1877 did the U.S. Army replace their "fluid," if not unreliable, estimates of Lakota villages and resident warriors with hard counts. For example, the May 6, 1877, surrender of Crazy Horse's village at Camp Robinson, Nebraska, revealed 899 persons living in 145 lodges, and of these, 217 were warriors, a far cry from the earlier ten Indians per lodge with three of them men of fighting age. Thomas R. Buecker and R. Eli Paul, eds., *The Crazy Horse Surrender Ledger* (Lincoln: Nebraska State Historical Society, 1994), 157–64. For a contemporary "fur trader" map that influenced Lieutenant Warren's topographic work, see Hanson and Walters, "Fur Trade in Northwestern Nebraska," 294–95. Before he set out in 1855 against the Sioux, Colonel Harney took Hoffman's advice and tried to recruit Indian scouts—the Delawares, in particular, were renowned for their familiarity with the North American continent—but to no avail. Paul, *Blue Water Creek*, 61.

52. "M. M. T.," anonymous correspondent, December 1, 1854
My informant was at Fort Laramie when the massacre took place.

The as-yet-unidentified "M. M. T" contributed a heated but enlightening contribution to the literature, the facts apparently coming from another unknown Fort Laramie source, along with its forwarded opinions and fault-finding. Coincidentally writer "M. M. T." hearkened to the same recent officer fatalities at the hands of Indians— Gunnison, Maxwell, and Van Buren—that Captain Winship had referenced in his inspection report, a fact that may tell us less about possible authorship than about mid-nineteenth-century political talking points.

Editor of the *Republican:* There has been a great deal said and written concerning the massacre at Fort Laramie by persons who know nothing about the matter, and having come in possession of facts concerning this affair I thought a statement of these facts might be interesting to yourselves and numerous readers, and at the same time I shall add a few remarks of my own. My informant was at Fort Laramie when the massacre took place, and therefore I think can be relied upon as giving a clear, unvarnished, and fair statement. The Indians were camped a few miles below the fort between the road and the Platte River—the Ogallalah camp being nearest the fort, then the Brule, Wazh-ah-zhie and Min-e-cau-gu camps. The Indian who committed the depredation not only killed the cow but first tried to kill the emigrant, but failing in this said, "I will leave you to God Almighty (this time) but will kill your cow." Now if such depredations are to be tolerated in the vicinity of a government fort, then it is high time they were abolished. The offender was a Minecaugu, and there were about sixteen lodges of that band camped with the other Indians at the time. The government was on the best terms with the other bands, and the troops sent down to receive the offender, whom the chief had promised be given up, were sent only, if necessary, to act against these sixteen lodges.

The Minecaugu band belonged on the Missouri River and receive their goods from [the] government there but make yearly expeditions to the Platte during emigration for the purpose of stealing horses and murdering defence-less emigrants. Last year the troops had a skirmish with eighty lodges of the same band, in which several were killed and two taken prisoners; this summer they have been on the ridge, one hundred and twenty miles above the fort, levying black mail, stopping trains by beating animals over the head with their spears, and among all their other outrages shot one or two men. This, you see, was not the first depredation, nor the second, nor the third, but one of a series of like nature, which this band has been committing for the last two years. My informant thinks the disastrous termination of this affair may in a great measure be attributed to the early death of Lieut. Grattan, for, had he survived, the men would have rallied round him, and, had they not repulsed the Indians, at least, a large number of them would have been killed. The Brules and Wazh-ah-zhies were in the commencement of the massacre, but the Ogallahs, the largest band, took no part in it till after the soldiers were retreating, and then some of the young men joined in to help kill the defenceless few. Indeed it appears they stood by to join the victorious party; it seems quite probable this was the case, as it corresponds exactly with the nature of these blood-thirsty demons. Some may say Lieut. G. trusted the treacherous wretches too far, and this I readily grant, but at the same time such persons must recollect that with so small a force as has been stationed at Fort Laramie in the Indian country surrounded by thousands of Indians, it becomes absolutely necessary to place confidence in some of them, even for the safety of the garrison itself. That the garrison should have been five times as large as it was at the time, no one will pretend to deny and in support of this statement I will quote the following from Major [Thomas] Fitzpatrick's report in 1851. The Major was Indian Agent at the time. . . .

It appears from this that the Major, who had lived among the Indians the greater part of his life, understood the subject far better than some who occupied high places, sat in their easy chairs, built castles in the air, and transformed these "noble sons of the forest," I should rather say these blood-thirsty red devils of the prairies, into gods. The Major knew they would not keep the treaty, however solemn the engagement, and they never have, and they never will. Some very philanthropic and sensible persons have a great deal of sympathy for these "poor wronged beings," and why? I think this will be fully answered by simply saying—they know nothing about them. After such persons have seen them, understood their motives, or had their houses burned over their heads, their wives killed or carried away captive to endure a life more intolerable than death itself, had their infants' brains knocked out against the walls, or perhaps some innocent and helpless relative put to the torture and burned at the stake, then their sympathy is changed into the most bitter undying hatred. For my own part I never saw one redeeming trait in their character and am really at a loss to determine how, after considering all the cruelty and barbarity they have practiced towards the whites, and the many valuable lives taken by them, any one can have the least spark of sympathy left for them. Ask any gentleman who has been among them and knows them, and he will tell you that, the best you can make out of them, they are nothing but cunning brutes.

My informant says the goods designed as presents for the Indians, instead of being delivered at the fort, where they could have been protected, were left at the house of the American Fur Company, five miles below the fort. The

Indians knew the goods were there, and there without any protection whatever, that they could take them when they chose, and thus were emboldened to commit depredations without the least fear that their presents would be withheld from them.

Who was at fault in reference to this matter? I do not know, but to say the least of it, it seems very strange that any government officer, whether in the Indian Department or any other, should store public goods in the Indian country at a private establishment when there was a government fort only five miles distant. Of their motives in so doing, I have no right to judge but leave such officers to settle this matter with their own consciences and the Indian Department.

Last August, while assembled on the Arkansas River, the Indians told the Agent [John Whitfield] not to bring them any more goods but in lieu thereof made a positive demand for money, horses, and one hundred white women. The demand for white women is no idle tale and if necessary can be proven by the Agent himself.

That Lieut. Grattan was treacherously dealt with I think there is not the least doubt, but he fell a brave, fearless, and good officer, and we can only say perhaps he trusted to the fidelity of the treacherous savages too much. My informant says he was the only son of fond parents, who now mourn his untimely loss.

Among those recently killed by the Indians are Captains [John Williams] Gunnison and [Michael E.] Van Buren, Lieutenants [Joseph Edward] Maxwell and Grattan, besides many other good men in and out of the service, and I hope I shall see the day when the slain are avenged and the savage humbled in the dust. Now, to me, there appears but two courses in this matter for the government to pursue—either send force sufficient to guaranty [guarantee] perfect safety, where they pretend to protect, or say, "We have not the means to afford you protection; therefore, protect yourselves."

Our Secretary of War had broken up all the eastern forts—removed the troops where they see actual service—and considering the means of his command the country has no reason to complain. Government, we are all well aware, has very few troops with a wide extended frontier, but it would be far better to protect perfectly a part than to undertake the whole and afford only nominal safety. An Indian never did, and never will, respect a white man, except through fear. If you will look at all the tribes with whom we are at permanent peace, you will see they never have respected the power of the government until they have been made to feel that power and been whipped to their hearts' content. I think the Chickasaws are an exception to the above, which conclusively proves the rule. He may live on your bounty for years and years and then as a compensation turn round and murder you for your kindness. Although our wise men in Congress assembled passed "An act to regulate trade and intercourse with the Indian tribes, and to preserve peace on the frontiers," and also an amendment to said act, yet without force to put those wise laws into execution I can inform such persons as cross the plains that said news will not save their scalps, nor prevent the savages from stealing their horses and cattle. Very respectfully, yours, &c.—"M. M. T."

"M. M. T.," "Massacre at Fort Laramie," Dec. 1, 1854, in *Missouri Republican*, Jan. 3, 1855.

53. William Hoffman, December 4, 1854
I send this to overtake the express.

Major Hoffman at Fort Laramie realized the military importance of the earlier reproduced civilian accounts by Galpin and Vaughan and the urgency of relaying them to his superiors with a brief comment.

I have this moment received the accompanying letter from Major Vaughan, the Indian Agent at Fort Pierre, and I have been permitted to make an extract from a letter to Mr. [J. P. B.] Gratiot of the Amer. Fur Company, which I also enclose. Both of these papers contain information of interest in relation to the present attitude of the Sioux, and I send this to overtake the express which left yesterday with my report of the 29th ult. [Nov.]

The messenger from Fort Pierre contradicts the report from the Ogalallahs of the large encampment of various bands on the L'eau-qui-court and the camp of Brulees where the Bear is buried. It is impossible for a large number of lodges to remain together any length of time during the winter on account of the difficulty of procuring subsistence.

The information contained in my report of the 29th in relation to the country of the Sioux &c. &c. was obtained from the best authority within my reach.

Maj. William Hoffman, headquarters, Fort Laramie, N. T. [Nebraska Territory], to Col. Samuel Cooper, adjutant general, Washington, D.C., Dec. 4, 1854, received at department headquarters Jan. 8, 1855, Letters Received, Department of the West, RG 393, NARA.

54. Peter Grattan, father of John Grattan, December 5, 1854
my son's remains

Peter Grattan, the father of John, was born in Ireland in 1800, came to the United States in 1822, and was naturalized in the Court of Common Pleas, Laconia, New Hampshire, in 1846. The 1850 U.S. Census listed his occupation as a carpenter. An emigrant craftsman of modest means, there should be little wonder why he expressed in this letter such interest in his son's personal possessions or "remains," nor why he voiced his low esteem for the anti-emigrant, anti-Catholic Know Nothings. Later in old age, totally disabled and impoverished, Peter Grattan petitioned Congress for a government pension, citing as the reason the loss of son John, who had financially supported the family during his brief life.

His son's physical remains never returned home. The corpse was transported to Fort Leavenworth, where it was buried with military honors in November 1855. One attendee observed, "It was a great satisfaction to us to feel that his fall had been already avenged."

I called on Mr. [John?] Bedel. Since you left, he says he has not learned anything about my son's remains since he wrote to me Oct. 7th. Therefore I hope you'd be so kind as to make an inquiry of the President [Franklin Pierce] or Secretary of War [Jefferson Davis] on the subject and let me know what the prospect is. My son carried off from home one year ago last Sept. over three hundred dollars worth of clothing, and after leaving home he bought sword, sash, epaulets, cap, six barrel pistol, one shot gun, one rifle and besides his gold watch and military cloak that cost forty or fifty dollars, trunk 23 dollars, one chest containing all the books which he used at West Point besides a number of historys both ancient and modern. He owned two or three horses at the fort besides part of a melodion [melodeon] which cost about one hundred dollars. If his trunk is not [sold?], a memorandum will be found in it of all his property. Now, my friend, I feel as if the government ought to pay for or return these things. As my son was murdered not killed in Regular War.

How he stands with the department in money matters or how much he had at the fort, I cannot tell. But I am certain he had between one and two hundred dollars from his own letters. He also wrote to me that he was acting as commissary and quarter master ever since Capt[ai]n [William Scott] Ketchum left the post for which he expected extra pay. I suppose Captn Ketchum can give all the facts on that point, and the quarter master department at Washington can tell how he stands on the books. When Mr. Bedel returns to

Washington, he will lend you all the assistance he can which will be in a few weeks. I don't know as I can give you any further information at this time.

My dear friend, we are, I am sure, approach[ing?] a terrible time in this State. Report says that Governor [Nathaniel B.] Baker is Knownothing [a member of the Know Nothing political movement] and also that President Pierce is the [same?]. I don't believe, but the former I have my doubts as the *Patriot* [a Concord, New Hampshire, newspaper] is mum on the subject. If Baker is a Knownothing, I will not support him, and I will do all I can to have all foreigners in this State do the same. I never will support any man that is tainted with such a band of midnight cut throats if I know it.

I hope you know me well enough to know that common reports don't affect me, but our Governor will have to come out or be mum before our elections. You may depend on that. We as adopted citizens will vote for no man that is opposed to granting us equal rights in accordance with the principles of the Constitution. I for one don't believe any man a democrat who would directly or indirectly endeavor so to deprive us of our just rights as laid down in the United States bill of rights. Nor do I believe you do. As for the President, I believe him to be what I always knew him and his Noble Father [Benjamin Pierce] to be—true to the core on democratic republican principles. Therefore you may depend on it. I for one humble individual approve to the letter his whole course since he became president and wish from my heart I could give him another election. If we get anything new on New Hampshire politics, you shall be informed.

Letter of Peter Grattan, Lisbon, N.H., to Harry Hibbard, member of the United States Congress, Washington, D.C., Dec. 5, 1854, McDermott Collection; "The Committee on Pensions, to Whom Was Referred the Bill (H.R. 1830) Granting a Pension to Peter Grattan.," *Senate Reports*, No. 931, Mar. 3, 1881, 46th U.S. Congress, 3rd session, Serial 1948. At this time John Bedel, possibly the "Mr. Bedel" of whom Grattan spoke, was a member of a prominent New Hampshire family and Hibbard's law partner. The quote from the Grattan burial came from Lieutenant Warren's diary. Emerson Gifford Taylor, *Gouverneur Kemble Warren: The Life and Letters of an American Soldier, 1830–1882* (Boston and New York: Houghton Mifflin, 1932), 30.

55. Big Partisan, Brulé Lakota leader, December 7, 1854
I saw the Bear fall.

Two of the three Lakota eyewitness accounts—critical for piecing together and understanding the events of August 19—follow. Recorded on December 7, 1854, neither has been published before in its entirety.

After Grattan arrived at the Bordeaux trading post, Conquering Bear joined the party, along with the Brulé Lakota leaders Big Partisan and Little Thunder. Big Partisan noted exactly where he was—in his lodge—and why he thought the soldiers had come—"they were bringing us word that the agent had arrived." He soon realized that this was not a friendly visit.

The day after the cow was killed the Bear went up to the fort. What was said to him there I did not here [hear] him s   ay or [n]either did I here what he said on his return. I was in a lodge, and the first news I heard of the soldiers coming, they was close to this place, and we all thought that they ware [were] bringing us word that the agent had arrived.

I saw August [Auguste Lucien] riding behind the Bear, and, as he passed, he took four [rifle or musket] balls from his mouth and said that they were to kill the Minneconjous, and that they were all women, and that all the Sioux were women.

The Bear went to the Indian's lodge that killed the cow [High Forehead]. The Indian said that he did not think the whites wanted to kill him for a poor lame cow that was left on the road and could not travel any farther, that he had killed the cow because he was hungry. And that the soldiers had killed three of them the summer before and that they had never said anything about it, and that he had started a few days ago from his chief, the Little Brave, who was moving towards the fort but died on the way, and that he was crying for him and wanted to follow him.

The Bear returned and said to Mr. G. [Grattan] that everything he had the whites had given to him, and that he did not think that he would place his cannon there as he might shoot some of his people, as all the lodges in the ring was his, and then said to him, "Now for once, take my advice, and go back to the fort and tell the chief to think the matter over, and I think he will decide otherwise." This he repeated twice.

In a short time the soldiers, one of them a tall man, fired and shot an Indian in the mouth and another in the hand. After that two others fired, and then all the small arms, or most of them, were fired and wounded two, also the Bear and his brother, the Red Leaf. When I saw the Bear fall, I ran up to him and caught him by the arm. He said to me to let him go as his arm was broken. I then put my arm under his head and raised him up. He said that he hoped that they had killed them all (the soldiers) as he loved the whites and wanted to go with them. He then laid down, and I again raised him up, and he said to me to bring him the wagon and put him in as his arm was only broken, and that he might live, and that he wished to go to the fort with them.

I then unbuttoned his coat and found that he was shot through the body. He then said that he could not live and wanted all the soldiers to go with him. I do not think he was out of his mind but knew everything he said.

After the cannon was fired, the first Indian I saw fire was the one that killed the cow. He shot a soldier, which staggered for some distance and fell. All the other soldiers threw themselves on the ground, and, when they raised, they commenced getting into the wagon and started and went about four hundred yards and stopped and then got out and started afoot up the road. This was the last I saw of them. After this I returned to the front of Bourdeau house and remained there until we moved across the River.

The next morning on the other side of the river some man harangue[d] the village for them to go and get there [their] goods as it was on there account that this first commenced and was the cause of all there trouble.

The Brulees were not alone in this affair. Some of all the Sioux was engage[d] in it. I do not attached more blame to one than the others. (signed) Big Partisan.

Big Partisan, statement, n.d., in "A True Copy: O. F. [Oscar F.] Winship, A. A. G.," Jan. 8, 1855, Letters Received, Department of the West, RG 393, NARA. See also Paul, "First Shots," 25–26, 28; Paul, *Blue Water Creek*, 20–24.

56. Little Thunder, Brulé Lakota leader, December 7, 1854
I was with the Bear and Mr. Grattan.

After a lengthy sketch of his people's movements *after* the Grattan fight and the mail party killings in November, Little Thunder described the debacle's final moments. Neither he nor Big Partisan, whose accounts were saved as "true" copies, meshed with the official narrative that Captain Winship and others had crafted. Their eyewitness testimony was never formally published, although evidence exists that it was circulated in official circles. (The officer testimony accumulated by Major Hoffman, on the other hand, probably did more to tarnish Lieutenant Grattan's reputation and hurt the government's argument for punitive action.)

These important Native American documents lay undisturbed by scholars in departmental military records and later in the National Archives until unearthed in the twenty-first century.

After we left here, we moved towards the Missouri as far as the point of the Black Hills. There we met the Two Kettle Band of Sioux, about 20 lodges, and there was a part of my lodges, not exceeding 10, went down to the Forks of the Cheyenne River to the Missouri traders, and they made them a feast and gave them a present consisting of knives, powder, &c. and told them that the whites on the Platte would give them the small pox and that the snow would fall very deep and they would loose [lose] all their horses, and that the soldiers next summer would kill them all. They had better remain on the Missouri where they would be taken care of, and that they would do all in their power to protect them, that the whites on the Platte were deceitful and would not tell them of their danger.

None of the Brulees has stolen horses from Fort Kearney, or any of them went to war to the Pawnees this winter, or have stolen any horses except those from the mail, and 11 from Mr. [Geminien] Beauvais; the latter we took away from the young man that stole them and gave them to Robadiux [Robidoux's] brother-in-law to take back.

After the Bare [Conquering Bear] died, Mr. Bordeau['s] father-in-law [Lone Dog] left the village with five lodges and moved to the Sand Hills. A short time afterwards the Bear's family, about 10 L. [Lodges], joined him. The Red Leaf, Big Chin [Long Chin], and there [their] two brothers and nephew then started, as they said to come to the Platte, and intended to go direct to the fort, but previous to there starting Mr. B.['s] father-in-law learned that they were going to war; he then used all of his influence to stop them but could not succeed. They at the same time saying that they ware [were] going to the fort.

They reached the Platte opisite [opposite] the old mail station; they there discovered a wagon coming down the road. The Big Chin commenced calling the Red Leaf a coward, and saying to him that the soldiers had kill[ed] his brother and wounded him and that, if he was brave, he would take pay for his wounds today. The Red Leaf said that he was no coward, but, if he wanted to injure him and make him kill the whites, he would do so, and that he would show that he was no coward. He then started and killed the two first. The Big Chin then killed the other; his two brothers and his nephew wounded Mr. Kinkhead [Kinkead]. They brought in 7 mules and some money. I do not know how much. They are camped about 2 miles from my village. There is in my village nearly 200 lodges; we are on the Running water [Niobrara River]. The lower Brulees are in 5 different bands at present out making meat, but they intend to move together as soon as they get a plenty of meat to move together below the Running water.

I was with the Bear and Mr. Grattan. The Bear went to the man that killed the cow, and he said to him that he would not be taken, that he wanted to die; the Bear returned and said to Mr. G. that there he was and pointed him out and said that he could not take him as he was determined to die and would kill any person that would approach him.

I then pointed him out again and told them to go and take him. Mr. G. and August [Lucien] then started and made a few steps and returned; he [Grattan] then put his hands up to his mouth and said something. I did not understand, but I think he told the soldiers to fire as they commenced firing immediately. After I had pointed him out, instead of shooting him, he turned and fired on all that was near him; if had have fired [on] and killed him, there would not have been a word said about it, and we all would been glad, as he was the cause of all the fuss, and is yet living and we are to suffer for him. (signed) Little Thunder.

Little Thunder, statement, n.d., in "A True Copy: O. F. [Oscar F.] Winship, A. A. G.," Jan. 8, 1855, Letters Received, Department of the West, RG 393, NARA. The Indian accounts of the Grattan fight were mentioned in passing on the floor of the U.S. Congress and referenced in *Congressional Globe*, Mar. 1, 1855, 1026.

57. Little Thunder and Big Partisan, December 8, 1854
Our hearts entirely failed us.

The two previous accounts and this letter indicate the mantle of prominence that Little Thunder and Big Partisan took on after the death of Conquering Bear. The former clearly appeared as an advocate of restoring the peace between the Brulé Lakota tribe and the American government, but to no avail. Major Hoffman subsequently refused the overtures of the Little Thunder–Big Partisan deputation, as indicated in the following account, and Colonel Harney did the same face-to-face and more demonstrably with Little Thunder along Blue Water Creek the following year.

In a February 21, 1855, letter by Major Hoffman, he wrote of Big Partisan's continued efforts: "Two days since the Big Partisan with a small party of Brules brought in to Mr. Bordeau's trading house all the animals recently stolen from the traders near us.... He is still very anxious to have peace and will do any thing to obtain it." Remarkably both Brulé leaders survived the First Sioux War, Big Partisan being a signatory to the Fort Laramie Treaty of 1868 and Little Thunder living well into the 1870s.

Before leaving the village we had a general council of all the Brulees after they had assembled. (I the Little Thunder) asked them what were there [their] feelings towards the whites; the old chiefs answered that they had nothing to say. That the five chiefs setting together, naming us all—Little Thunder, Big Partisan, Black White Bird, Iron Shell, [and] Eagle Body—was that they depended on to do everything with the whites that was good for their nation. We then told them that we would start to the fort the next day to see our Father and see if he would not take pitty on us as it was our wish to live and have peace if possible and that, whatever he told us to do, we would listen to.

It was our intention to have gone to the fort when we left the village, but, on seeing the ground where we had killed the soldiers, our hearts entirely failed us, but after reflecting one night we concluded if you would allow us to come up and see you; we feel that you will do us justice, and we could then explain to you our feelings. If at any time you may conclude to see us, we will willing[ly] come in as we are willing to throw ourselves on the mercy of our great Father.

Again we hope you will take pitty on us as we think it hard that our nation should suffer for what five has done; it is true that they are camped near us, and, if we could only see you and you would tell us how to act, we would do so.

You need not be afraid of any of the Brulees disturbing any of the whites or any person on the road or anywhere in the country as we are determined to show by our future conduct that we wish to have peace. (signed) Little Thunder, Big Partisan

Little Thunder and Big Partisan to "Father" (Fort Laramie commanding officer), "Sarpies [Sarpy's] Point," Dec. 8, 1854, in "A True Copy: O. F. [Oscar F.] Winship, A. A. G." Jan. 8, 1855, Letters Received, Department of the West, RG 393, NARA; Maj. William Hoffman, Fort Laramie, to O. F. Winship, A. A. G., Feb. 21, 1855, Letters Received, Department of the West, Fort Laramie Collections. See also Paul, *Blue Water Creek*, 76–79, 156–57.

58. William Hoffman, December 12, 1854

They are perhaps not far from the truth.

Even the level-headed Major Hoffman, commander of Fort Laramie, could contradict himself within the space of two paragraphs. On the one hand he opined about the truthfulness of the aforementioned Big Partisan and Little Thunder accounts but countered with a general comment about the unreliability of an Indian's word. He correctly wrote, however, that the Brulé Lakota considered their role in the Grattan fight an act of self-defense.

I have the honor to report, that on the 7th inst. [December] a deputation of nine chiefs and warriors of the Brulees came in to the trading house of Mr. Bordeau and through him sent a message to me, requesting an interview. I declined seeing them, and the chiefs then addressed to me the accompanying letter by the hands of Mr. [Seth] Ward, a trader.

I enclose also statements made by two of the chiefs [Big Partisan and Little Thunder], taken down by Mr. Ward, in relation to the affair of the 19th August and the murder of the men with the mail. They are perhaps not far from the truth as they make no attempt to palliate their conduct, and their account of what occurred in the camp does not differ much from what we have heard from other sources.

No reliance whatever can be placed on the word of an Indian when his interests or his feelings prompt him to deviate from the truth, and his promises of future good conduct can be depended in only so far as his fears govern him.

I have now no doubt that the Sioux of this section of the country are very desirous to have peace and to escape the retribution which they feel should be demanded of them for their recent hostilities; the chiefs will promise to restrain their people from further depredations, but they have very little control over the young warriors, and the safety of the mail or small parties on the road will depend on the chance of their not meeting war parties or on their power to defend themselves. Until these difficulties are settled, I do not think a party of less than eight men well armed could travel with safety between this post and Fort Leavenworth.

To obtain peace I believe the Brulees would undertake to surrender the murderers of the mail party, though it might cost them several lives as they are said to be desperate men. They look on the massacre of Lieut. Grattan's command as an act of self defence for which they will not be held accountable.

The Sioux, Cheyennes and Arrappahoes have committed so many depredations of late years, with impunity, that they now laugh at the threats made to them by the commanders of these small posts, that a sufficient number of troops would be sent out to punish them, and they go on year after year increasing in the number and enormity of their outrages on our people, and this state of things will continue until some of them suffer the punishment they have so long been threatened with.

The traders on the Platte experience a serious injury by the prohibition of their trade with the Sioux, and, unless the Missouri traders are brought under the same rule, the prohibition here does not accomplish all the purpose intended. I therefore respectfully recommend that the trade on the Missouri be stopped or that the injunction on the traders of the Platte be removed.

I deem this a matter of much importance, and I desire to receive the General's instructions in relation to it, at his earliest pleasure.

Maj. William Hoffman, Sixth Infantry, Fort Laramie, to F. N. [Frank N.] Page, assistant adjutant general, Department of the West, Jefferson Barracks, Mo., Dec. 12, 1854, in "A True Copy: O. F. [Oscar F.] Winship, A. A. G.," Jan. 8, 1855, Letters Received, Department of the West, RG 393, NARA.

59. Converse, Mitchell, and Harley, civilian travelers, December 9, 1854
the unfortunate mail party

This account identified the three fatalities of the raid on the U.S. mail party but provided no other biographical details. The "particulars" of the event, such as the number of raiders and the amount of gold stolen, may vary from other sources, but the general consensus remained among the American public: this was an act of Indian treachery against government representatives that had been long expected.

Another Indian butchery to record. The noble and brave hearted John F. Jamerson [Jamison], conductor of the November Salt Lake Mail, and his brave companions, Thos. B. Hackney and James Wheeler, were murdered by the S[i]oux Indians on the 13th [Nov.] ult.

The particulars are given by Messrs. Converse, Mitchell, and Harley, who went out with the October mail and returned on the 5th [Dec.]. The unfortunate mail party was on its way in, got to the "Sand Hills," 26 miles this side of Fort Laramie, where they were fired upon by a band of S[i]oux, supposed to be about twelve in number, and the mail carriers all killed, and Charley Kinkead, of the firm of Livingston & Kinkead, Salt Lake, badly wounded. Kinkead was in the wagon when the attack was made but was wounded. He undertook to save himself by flight, mounted a mule, but the mule being jaded by travel, and not disposed to leave the mail wagon, he was soon overtaken, and after having six arrows lodged in his body and a ball shot through his arm, which glanced and come near passing through his throat, he was finally beat down off his mule by guns being clubbed over his head. The Indians left him for dead and returned to plunder the wagon, except the mail which they emptied out of the bags, including the mules and about $12,000 in gold of Charley Kinkead's.

After Kinkead revived, he had to walk several miles through sand before he got any assistance.

This occurred in six miles of Dripsey's [Drips's] Trading Post. Kinkead, at the latest accounts, was at Laramie doing well. The mail will most likely be sent in by an escort of soldiers, with whom Kinkead will most likely come.

This massacre was not unexpected to us, as the mail carriers have been menaced so often by the Indians, we expected butchery after awhile; it has come—poor Jamerson sleeps upon the plains and his two comrades by his side.

"Massacre of the Salt Lake Mail Party by the S[i]oux Indians," *Occidental Messenger* (Independence, Mo.), Dec. 9, 1854, reprinted in *Weekly Brunswicker* (Brunswick, Mo.), Dec. 16, 1854; Barry, *Beginning of the West*, 1187 (Converse, Mitchell), 1211 (Jamison). An unsigned article with a dateline of Independence, Mo., Dec. 5, 1854, appeared simultaneously in the *New York Herald*, *New York Daily Times*, and *New York Daily Tribune*, Dec. 7, 1854. Presumably from the same source, it differed in some of the details: Kinkead shot with three or four arrows, $10,500 in gold taken, and seven mules driven off and one killed "on the spot." More poignantly, this article stated that the returning party brought "the sad news to the families of those who were murdered residing here."

60. Charles A. Kinkead and C. L. Barnes, civilian travelers, December 12, 1854

two arrows in his breast, two in his hips, and two in his back

What a tale told by Kinkead, the mail party passenger wounded by six arrows but who somehow survived the ordeal! Fortunately his secondhand version appeared in a Missouri newspaper that added more details to the deadly event. One wonders, though, if Kinkead ever appreciated the historical significance of this run-in with the warrior who later became the famed leader Spotted Tail of the Sicangu or Brulé Lakota.

We have been permitted to examine letters from Mr. C. A. Kinkead and Mr. C. L. Barnes, from which we learn some particulars of the recent massacre and mail robbery by the Sioux Indians near Fort Laramie.

It appears that Mr. Kinkead left Fort Laramie on the 13th of November in company with Mr. Jamison, the conductor of the Salt Lake mail, and his two assistants, one of whom was named Wheeler; the other's name is not stated. When the party had reached a point about twenty-two miles from Laramie and six miles from Major Dripps' [Drips's] station, they were attacked by fifteen Sioux Indians, and at the first fire two of the party were killed and a third mortally wounded. When Mr. Jamison, who was about 100 yards in advance, was shot, his mule ran back to the wagon in which Mr. Kinkead was seated, as yet, unhurt. Mr. K. concluded to mount him and escape, but, as he emerged from the wagon, a ball grazed his neck, and he had hardly mounted the mule when he received two arrows in his breast, two in his hips, and two in his back. He fell senseless to the earth, but recovering soon he saw two Indians making off with his mule. They made signs for him to go back from where he came, and he started for Dripps' station. Fortunately Major Dripps was out engaged in scattering arsenic to poison wolves, which abound in the region. He met Mr. Kinkead and assisted him to the house. Arrived there, Mr. Kinkead despatched a messenger to Fort Laramie, and an escort was sent forthwith to bring him to the fort.

He is now staying at Fort Laramie and is rapidly recovering. At the time the attack was made, he had with him about $20,000, one-half in coin and the rest in drafts. The coin was carried off by the Indians, but he succeeded in saving the drafts. The mail bags were cut open and ransacked, but according to Mr. Barnes' statement the letters were recovered and will be forwarded as soon as possible.

"The Indian Murder Near Fort Laramie," *Missouri Republican*, Dec. 12, 1854. An anonymous wag writing to a newspaper from Fort Laramie teased: "Give my kind regards to Kinkead. I hope he has long since recovered. I have heard his money is still in the Brule camp, that they made a big feast after the robbery, and in the pan of each woman, child, and man they put some pieces of this gold, that the little children have lots of $10 and $20 pieces strung around their necks." "From Fort Laramie" by "a reliable gentleman," Jan. 23, 1855, *Liberty Weekly Tribune* (Mo.), Mar. 16, 1855.

61. Charles A. Kinkead, December 12, 1854

At the first fire everyone in the mail wagon was either killed or badly wounded.

The *Missouri Democrat*, the partisan competitor in St. Louis to the *Missouri Republican*, provided another version of the attack on the U.S. Mail and neatly folded this event into the Grattan massacre as yet another Indian outrage. The Sioux warriors were apparently well-armed and good shots with both their native weapons and trade guns.

By private letters which have been received in the city we are placed in possession of further particulars of the late terrible massacre of the mail party near Fort Laramie.

The U.S. Mail, it seems, had left the fort and proceeded some twenty miles this side without molestation. The party consisted of the mail agent, Mr. Jameson [Jamison], and James Wheeler and Thomas Hackett, and one passenger, Mr. Kinkaid [Kinkead] of Salt Lake. They had reached a small creek which flows into the Platte and passing through the bed had ascended the opposite side, when, just as they gained the summit, they were fired upon by a numerous party of Indians who were lying concealed in the grass.

At the first fire everyone in the mail wagon was either killed or badly wounded, with the exception of Mr. Kinkead. He, so soon as he saw the result, jumped out of the wagon and, seizing upon one of the mules, mounted it and attempted to disengage it from the traces. While doing so several arrows were shot into his body, which he pulled out as fast as they pierced him, and was getting clear when a pistol ball struck him on the side of the neck and disabled him.

An Indian then ran up and felled him to the ground with the butt of a northwest gun, and he became insensible. After a few moments, however, consciousness returned to him, and raising himself on his elbow he saw that the Indians were engaged in robbing the mail wagon. An Indian who saw him at this moment beckoned to him to mount and clear out, but he was too enfeebled to stir and sank back again prostrate from loss of blood.

The Indians pillaged everything in the wagon, amongst which was a box of coin ($10,000), which Mr. Kinkead had in his possession. They after that ripped open the mail bags with their knives, scattering the mail and letters, and then, cutting the traces of the mules, trailed off across the Platte.

Mr. Kinkaid [sic] lay in a very critical condition for some time until he was so fortunate as to be discovered by a soldier from the fort, who was out wolf hunting and who was attracted thither by seeing those animals moving towards the spot. Their unerring scent told them where the dead bodies lay, and they no doubt were preparing for their feast. The soldier at once made the best of his way to the fort and soon brought assistance, when Mr. K. was conveyed thither and cared for. The bodies of those who were killed were interred on the spot. Fortunately Mr. K.'s person was not searched by the Indians when they left him as dead, and he thus preserved some ten thousand dollars which he had in the shape of drafts with him.

The party of Indians who made the attack were Sioux, most likely of the Brulie band and seemed to be bent solely on plunder and to have laid their ambuscade for that purpose alone.

We have thus given more in detail than has yet been made public, the particulars of this horrid tragedy. Mr. K., we understand, will be in the city himself in two or three days, when, if any further facts transpire, we shall give them to the public.

Comment is useless. The murder of our own brave voyagers and citizens by a blood-thirsty tribe of savages glares us in the face, and yet the government at Washington have not taken any effectual steps to wipe out the offence or to afford protection for the future. This last occurrence, too, like the one which preceded it, happening in the very vicinage [vicinity] of a U.S. fort, shows that United States troops are perfectly useless and unservic[e]able in that country and that the only adequate means of defence would be to make a change from the regular army to mounted rangers. Let Congress but give us a regiment of frontiersmen, and we are satisfied they will keep the peace of the plains without fail. Let them put the regiment, too, under the command of some western man who has some knowledge of Indian warfare and the countries they inhabit, and then may we expect safety and security upon the border and in the interior—but not until then.

"Further Particulars of the Massacre Near Fort Laramie," *Missouri Democrat*, Dec. 12, 1854.

62. William M. F. Magraw, civilian traveler, before February 3, 1855

These barbarous and wanton atrocities give a flat contradiction.

In early 1855 from the floor of the U.S. House of Representatives, Congressman Harry Hibbard of New Hampshire championed John Grattan, proclaiming "I knew Lieutenant Grattan well. He was a citizen of my State, my constituent, and my neighbor." In his remarks about the destruction of the Grattan command, which were given during the especially acrimonious debate over an army appropriations bill, Hibbard assigned nearly all blame to the Indians and some to the drunken interpreter. He submitted as an exhibit, "to show that the massacre was probably preconcerted," a letter from William M. F. Magraw, a citizen who held the mail contract between Independence, Missouri, and Salt Lake City, whose employees had been attacked on November 13, 1854, and who was now in Washington lobbying for more government funds to address such dangers. Magraw's charges and Hibbard's arguments in this account were immediately and ably countered in detail by former agent, now representative of Kansas Territory, John Whitfield in his own account that followed later.

To the Editors of the *Agrarian:* I perceive going the rounds of the newspaper press (yours amongst others) statements of facts and comments upon them in reference to the late lamentable affair at Laramie, which in my opinion are calculated to do injustice both to the living and the dead. I have recently been on the ground of the disaster, claim to be well informed of the matters of which I shall speak, and am also able to substantiate by proofs any statement of mine which may be called in question. I have no interests to subserve other than such as are common to the whole country, and I may therefore expect a candid hearing from your readers and the public.

It will be borne in mind that, with the exception of the official report of Lieut. Fleming, all the statements of facts upon which the public has been so prompt to form an opinion have been made by Canadian French traders, men who have married Sioux squaws, constitute a part of the Sioux nation, and have no interests in common with the American Government or people. It is questionable whether a single one of them ever acquired or exercised the right of American citizenship. It will be readily perceived that any facts stated by them, with a view to the exoneration of their tribe, should be received with a great deal of caution, or rather they should be rejected as false.

It will also be remembered that about a year ago an encounter took place between Lieut. Fleming and a band of these Indians, in which the latter were worsted and lost four of their number. A desire for vengeance has actuated the tribe ever since, and in consequence the last season has been one of constant annoyance and outrage to emigrant and trading trains. Not a train has crossed the plains, unless it was so strong as to overawe these savages, without being laid under contribution and having stock stolen or openly seized. Men have been killed and left upon the plains, their families being in the mean time destitute of the means of transportation or subsistence. Their hostility to the government and those in its service was evinced in their conduct towards the Mail Company, whose establishment at Ash Hollow was broken up in the manner described in a later number in your paper. This outrage was, I understand, most detrimental to the interest of the company and has caused the fulfillment of its contract to be attended with great additional expense.

Such being the state of feeling on the part of these Indians, and such their desire of vengeance against the force stationed at Laramie, it is easy to conceive, and such, indeed, is the fact, that they resorted to false pretenses for the purpose of luring a detachment of troops into their power. They had no intention of surrendering any one of their men into the hands of the

United States, and they had made ample preparation for the massacre which ensued. An evidence of this is the fact that they had removed their women and children to the cotton wood, six or seven miles distant, and that they were in a state of complete readiness for action. When Lieutenant Grattan found that he had been trifled with, and that there was no intention of giving up the Indian he went to receive, he thought he had gone too far to retire without an assertion of the dignity of the government. He, therefore, in the hope of intimidating the Indians into a compliance with his demand, fired two field pieces into the tops of their lodges, doing no injury to any one. This was instantly followed by a flight of arrows, which struck down all of the party except five, as is supposed, before preparation for firing in return had been made and before the danger had been perceived. Some of the troops—how many is not known—fired upon the Indians, and one chief received three wounds, but whether they were all inflicted by gun shots or some of them by the arrows of the Indians is uncertain. The whole was the work of an instant. Most of the slain received many wounds, and Lieutenant Grattan had no less than twenty-four. The whole party was scalped; those who wore beards had their chins scalped, and the bodies were otherwise horribly mutilated. These barbarous and wanton atrocities give a flat contradiction to the pretense set up on behalf of these Indians that they were acting in self-defense and sought to avoid the conflict. Further proof, if it were needed, may be found in the fact that, when the affair was over, they retired to a trading post in the neighborhood of the disaster and there flourishing the trophies of their victory boasted that they had been lied to and deceived, that they had been told that one soldier could kill ten Indians, but now it was seen that one Indian could kill ten soldiers, and that the big guns were no account.

A Traveller, "Frontier Affairs," *National Intelligencer*, Feb. 3, 1855, from the *Agrarian* (Independence, Mo.), later excerpted in *Congressional Globe*, Mar. 1, 1855, 1026, 1067–68. For more on Magraw, see *Appendix to The Congressional Globe*, 33rd Congress, 2nd session, 397–98; Barry, *Beginning of the West*, 1207.

63. Man Afraid of His Horses, Oglala Lakota leader, February 13, 1855

Look, my friend, do you not see a heap of lodges?

Man Afraid of His Horses, a preeminent Oglala leader present at Fort Laramie on another matter, witnessed the entire day's events: the initial council between

Lieutenants Fleming and Grattan at the fort, the fateful march of the detachment to the Indian village, the botched negotiations to surrender the man who had killed the cow, and the soldiers being killed. Other than he and Obridge Allen, no one survived who saw the entire panorama unfold. Nor could any other Lakota have left us so much of the Indian give-and-take dialogue spoken that day.

As with the other narratives of Lakota leaders, Man Afraid's did not get printed in an official government publication. Unlike the others, though, this lengthy document and critical piece of testimony became known to later historians and figured prominently in their interpretation of the Grattan fight. The statement of Man Afraid, who subsequently would be considered by the federal government as Conquering Bear's successor as head chief, left no doubt of the culpability of the deceased officer or his interpreter.

I was encamped at Bissonette's at the time of first occurrence, heard of the close proximity of the agent [John Whitfield], and moved down to the Ogalalah camp; they and the Brule were encamped close together. When I got there, they told me that a Minniconjou had killed an emigrant's cow. I went to Bordeau's with a Crow Indian; the clerk gave a paper to the Crow to go to the fort. I went to the fort with the Crow. We came to the fort, and the Comd'g [Commanding] Officer [Hugh Fleming] was asleep; we sat in the store some time when he came in, and the Crow gave him the paper; he then gave the Crow some provisions and gave me some also.

The officer then took out a large paper and was looking at it a long time and mentioned my name, and the interpreter [Auguste Lucien] who was there pointed me out to him; he then turned to me and asked why I had not told him my name when I came in, for, had he known me, he would have given me more provisions; he told me to look for the arrival of the agent as he was close.

After he said this to me, he looked at the paper the Crow had given him, and while looking at it two men came in in a great hurry and gave him another paper; he read it, and I heard him say "Minniconjou." The interpreter asked me if I knew of a cow having been killed; at first I said no but then recollected that a cow had been killed. I then said yes. I had heard of a cow having been killed by a Minniconjou Indian.

The officer then went out, and I saw him go to the big house; he then came back to the store and talked very loud. I do not understand English and do not know what he said. The young officer (Mr. Grattan) then went to the

Soldiers' House, and the next thing I saw was a wagon go over to the adobe fort, and next I saw the soldiers draw a cannon out of the fort. I went out of the store and stood by the cannon, saw the soldiers taking a great many things out of the house; then I saw them clean out the cannon preparing to load it. The officer then went to the store and talked very hard; the interpreter said to me, "it is my place to do as the Captain tells me, and I suppose the Sioux will want to kill me or think hard of me," that they were going to get the Indian who killed the cow.

The officer then said to me, "I will give the Bear forty soldiers today," that the Bear [Conquering Bear] had been Chief of the Sioux for three years and had always done something foolish. I then told the Commd'g Officer I would go, but he said to me, "no, do not go; if you get there and tell the news, the Indian who killed the cow will run off," and to let the soldiers go first, and then for me to go afterwards.

The two officers talked a great deal together; the wind was blowing very hard at this time; the interpreter said to me that he believed he had to die; at this time the young officer was playfully sticking at the interpreter with his sword telling him to make haste; the interpreter said to me, "I am ready but must have something to drink before I die." They gave him a bottle, and he drank; by this time his horse was saddled for him; the horse belonged to the storekeeper. I said to the officer, "you had better not go tonight [actually the afternoon]," that there are a great many Sioux; the officer said to me, "Yes, that is good."

The wagons and cannons by this time had crossed the river. I started to go [to?] the river, and the interpreter called me; the officer, interpreter, one white man who was not a soldier [Obridge Allen], and myself started together and went ahead. When we got on the hill, I told the officer that there was a heap of lodges, and he said it was good as he was going to war to [on?] them; he told me if any other Indians wanted to interfere for me to tell them to stay to one side. We then got in sight of the lodges. I told him again, "look, my friend, do you not see a heap of lodges?" By this time the interpreter was drunk and talking a great deal; he said the soldiers had killed three Minniconjous last summer and that all the Sioux were women; he was drinking all along the road, did not see the officer drink on the road; the soldiers in the wagon were drinking out of a bottle; by this time they were in a fullness; we met a man standing by the side of the road holding his horse; the officer said to me that he took all persons prisoners whom he met on his way to war. We got to

Gratiot's houses, and all the soldiers went in; some whites who were in the house came out and asked me what was the matter. I said to them that they were white and for them to ask the soldiers. The soldiers came out of the house, and some loaded their guns and fixed bayonets. I went into a lodge. Interpreter and the officer called me out and said that the Ogalalahs had nothing to do with this business. "We are going to the Bear's [Conquering Bear's] camp as the Minniconjous are camped with him, and we will ask the Bear for the Indian, and we will get him." They wanted me to go with them so I could tell the Bear what they had come after. As we passed my lodge, I wanted to stop as my horse was tired, but the interpreter said, "No, there are your horses; catch that white one and come with us." He and the officer then helped me catch a horse, not the white one as he was too wild. I started without my bow & arrows, but the interpreter said for me to take them with me as I would see something that would be strong. We started in a full run again and got opposite the Brule camp.

We went to Bordeau's houses; they told us Bordeau was in Reynald's lodge; the officer went to Reynald's lodge and came back with Bordeau and Reynald [Antoine Raynall]; by that time all the soldiers stood in a row or column. Bordeau called me; the Little Thunder came and stood by us; the officer asked for the Bear. Bordeau sent an Indian for the Bear; he came to us riding behind the Indian who went for him; he got off and stood by us; the officer said to the Bear that he and all the soldiers loved him, that he had been sent to get the Indian who had killed the cow. "I want to take him to the fort and keep him until your Father, the Agent, comes, and then will send him back to you." The Bear said to me, "you are a brave; what do you think of it?" I said to him, "you are the Chief; what do you think?"

The interpreter was a short distance off charging about and showing a ball [?] to us saying, "today you are all women," and that he was going to kill a Minniconjou; he was quite drunk; the officer asked to be shown the lodge of the Indian who had killed the cow; the Brules all said, "he is with the Ogalalahs," but one Wazaszie stepped up and said no, that there was his lodge, at same time pointed to it. The Bear then went off and returned; the officer asked if he had been to the Indian's lodge; he said no, that he had started to go but had turned back. Bordeau asked me to speak and repeat well what had been said. I asked the Bear why he did not go. The officer then asked me to go to the lodge.

I and one other Ogalalah started and went into the lodge of the Minniconjou; there were six of them; they were naked, and their hair tied up and were loading their guns; as we went in, I said, "light the pipe; let us smoke." I asked if they had killed the cow and why had they done so; one said, "it is the fact. Last year the Soldiers killed three of us, and again this year, as we sat by the side of the road, an emigrant shot at us and hit a child in the head with a small ball; the child still lives. Our chief, the Little Brave, is dead, and we want to die also."

I went back and told the officer that there were six of them, and "if you go, they will shoot at you." I stood in the ring with the Bear, Little Thunder, and Big Partisan. The officer told the Bear to go himself to the lodge and speak to the Indians; the Bear went to the door of the lodge and spoke and came back and said that they would not give themselves up. The officer said, "show me the lodge;" the Bear pointed it out to him and said it was hard as it was a poor cow and that today the soldiers had made him ashamed, that he was made chief by the whites, and "today you come to my village and plant your big guns."

The officer got down and sat with a chief of the Brules and me; he said, "go after Bordeau, as the interpreter talks so much I cannot understand him;" the interpreter said to me, "yes, go and get him." I went to Bordeau and told him to come quick as I was afraid it would be bad; as I came back, I said, "stop. Bordeau is coming."

The Bear was speaking very loud and said, "today there is one lodge of the Minniconjous with us, and if I give him up, all the village will blame me for it." He said to the officer, "for all I tell you, you will not hear me; today you will meet something that will be very hard. I would strike you were I not a chief, but as I am a chief and am made so by the whites, [I] will not do it. But you will meet something very hard."

I then said to the Bear, "you are talking very bad. The Brules have a great many soldiers; why do you not get them together and do something that will be good? Today you are acting the fool."

At this time the Minniconjous stood in front of their lodge loading their guns. The interpreter said something to the officer, and he answered, "How! How!" and then one soldier came out and fired his gun, and I saw one Indian fall; as the gun was fired, Bordeau started off. The interpreter went after him and came back and asked me to tell the Sioux to stop. I said to him, "yes, but you have killed one of us."

The Indians at this time moved back a little, but the Minniconjous still stood looking at the soldiers. The officer was going back and forth on his horse talking to his soldiers; he then got off and stood with me and the interpreter; a Sioux came and told me to come away as the soldiers would kill me. I said if they killed me, it would be good, that I would stay. The interpreter told me to stop the Sioux, and he would give me a horse. I did all I could to stop them.

I saw the Bear walking off and looking back; at this time the Minniconjous fired. The officer pointed towards the Bear and talked a great deal; the soldiers turned and fired at the Bear; the officer turned his cannon towards the lodge of the Minniconjous, and, as I saw the fire lighted, I went around it and stood off a little distance. I was in between the two fires and saw the soldiers and the Brules firing; the Brules shot at me but did not hit me.

The chief [Grattan] and five others [soldiers] were dead; the other soldiers got into their wagon; the interpreter and a soldier who had got on the officer's horse when he fell started off; the rest of the soldiers were in the wagon, and one was driving off very fast. No Indians were after the wagon, but all were after the interpreter and the one who was on the officer's horse. I then got on my horse and went to the Ogalalah lodges. I looked back and saw that they had stopped the wagon; they asked me what was the matter; they all stood in a row. I said to them, "they are killing all the soldiers."

I caught another horse and got on him, and the Ogalalahs were standing in a row of about six hundred yards. I said to them, "have we no brave men? Do you not see they are nearly all dead, and are you going to let them all die?"

I started to go, but they caught my horse and stopped me until the last soldier had fallen; they then let me go, and I started to kill a Brule as they had shot at me also; a good many went with me, and, as the Brules came back, I struck three of them in soldiers [see note below]; at this all the Brules stopped, and they and the Ogalalahs spoke angrily to one another. The Brules asked me why I had done this. I said, "because you shot at me, and, had you wounded me, I would kill one of you."

Man Afraid of His Horses, statement, Feb. 13, 1855, Letters Received, Department of the West, RG 393, McDermott Collection. Significant portions were published in McCann, "The Grattan Massacre." From personal communication with Kingsley Bray, biographer of Crazy Horse and noted ethnohistorian of the northern Plains Indians, regarding the term "in soldiers" that appears in the last paragraph, "This must be an example of trader French—*en soldat*, i.e. to strike in the manner of a soldier (*akicita*)."

64. Fort Laramie Orders, February 17, 1855

the effects of the late . . . J. L. Grattan

This example of crime and punishment at Fort Laramie, involving the late Lieutenant Grattan's personal effects, revealed that the structured life and good order of the frontier army deviated little, even during difficult circumstances and an environment of great stresses.

Orders No. 13. Headquarters, Fort Laramie, N. T., Febr. 17, 1855.

At a Garrison Court Martial which convened at this Post on the 24th of February 1855, pursuant to Orders No. 11 of February 23rd, 1855, and of which Capt. and Bvt. Maj. Ed. [Edward] Johnson, 6th Infy. [Infantry], is President, was tried Private Simeon Covington of Compy. [Company] "D," 6th Regiment of Infantry, on the following charge and specifications, viz: Charge—Conduct to the prejudice of good order and military discipline. Specification—In this, that the said Simeon Covington, a private of "D" Compy., 6th Regiment of Infantry, did feloniously take and appropriate to his own use or dispose of, certain articles of property, viz: one Bible, two pairs of Shoes, one Shawl, and two volumes of *Infantry Tactics,* all of which were a portion of the effects of the late Bvt. 2nd Lieut. J. L. [John L.] Grattan, 6th Regt of Infantry. This at Fort Laramie, N.T., on or about the twentieth of November, 1854.

To which charge and specification the prisoner pleaded as follows: To the Specification, "Not Guilty." And Not Guilty to the Charge.

The Court after mature deliberation on the evidence adduced finds the prisoner, Private Simeon Covington of Co. D, 6th Regiment of Infantry, as follows. Of the Specification, Guilty, except the words "One Bible," and Guilty of the Charge. And the Court does therefore sentence him, Private Simeon Covington of Co. D, 6th Infantry: "To walk or stand in front of the Guard House for seven consecutive days, from the promulgation of this sentence, in charge of a sentinel, from Guard Mounting until Retreat, with an intermission of one hour for dinner, and to have a board suspended from his neck labeled 'Thief' on it in large letters. Then to be confined at hard labor in charge of the Guard with a ball and chain attached to his leg for twenty-three days and to forfeit one month's pay."

The proceedings, findings and sentence in the foregoing case are approved, and the sentence will be carried into effect.

The Garrison Court Martial of which Capt. and Bvt. Maj. Ed. Johnson, 6 Infy., is President is hereby dissolved.

By Order of Bvt. Lt. Col. [William] Hoffman, John T. Shaaf, 2nd Lieut., 6th Infy., Post Adjutant.

Fort Laramie Orders, 1854–55, typescript, Records of the War Department, United States Army Commands, RG 393, Fort Laramie Collections. For details on the daily life and difficult times of the frontier soldier, see John D. McDermott, "Crime and Punishment in the United States Army: A Phase of Fort Laramie History," *Journal of the West* 7 (Apr. 1968): 246–55; Don Rickey Jr., *Forty Miles a Day on Beans and Hay: The Enlisted Soldier Fighting the Indian Wars* (Norman: University of Oklahoma Press, 1963), 137–84; and Durwood Ball, *Army Regulars on the Western Frontier, 1848–1861* (Norman: University of Oklahoma Press, 2001), 56–60.

65. John W. Whitfield, March 1, 1855

I am satisfied that there was no premeditation on the part of the Sioux.

Former agent John W. Whitfield and the current congressional representative for Kansas Territory now stood on a larger soapbox to offer his observations on Indian affairs. On the floor of the U.S. House of Representatives he astutely predicted the outcome of the unfolding military actions. The mail party murderers, he said, would surrender to authorities after the army had chastised the Lakota tribe, and this is indeed what happened in fall 1855.

Whitfield's later years continued to be colorful. During the Civil War he served as a general in the Confederate army, afterward settled in Texas, and lived until 1879. He made enough of a mark on that state's history to warrant a modern entry in a Texas encyclopedia.

As much has been said recently in relation to the Indians in Kansas, and as it is known to most of the members of this House that for some time I acted in the capacity of agent, and reference having been frequently made to my last annual report, I deem it to be my privilege and duty to state what I know from personal observation to be the condition of the tribes to which I sustained the relation of agent, as well as of other tribes through which it was necessary for me to pass in going to and returning from my agency.

[Not included here is a brief account of his 1854 summer travels among the Indians of Kansas.]

In a special report which I submitted to the Commissioner of Indian Affairs in relation to the unfortunate affair of the 19th August last between Lieutenant Grattan and the Sioux Indians, I stated what were my conclusions from all the evidence I was enabled to obtain. Whilst I have no desire to cast any reflection upon the memory of Lieutenant Grattan (for what he has done is passed, and, if he committed an error, he has made atonement with his life), I am aware that there is some discrepancy between my report and that of the offices of the military department. This discrepancy arises from a difference of opinion as to the circumstances which led to the unfortunate affair referred to, and, while I concede to these officers the right to freely exercise and express their own opinions, I hope that candor will accord the same privilege to me. On one point we are fully agreed and that is that Lieutenant Grattan's interpreter [Auguste Lucien] was drunk and went into the village of the Sioux, using threatening language, and such epithets as were calculated to provoke the Indians to fight. In regard to the statements of Mr. Bordeau and others which accompanies my report, I place entire confidence in what he says—his character being without reproach, his credibility unimpeached and unimpeachable. The charge against the Sioux is that they provoked the combat between themselves and Grattan's command, which led to the massacre, by shooting the ox of an emigrant whilst in the yoke and attached to the wagon. The facts are that the animal killed by them was a lame cow, which had been either designedly abandoned by the owners or had escaped from them and wandered into the village.

I am satisfied that there was no premeditation on the part of the Sioux. Any one acquainted with the Indian character and habits knows that they never admit an enemy into their camp, amidst their women and children, for the purpose of bringing on a conflict. Indians never permit their women and children to approach a battle field during the time of an engagement—their custom being to remove them as far as possible for safety. In this case, if the Sioux had desired to attack the soldiers, they had every opportunity to do so as about twenty of the soldiers were at the time twenty miles distant from the fort cutting hay. This small party could have been easily destroyed by the Indians, and it is much more consistent with their character to suppose that they would assail this small party with the certainty of an easy victory than that they should invite Lieutenant Grattan and his command, armed with muskets and two howitzers, into the midst of their village. As far as the various trading posts are concerned, they are entirely at the mercy of the Indians but remained unmolested up the time of the affair at Laramie. Besides, the government has kept at Fort Laramie a herd of four or five hundred cattle, which have been frequently sent off several miles for pasturage. The cattle could at any time have been taken by the Indians, if as is alleged they were disposed to plunder public and private property.

I have heard of but one other instance in which the Sioux have been charged with theft or robbery. It has been alleged against them that they killed two cows belonging to the interpreter at Laramie. But there is no certainty whether this depredation was the act of the Sioux or the Cheyennes.

I am not here, sir, as the apologist or advocate of the Indians. But I wish to see justice done, and I defy any man to show any act of the Sioux, prior to 19th August last, evincing any hostility to the whites or showing that they premeditated acts of outrage. As I have stated, better opportunities were often presented than that afforded by the presence among them of Lieutenant Grattan and his company. Emigrant trains were passing daily, frequently no more than three or four persons being together in one party. Large herds of cattle, attended by not more than ten or fifteen men, were also daily passing, and the Salt Lake mail, guarded by only three or four persons, passed monthly without any interruption or molestation. In addition to all these circumstances, the important fact must not be overlooked that at the time of the destruction of Lieutenant Grattan and his company the Sioux were encamped on a spot where they had been in the habit of encamping for several years. They were there peaceably and lawfully, awaiting the arrival of the agent. No hostile feeling, not the slightest, had been previously exhibited by them towards the whites, and it may be added that, if the Mormon emigrant whose cow was killed had made proper exertions, she might have been recovered or at least her value in money, and the subsequent unfortunate collision would not have taken place. By the act of Congress known as the intercourse law, the Mormon should have presented his account to the agent of the tribe, and by him payment should have been demanded of the chiefs, and in case of their refusal to satisfy their demand it would have become the duty of the Commissioner of Indian Affairs to deduct the amount from the annuity of the tribe. Thus the difficulty might, and should, have been peaceably adjusted, and the unfortunate catastrophe which followed, a catastrophe which brought so many gallant men to an untimely end and now threatens to plunge the nation in a long and bloody Indian war, would never have occurred.

On the 13th of November last, five of the Sioux, brothers and nephews of the Bear Chief [Conquering Bear], who was mortally wounded on the 19th of August in the affair at Laramie, attacked and killed the three mail carriers and wounded Mr. Kincaid [Kinkead], who was traveling in their company from Salt Lake. This massacre was committed in revenge for the death of the Bear Chief. I have recently received a letter from Mr. [Seth] Ward, who resides near Laramie, inclosing a statement of two of the Sioux chiefs and detailing the circumstances of the murder of the mail party. The chiefs state that they are willing to surrender the murderers. I have no doubt that the chiefs are now sincere, but I believe that the murderers will not be surrendered unless a respectable military force should be sent into the country.

[Other examples of tribal conflicts or, as Whitfield termed them, "collisions," are omitted here.]

Sir, the great question which this government must soon decide with respect to the Indians of the plains is: what is to be done with them? The tide of civilization rolling resistlessly onward is driving them further and further towards those vast, sterile wastes which separate the eastern and western slopes of the continent. Hitherto the Indian has depended for subsistence mainly upon the buffalo, which in countless herds roamed over the vast plains between the Missouri River and the Rocky Mountains. But these herds are seen no more or in greatly diminished numbers, and soon this noble animal, so long the pride of the prairies, will have ceased to exist. What then becomes of the Indian, when, pressed by hunger and no longer able to subsist on the buffalo, he is driven to the dreadful alternative of starvation or robbery? Can anyone doubt that their depredations on the whites will increase until both races, exasperated by mutual injuries, shall wage against each other a war of extermination? To avert this direful calamity, which from the great superiority of the whites in numbers and discipline must necessarily result in the extinction of the Indian race, what course shall the government pursue? Shall it provide the means of subsistence which nature seems about to deny them? Shall it permit them to continue in their present barbarous state or attempt to reclaim and teach them the arts of civilized life? These are questions which I leave to the statesman and philanthropist. I confess myself unable to arrive at a satisfactory solution.

In this connection it may not be inappropriate that I should say a word in relation to the policy of the government of paying the Indians annuities in money. Observations of the prodigal and wasteful habits of the Indians have convinced me that these annuities are attended with no benefit to either party, the great receiver; on the contrary the Indians regard these bounties as an annual stipend paid to them to appease their anger and prevent them from exterminating the whites, which in their rude simplicity they imagine they have the power to do. Tell them of the power of the government—of the number of soldiers which their Great Father can send against them—and they will laugh derisively, telling you they have heard such talk before. The meagerness of the force usually employed by the government on the frontier, the frequent threats (never executed) with which they are so familiar, the late unfortunate affair at Fort Laramie have powerfully contributed to deepen this feeling of contempt for our supposed weakness, while their ideas of their own prowess and invincibility have by the same causes been proportionably heightened.

My own opinion of what should be the policy of the government at this time is that a force should be sent into the Indian country sufficient to over-awe them and prevent a bloody and expensive war. While, for the purpose of vindicating the truth of history I have shown that the massacre at Fort Laramie was unpremeditated, yet I believe the exasperation growing out of that affair, and other collisions to which I have referred, renders a general outbreak very probable, unless the government take[s] proper precautions to avert it. I do not advocate a war of extermination. I do not say that there should be any war. But I do say that something must be done to avert it. I have been taught to believe that in the treatment of disorders of the body, "an ounce of prevention is worth a pound of cure." Apply this maxim in the management of our Indian affairs, and all will be well. Disregard it, and I fear that thousands of lives and millions of money must be the penalty we must pay for our culpable and suicidal apathy.

John W. Whitfield, *Congressional Globe*, Mar. 1, 1855, 1025–26. See also Patricia L. Faust, ed., *Historical Times Illustrated Encyclopedia of the Civil War* (New York: Harper and Row, 1986), 822; Kristl Knudsen Penner, "John Wilkins Whitfield," Handbook of Texas Online, Texas State Historical Association, Denton, modified Nov. 17, 2011, https://tshaonline. org/handbook/online/articles/fwh38.

66. "O-yoke-e-se-cha," March 12, 1855

There lies the whole secret.

Yet another anonymous correspondent from Fort Laramie, one seemingly writing from the trader perspective, submitted a version of events that saw print in the influential *Missouri Republican*. This time the author used a colorful but woeful nom de plume, one that bears similarities to the Sioux words for "dreary," "grievous," "pitiful," and "sad." As much commentary as narrative, he defended Conquering Bear, dispelled the notion of Indian premeditation, and understood the concept of revenge killing as it pertained to the mail party. If only a more experienced officer, such as Lt. Richard B. Garnett, had been in command of the post and not away on leave.

A great deal has been said and written about the massacre of the troops near Fort Laramie last August, and, as I have been living in this country for many years, am well acquainted with the habits of the Indians, and have taken much pains to inform myself of the particulars relative to this massacre, I hope it may not be deemed irrelevant in making a few remarks.

You have already learned that the annuity goods were deposited at the houses of the American Fur Company, about five miles below Fort Laramie, and the Indians had assembled near there awaiting the agent to distribute them and that a Mormon train in passing their encampment had a cow killed and eaten by them, that the Mormon reported it to the commanding officer at the fort.

Up to this point all the information I can gather and all the reports I have read agree. I will now commence with my version.

Some time elapsed between the report of the Mormon and the sending of the troops, and in the interim the Bear (head chief of all the Sioux) came to the fort and told the commanding officer what had taken place and said, if he sent some soldiers down for the Indian, he would be given up. Lieut. Grattan, with twenty-nine soldiers and an interpreter, were sent (with what instructions, I have never learned, and I believe no one else). When they appeared in sight, much joy was manifested in the Indian camp, supposing, as they said, that the agent was coming to distribute their presents. They arrived at the house of Mr. Burdeau [Bordeaux], within four hundred yards of the Brule lodges, where the Indian was that killed the cow. Lieut. Grattan sent for the Bear, who came with some of his braves; they then had a talk, Mr. Burdeau interpreting.

The Bear said he had talked with the Indian and tried to get him to give himself up, but he said he would not and was ready to die and would shoot the first Indian or white man that attempted to take him. Mr. Burdeau then said to Lt. Grattan that, if he would make his interpreter not talk any more but remain at his house, he would settle the difficulty in a few minutes, that the interpreter was drunk and charging round on his horse, calling the Indians cowards, women, and all the insulting epithets he could think of.

Lt. Grattan, with his interpreter and soldiers, then moved and placed himself in the centre of the Brule village and commenced a talk with the Bear. I have the evidence of three men that the Bear there said, "I cannot take the man; you take him; you shoot him; there he stands." And it is a fact that the Indian stood at his lodge door leaning upon his gun with his bow and arrows in his hand, about sixty yards off. At this time a large number of Indians were close up round the men in great confusion. Lt. Grattan gave some command, when a tall soldier fired, in a few seconds another; the Indians then began to run (those that were close to the men), when the cannon was discharged and almost immediately another. The Indians then began their slaughter, and in less than ten minutes there was but one left alive and he so badly hurt that he died in three days and unable during the time to give any account of it.

I will now make a few comments. Some contend that the whole affair was premeditated and a deep laid scheme on the part of the Bear to betray the troops into the village. I do not think so.

The Bear has always stood high with the whites, and it is well known that, previous to his being made head chief of the whole nation by [the] government, he had killed several of his own people on their account and has always assisted and taken sides with the white man. All who know the Indian character are well aware that they are great cowards. They will never run the risk of losing life, and, knowing as they did that in the attempt to take the Indian some one of them would be killed, no man could be found to undertake it and hence with them the impossibility.

It is the opinion of nearly all the people in this country and, with one or two exceptions all the officers at the fort, that the censure for all this loss of life belongs to the power that removed an officer from the command of the fort who was universally beloved and respected by whites, Indians, and all who had occasion to experience his authority or his kindness and leave in command an inexperienced second lieutenant.

There lies the whole secret. Had Lieut. Garnett been here, or Capt. [William S.] Ketchum, the difficulty would have been readily settled without the loss of a drop of blood. It was noticed by everybody here and by those who spoke to me on the subject in the States (before the trouble) that Fort Laramie was too important a post to be left in the hands of an inexperienced young man, not two years from the military academy when he took command (16th May, 1854). I hope, therefore, that this oversight in the "powers that be" will prove a warning for the future.

I will now proceed to the killing of the mail party. Poor frail humanity was not created without revenge, which in the untutored savage is the predominant trait.

It is known, when the soldiers fired, they wounded the Bear in three places, of which he died after six days. The brothers and near relatives of the chief, desirous of revenging his death, started out to steal and kill; they saw the mail party coming, laid in wait, and you know the result.

The village of which they were members have offered to give up these murderers (five in number), and the murderers themselves say they have revenged the death of their chief and are willing to die and will go to the fort whenever their Father calls for them.

All the Sioux I have talked with since the difficulty say that the whole nation is sorry for what has been done; they feel that they are to blame in the killing of the mail party, but in the other instance they acted in self-defence.

The present situation of the Indians is distressing; they have been so long accustomed to sugar, coffee, and other luxuries of the white man that they cannot well be suddenly deprived of them without seriously experiencing their want.

The course pursued in stopping all trade with the Sioux and not holding any intercourse with them whatever is thought not to be a very judicious one and is certainly a very hard one upon us traders who make a living in that way. If the Indians could get no ammunition, sugar, coffee, &c., from any other place than the traders on the Platte, I would willingly submit to lose what little I have, to starve them out and bring them to terms, but they have only to travel a few hundred miles to Fort Pierre, where they can get guns and ammunition in abundance, and I have been informed that the traders from Fort Pierre are on the Cheyenne and White rivers, waiting for the Platte Indians to come and trade with them; therefore it is that I think it peculiarly hard for us here to be made to suffer, when it effects not the object for which it was intended. I hope, soon, relief will come to us in the shape of opening the trade, for the poor people of the country are in a destitute situation, having no employment nor means of support, and, after the buffalo are gone, it will be tolerable tough times to live.

The people in this country are entirely dependent upon trading with Indians for a support, and, when we have no trade, there is no employment to be given, and consequently they have no means of making money to purchase meat and bread. Every trading post has its full complement of destitute men, whom they have known for years and cannot refuse the actual necessities to sustain life, and scarcely a day passes that you do not see men seeking employment and something to eat; one poor fellow, who came from the Arkansas river, destitute of money, applied to me for employment, which I had not to give him. He had applied at the fort without success, and a short

time afterwards he was found a few miles up the Platte dead and no doubt
starved to death, for he had no wound or bruise to indicate violence, nor had
he anything about him—gun, matches, knife, or anything to make a fire or
cover himself with.

The Indians have all left the Platte and gone to White river and L'eauquicourt
[Niobrara River]; they have been anxiously waiting to hear from their great
Father at Washington, to see if the whites are determined to fight. They now
begin to think it "all day" with them. They say they are determined not to
fight the whites. But I should not be surprised if they moved to the Missouri,
to hear of murders and thefts whenever they have a chance. I believe we
all (outside of the fort) have serious cause to be alarmed for our lives and
property.—O-YOKE-E-SE-CHA.

O-yoke-e-se-cha, "A Letter from the Plains," Platte River, Mar. 12, 1855, in *Missouri Republican*, Apr. 13, 1855; John P. Williamson, *An English-Dakota School Dictionary* (Yankton
Agency, Dakota Territory: Iapi Oaye Press, 1886).

67. Anonymous soldier at Fort Laramie, March 12, 1855
She rushed . . . to protect him.

The credibility of this account, a so-called "romance of Indian life," should be questioned. Its author is anonymous, and its "Pocahontas and John Smith" scenario
cannot be substantiated elsewhere in the historical record. To its narrator's credit,
though, two soldier musicians did die with Grattan, Henry A. Krappe (also spelled
Crabbe) and Henry E. Lewis. Also the term "owned or married a squaw" rings
surprisingly true. Many soldiers at Fort Laramie took Indian wives, the most famous
liaison being that between Lt. Richard B. Garnett and Looks-at-Him. The result of
their union was William "Billy" Garnett, born in 1855, who went on to become one of
the great mixed-blood figures of the late nineteenth century American West.

A private soldier, writing from Fort Laramie, March 12th, mentions the
following incidents of the massacre of Lieut. Grattan:

I will give you two facts connected with the massacre, which I have never
seen in the newspapers. A musician, one of the party, owned or married a
squaw, and, on the unfortunate day when she saw danger threatening the
troops, she rallied her father and her brother to preserve her lover. When he
fell wounded, she rushed to him to protect him from the arrows or perish with
him. Her father shot several arrows at the other Indians and was wounded

himself in the zealous defense of the soldier. Then he sat down and wept, as he could do no more. The hostile Indians then rushed on the wounded soldier, tore him from the embrace of his faithful squaw, and scalped him before her eyes. After this she could not be prevailed upon to eat or drink and starved to death, dying in nine days, and glad to go to regain the presence of the spirit of one she loved so dearly.

The only soldier that reached here alive was found by an Indian, who, instead of scalping him, ministered to his wants, carried water to his hiding place, and endeavored to bring him into the fort during the night, but being unable and afraid to accomplish his purpose he turned back to Mr. Bordeau's house, bearing the soldier, and four Indians overtook him and wished to kill the wounded man, or, as they said, "that dog." The reply of the noble, friendly savage was "This white man must live, or I must die," and he bore him off in safety. Such generous deeds should be remembered.

"Romance of Indian Life," *Herald of Freedom* (Lawrence, Kans.), Aug. 4, 1855. The editors first encountered this story in the pages of a Kansas newspaper and subsequently found it in an Ohio paper dated a month earlier, indicating a wide distribution. *Western Reserve Chronicle* (Warren, Ohio), July 4, 1855. Its first appearance in print is yet unknown. For more on the life and career of William "Billy" Garnett, see Thomas Powers, *The Killing of Crazy Horse* (New York: Alfred A. Knopf, 2010).

68. John Didier, trader, March 13, 1855
a most shameful waste of property

John Baptiste Didier was born in France in 1827, immigrated to the U.S. in 1847, and five years later came to Fort John—otherwise known as the Gratiot House(s)—to become a clerk in the fur trade. His mercantile interests mandated that his greater concern be for the property lost to the Indians under his watch.

Red Leaf, whose assistance Didier mentioned in somewhat confused but positive terms, was Conquering Bear's brother and later was implicated in the mail party killings. The intriguingly named "Man Who Hates Women" does not appear elsewhere in this volume, except in Didier's accounts.

Engaged at Fort John on north fork of the Platte about 5 miles from Fort Laramie as carpenter and later clerk. July, Mr. [J. P. B.] Gratiot left to return to the states and gave me charge of all the property. August 20, the day after the massacre of the soldiers at Fort Laramie by the Sioux Indians, a large number of said tribe came to Fort John and demanded the goods which had been stored in said fort, on or about August 10, for distribution to the Indians by the government of the United States as their annuities. I told them their annuities were locked up and that the door could not be opened except their Father, General Whitefield [Whitfield], the Indian agent, gave permission. The Indians said they had waited three weeks, and the agent had not come, that they had nothing to eat and would not wait any longer, thereupon, notwithstanding our resistance, they broke open the door of the fort with force and sacked the fort of all the goods which had been deposited there as their annuities in separate apartments from the goods of Messers. P. [Pierre] Chouteau and Company and carried them on their animals across the Platte opposite Fort John.

On the following day, August 21, they again returned in very large force exceeding 200, demanding goods in my charge belonging to Messrs. P. Chouteau and Company, which I refused to give them, and they became very tumultuous and bold and with their axes and tomahawks broke open the door of the fort, and notwithstanding all the resistance it was possible for us to make with the assistance of the brother and son of the chief and the Man-who-hates-women, we were overcome by their great number and were compelled to flee from the fort to preserve our lives, and thereupon the pillage of the goods of P. Chouteau and Co. commenced by the Indians. I believe we would not have been permitted to escape and that we should all have been massacred had it not been for the interference of the Bear, Red Leaf, the brother and son of the chief, and the Man-who-hates-women.

I and the men employed at the fort returned next day and were witnesses to a most shameful waste of property. The shelves that were piled high with goods when we left were empty; piles and piles of cloth and other goods had disappeared; flour, sugar, coffee, and many other articles were strewed over the floor and around the yard in front of the fort and entirely destroyed. On the 23rd of August, the Indians left the river and went north, and on the 24th of August I examined the goods remaining and took an inventory of them. I know from my knowledge of the goods that were in the fort before the sacking by Indians and of what remained after they left, that all the articles mentioned in exhibit A hereto annexed [this document not included], were stolen, carried away or destroyed by the said Indians. (signed) J. B. [John B.] Didier

---

John B. Didier, deposition, Mar. 13, 1855, "Account of Goods Taken by Force of Sioux Indians on August 20, 1854, at Fort John and Laramie," Chouteau Miscellany, Pierre Chouteau Collection, Missouri History Museum, St. Louis; copy in McDermott Collection. See also

McCann, "Grattan Massacre," 22; Paul D. Riley, "John B. Didier," in Hafen and Hafen, *Mountain Men*, vol. 9 (1972), 137–38.

69. Thomas S. Williams, civilian traveler, May 10, 1855

They say that now they are satisfied with their revenge.

Overland travel during the off-season—late winter and early spring—was somewhat uncommon, even more so for west-to-east journeys. This "intrepid" informant, Thomas S. Williams, left Salt Lake on April 5 and arrived at Weston, Missouri, in early May. His account of Indian affairs is difficult to assess for trustworthiness. Nevertheless its publication by the local and national press at the commencement of the 1855 season indicated that any and all scraps of news relating to the Grattan aftermath and the security of the overland route were highly valued.

Indeed, the whole country is indebted to Mr. [Thomas S.] Williams for his intrepid daring and this successful trip. Mr. Williams had numerous "pow wows" with the Sioux chiefs; they told him that "Big Bear" [Conquering Bear] had fallen in the skirmish with Grattan and party, and the blood of Grattan and party had satisfied their thirst for his loss, but "Big Bear's" sister, having taken his death very much to heart, had grieved herself to death, and they called another "pow wow" and concluded that another slaughter of the whites should be had at the earliest opportunity. Hence the attack of [on?] the mail party. They say that now they are satisfied with their revenge for "Big Bear" and sister, and those who murdered the mail party are ready to give themselves up to [the] whites to be hung or shot, as shall be determined upon. They inquired particularly where all the whites were that they heard so much talk of, but never seen—why don't they come and fight and not talk so much! This is the severest rebuke the present [Pierce] Administration has received. . . . Mr. Williams also reports fires kindled upon the highest peaks of the mountains, which is a signal for a grand combination of all the tribes to adopt measures for their safety. They have quantities of furs and are busily engaged in making clothing, moccasins, &c. They have also been providing themselves with provisions—drying buffalo meat, &c, for a general campaign. . . . Mr. Williams reports that many of the old traders, who have lived in the mountains for twenty years and have Sioux wives and children, are in great fear of their lives. As his party came along, several of these traders had been robbed of all their stock. Should the war commence, they will flee to the States.

"Important News from the Plains," dateline St. Joseph, Mo., May 10, 1855, *Platte* (Mo.) *Argus*, in *New York Times*, May 23, 1855; see also "The Latest from Salt Lake," *St. Louis News*, May 18, 1855, in *New York Herald*, May 23, 1855.

70. Charles E. Galpin, May 19, 1855

The disposition of the Indians is to be at peace with the Whites.

Safety on the overland trail continued to be on the public's mind. Charles E. Galpin indicated that, in general, all was well, except, he wrote ominously, for the threat coming from the "Platte Brules." Travel on the Platte Valley route through Fort Laramie subsequently proved to be light in 1855.

Besides the political turmoil of the winter of 1854–55, Galpin personally faced more upheaval. He had to deal with the impending sale of Fort Pierre, the trading post he ran, to the federal government, which planned on transforming the modest compound into a grand military depot for the upcoming summer expedition against the Sioux.

We had a conversation with Mr. [Charles E.] Galpin, the chief of the [American Fur] Company's traders at Fort Pierre. He has long been a resident in the heart of the Sioux country, knows them well and spent the whole of last winter with them. He thinks that the number of Sioux represented to have been assembled at Rainy Butte [present North Dakota] is greatly magnified—that they could not exceed 600 lodges—and that the hostility manifested toward the whites, according to the report of the Yanctonnais, is not so general as is stated. For two months after the massacre of Grattan's command there was great excitement throughout the nation, but it died away, and the disposition of the Indians is to be at peace with the whites. The Platte Brules are an exception to this feeling; they are hostile to the whites. It was this portion of the Sioux that were concerned in the massacre of Grattan and his men. Although Mr. Galpin does not credit the reports of a determination to make war upon our troops and citizens, he still thinks that the proposed military expedition into that country will have an excellent effect and ought to be prosecuted. The agents of the United States have always represented that, if the Indians did not behave themselves, a large military force would be sent among them, but, as this has not been done, they begin to look upon all such statements with doubt of our ability to do it. Fort Pierre, it will be recollected, has been selected as one of the principal posts to be occupied by the proposed military expedition.

Charles E. Galpin, interview, "Arrival from the Falls of the Missouri," *Missouri Republican*, May 19, 1855; Wilson, "Old Fort Pierre," 284–85, 364–65; Merrill J. Mattes, *The Great Platte River Road: The Covered Wagon Mainline via Fort Kearny to Fort Laramie* (Lincoln: Nebraska State Historical Society, 1969), 18, 330.

71. Alden Sargent, army officer, May 25, 1855
I advised Grattan.

Here begins a series of accounts generated by Major Hoffman after his arrival at Fort Laramie. Alden Sargent, a junior officer, answered his commander's inquiries about J. H. Reed somewhat succinctly. Sargent's conversation with Reed, brief as it was, was potentially explosive because, not surprisingly, Grattan's former roommate had reported no such provocative statements in his own accounts.

In answer to your inquiries respecting my knowledge of the orders and advice which Lieutenant Grattan received from individuals at this post, a short time previous to his fatal engagement with a band of the Sioux Indians, in August last, I give the following as the substance of what I recollect to have been told by Mr. J. H. Reed, a gentleman from St. Louis, who was living here at the time of the unfortunate occurrence above alluded to. Mr. Reed says: Grattan came to my room a short time before starting for the Sioux village and declared to me his intention of not going for the Indian who had killed the emigrant's cow, unless he should receive orders from the commanding officer to take him "any how." I advised Grattan that if he went after the Indian not to return to the post without him.

First Lt. Alden Sargent, Ninth Infantry, Fort Laramie, N. T. [Nebraska Territory], to Maj. William Hoffman, commanding Fort Laramie, May 25, 1855, in *Senate Executive Documents*, No. 91. Prior to a May 1, 1855, promotion and transfer, Sargent was a second lieutenant in the Sixth U.S. Infantry. Heitman, *Historical Register* 2:860.

72. Charles Page, army surgeon, May 28, 1855
I think he was anxious to have an engagement.

Again, "in answer to your question," a member of the Fort Laramie garrison supplied Major Hoffman with additional, more devastating evidence of Lieutenant Grattan's impetuosity. Grattan's supposed quote, that "with thirty men, he could whip the combined force of all the Indians of the prairie," sounds eerily similar to the one attributed later to Fort Phil Kearny's Capt. William Judd Fetterman, an 1866 massacre victim of similar temperament.

Dr. Charles Page, the young medical officer of the post and an interesting character himself, was present as an observer at Lieutenant Garnett's 1853 skirmish, and shortly thereafter—to atone for the army's sins perhaps?—initiated the vaccination of seventy-five lodges of Lakota inhabitants. He served throughout the Civil War and was present at its conclusion at Appomattox. His military career in the U.S. Army only ended in 1893 after forty-two years of faithful, professional service, no indications to the contrary.

In answer to your question of what was my opinion of the impressions of Mr. Grattan in regard to the Indians, and what were his designs towards them when he left here by Lieutenant Fleming's order to bring an offender prisoner to the fort, I have to reply: It was Mr. Grattan's opinion, as expressed often and in earnest, that with thirty men he could whip the combined force of all the Indians of the prairie. He considered them arrant cowards and thought the discharge of a piece of artillery would scare them into a precipitate flight; and I think he made no difference between Indians in defence of their lodges, women, and children, and a roving band of bucks on a thieving expedition.

Mr. Grattan was a brave young man, impetuous, bold, and daring. He had the enthusiastic ardor of his race (Irish), and, when he was killed, it was unchecked by age or experience. He was proud of his profession and if it had been his fortune to have seen much service would have distinguished himself in the American army for bravery. With what design he went to the Indian village, I can form merely an opinion; of one thing I feel very certain, that he would have been very loath to have returned to the post without the prisoner because he had been laughing at several citizens in the vicinity for chasing a small party of Cheyennes, who had killed an ox of the post interpreter's herd, and halting (having accomplished nothing) three hundred yards from the Indians, who had taken a position for a fight, and another reason why I think he was very desirous to take the prisoner is that he had importuned Mr. Fleming, his commanding officer, to send him after this offender, and, if he had returned without him, he would have been the subject of a brother officer's jeers, to him more galling than death. I think he was anxious to have an engagement, not with Indians particularly but for want of a more noble foe even with them, to gain credit for himself and for his profession. He was very friendly with the Indians but was always very anxious to punish promptly any depredations.

I do not think Mr. Grattan was anxious to urge the Indians to fight but would have been pleased at the prospect of a skirmish in hopes of distinguishing himself and showing the Indians the power of the white man's arms. Instead of taking a regular detail from the company to perform a duty, he asked for volunteers on perilous service and was a volunteer himself to all intents, having solicited the order from Lieutenant Fleming, and I believe, but for his earnest solicitation, the offence would have been overlooked until the Indian agent, who was daily expected, should have arrived.

Hoping this may prove sufficiently comprehensive.

Assistant Surgeon Charles Page, Fort Laramie, N. T. [Nebraska Territory], to Maj. William Hoffman, Fort Laramie, May 28, 1855, in *Senate Executive Documents*, No. 91. Biographical details come from the Fort Laramie Collections. For the source of the Fetterman quote, see John D. McDermott, *Red Cloud's War: The Bozeman Trail, 1866–1868*, vol. 1 (Norman, Okla.: Arthur H. Clark, 2010), 174n30.

73. John T. Shaaf, army officer, May 29, 1855
in answer to your inquiries

An 1851 graduate of the U.S. Military Academy, John T. Shaaf arrived with the Hoffman relief column at Fort Laramie on November 12, 1854, in time to gather more hearsay tidbits from J. H. Reed. Shaaf later resigned his commission to join the ranks of the Confederate army.

In answer to your inquiries whether Mr. Reed told me that he had advised the late Lieutenant Grattan, previous to the affair of the 19th of August last, not to return to this post without the offender, I reply that Mr. Reed did tell me that he had given such advice or what conveyed to me that meaning.

Second Lt. John T. Shaaf, Second Cavalry, Fort Laramie, N. T. [Nebraska Territory], to Maj. William Hoffman, Sixth Infantry, May 29, 1855, in *Senate Executive Documents*, No. 91.

74. Ed Johnson, army officer, May 31, 1855
I heard Mr. Reed.

Capt. Edward Johnson joined Lieutenant Shaaf in sharing a portion of a past conversation with J. H. Reed, Grattan's confidante. Shaaf's and Johnson's accounts might lead one to conclude that they resisted entering the fray, but Johnson would dramatically expand his observations in the last account in this volume.

Some weeks since, in a conversation relative to the "Grattan massacre," I heard Mr. Reed make use of the following language: "It is better that he (Grattan) should be where he is than that he should have returned to this post without the Indian he went to receive," or words to that effect.

Capt. Ed. [Edward] Johnson, Sixth Infantry, Fort Laramie, N. T. [Nebraska Territory], to Maj. William Hoffman, commanding Fort Laramie, May 31, 1855, in *Senate Executive Documents*, No. 91. Gregg S. Clemmer, *Old Alleghany: The Life and Wars of General Ed Johnson* (Staunton, Va.: Hearthside, 2004), iii. Interestingly Johnson was the only narrator of these 1854–55 accounts to use the specific term "Grattan massacre," and that conspicuously in quotes.

75. William Hoffman, June 10, 1855

I have, therefore, obtained statements from officers of the army.

Major Hoffman, in his cover letter that accompanied the statements he had secured, directed his ire at Congressman Hibbard, the New Hampshire representative of John Grattan's father, Peter, and at Captain Steptoe, whose shaky source was Grattan's roommate, J. H. Reed. Hoffman wisely played up the credentials of Obridge Allen and damned with faint praise the character of the late lieutenant. The internecine bickering dragged on through the end of the year, at least, in the official military correspondence.

I have recently learned with much regret from various sources that my report of the 19th November, in relation to the massacre of Lieutenant Grattan and his command, does not meet the approbation of the War Department, and what I have heard is in a degree confirmed by the fact that a letter addressed by Colonel Steptoe to the Secretary of War [Jefferson Davis], based on a private letter from this place [Fort Laramie], giving what seems to be a more acceptable relation of the affair, was furnished to a member of Congress (Mr. [Harry] Hibbard) and quoted by him in a speech before the House (See "Globe [*Congressional Globe*]," March 3 [1855]).

I have, therefore, obtained statements from officers of the army, which— together with that of Mr. [Obridge] Allen, an eye-witness, whose veracity is not questioned by any one, forwarded with my report—not only clearly establish the correctness of the view I took of the affair but show also that Colonel Steptoe's information and inferences were erroneous in all essential particulars, and that his informant, Mr. [J. H.] Reed, advised Lieutenant Grattan not to return to this post without the offending Indian. In justice to myself I feel obligated, reluctantly, to lay these statements before the Secretary of War in confirmation of the accuracy of my report.

Lieutenant Grattan was unknown to me personally, but I am assured that he was a young officer of much promise, full of military enthusiasm, ambitious of distinction in his profession, and of undoubted gallantry, but without the experience requisite to conduct a delicate service. Unfortunately he was permitted to undertake a service of no trifling hazard, requiring much circumspection and self-possession, in the performance of which, urged on by injudicious advice and a mistaken apprehension of what his duty and the honor of the service required of him, he was led to take a course which resulted in the sacrifice of himself and his command.

Maj. William Hoffman, Sixth Infantry, commanding Fort Laramie, N. T. [Nebraska Territory], to Col. Samuel Cooper, adjutant general, Washington, D.C., June 10, 1855, in *Senate Executive Documents*, No. 91. The sniping continued, particularly regarding the veracity of Hoffman's witnesses. On July 8 the major defended Obridge Allen as "a young man of excellent character, who was sent here on business as the agent of a gentleman in California . . . in whom I was induced to place confidence by the favorable manner in which I heard Major [Oscar] Winship speak of him in Fort Leavenworth." The motives of James Bordeaux had also come into question, to which Hoffman countered defensively: "He bears here the character of an honest upright man, and, making allowance for his partialities for the Brules, his relations, his testimony is entitled to credence. At all events, I have heard nothing yet that contradicts its main features." Hoffman to Cooper, July 8, 1855, ibid. This elicited a swift response from Adjutant General Cooper: "I do not question the veracity of that gentleman [Allen] when I say that there is a difference between the two statements furnished by him, one to Major Winship and the other to yourself, in some essential points, so much so as to produce different impressions respecting the motives and action of Lieutenant Grattan," which prompted another impassioned rejoinder from the insulted Hoffman. Cooper to Hoffman, Aug. 20, 1855, ibid.; Hoffman to Cooper, Oct. 11, 1855, ibid. And so it went. Their back-and-forth bickering can also be found reprinted in Paul L. Hedren, foreword, and Carroll Friswold, introduction, *The Massacre of Lieutenant Grattan and His Command by Indians* (Glendale, Calif.: Arthur H. Clark, 1983).

76. John Didier, August 3, 1855

These three Indians saved our lives.

The dedicated John Didier amended his earlier deposition and, although he remained concerned about the major property loss suffered, now complimented his Indian protectors. An interesting note, he testified that the mortally wounded Conquering Bear remained conscious for a few days.

In the month of July 1854 Mr. [J. P. B.] Gratiot left said fort to return to the States and gave me the charge of all the property and effects of Messrs. P. [Pierre]

Chouteau, Jr., & Co. at that place until he should return. During his absence on the 20th day of August 1854, the day after the massacre of soldiers at Fort Laramie by the Sioux Indians, a large number of said tribe came to Fort John and demanded the goods which had been stored in said fort on or about the tenth day of August 1854 for distribution to the Indians by the Government of the United States as their annuities. I told them that their annuities were locked up and that the doors could not be opened, except [by] their father, General Whitfield, the Indian agent. The Indians said they had waited there three weeks, and the agent had not come, that they had nothing to eat and would not wait any longer, and thereupon notwithstanding our resistance they broke open the doors of the fort with force and sacked the fort of all the goods which had been deposited there as their annuities, in separate apartments from the goods of Messrs. P. Chouteau Jr & Co., and carried them on their animals across the river Platte opposite Fort John.

On the following day, the 21st of August, they again returned in a very large force, exceeding two hundred in number, and demanded the goods in my charge belonging to Messers P. Chouteau & Co., which I refused to give them and they then became very tumultuous and bold and with their axes and tomahawks broke open the doors of the fort and, notwithstanding all the resistance it was possible for us to make with the assistance of the brother [Red Leaf] and son of the chief [Conquering Bear] and "the man who hates women," we were overcome by their great numbers and were compelled to flee from the fort to preserve our lives and thereupon the pillage of the goods of P. Chouteau Jr. & Co. commenced by the Indians. I believe we would not have been permitted to escape or that we should all have been massacred had it not been for the interference of the Bear, Red Leaf, the brother, and son of the chief, and "the man-who-hates-women."

I and the men employed at the fort returned the next day and were witness to a most shameful waste of property. The shelves that were filled up with goods when we left were empty; piles and piles of cloths and other goods had disappeared. Flour, sugar, coffee, and many other articles were strewed over the floors and around the yard in front of the fort and entirely destroyed.

On the 23rd of August the Indians left the river and went north, and on the 24th of August I examined the goods remaining and took an inventory of them.

John B. Didier, deposition, Aug. 3, 1855, expanding that of Mar. 13, 1855, LR, Upper Platte Agency, Fort Laramie Collections.

77. Mr. Laframbeau, interpreter, August 31, 1855
a fair fight

The Missouri River steamboat *Grey Cloud* left St. Louis on June 7, 1855, to help move men and materiel to Fort Pierre as the U.S. Army prepared its summer expedition against the Sioux. John Radford, mentioned as a passenger on its return, was later the captain of this particular steamboat in 1856. Joseph LaFramboise and his progeny, likely candidates for being the "Laframbeau" mentioned here, had traded among the Sioux for four decades and often served others as interpreters.

Among the passengers on the *Grey Cloud*, yesterday, from Fort Pierre, was Mr. John Radford of this city [St. Louis]. He left the fort on the 18th inst. [August 1855], but brings no news of importance. . . . The Indians were quiet, and Laframbeau [LaFramboise?], one of the interpreters, reported having had a conversation with some of the Sioux Indians, in which they professed a willingness to give up the murderers of the mail party last fall but thought it not right to give up those who had killed Lieut. Grattan and his party. That, they contend, was a fair fight.

Mr. Laframbeau via John Radford, "From Fort Pierre," *Missouri Republican*, Aug. 31, 1855. See also Paul, *Blue Water Creek*, 65, 69; *Omaha Nebraskian*, Oct. 1, 1856; Wilson, "Old Fort Pierre," 296–97, 365–66.

78. William Vaux, October 4, 1855
acts which I conceived highly improper

Chaplain William Vaux used his estimable position as a highly reputable Fort Laramie insider and officer intimate to effectively nail the coffin shut on Lieutenant Grattan's character and motives. Adjutant General Cooper later regretted ever having defended the late, lamented officer.

In reply to your inquiry as to my knowledge of the character, &c., of the late Lieutenant Grattan, I beg respectfully to say that I was on terms of the greatest intimacy with him from the day of arrival at this post until the hour of his departure for the fatal mission, which I believe he sought and undertook. It is in connexion with this that I shall limit my opinion.

However unpleasant the duty, and the ungracious fact of censuring one who has so sadly fallen victim to his temerity, justice and truth demand an impartial testimony. Mr. Grattan, I know, had an unwarrantable contempt of Indian character, which frequently manifested itself in my presence and at my quarters, and often at the latter place have I reproved him for acts which I conceived highly improper, such as thrusting his clenched fist in their faces and threatening terrible things if ever duty or opportunity threw such a chance in his way. I have said to him again and again, "Mr. Grattan, if you choose to act in this way, I must beg you to indulge elsewhere than at my quarters." Indeed, so notorious was this trait that it was remarked to me by a trader here, "If ever G. gets into a difficulty with the Indians, I hope he may come out safe, but I doubt it," meaning by this remark that from his contempt of the Indians and an undue reliance on his own powers he would be led into conflict when there was no hope of success.

On the day of Mr. Grattan's departure I saw him when about starting and could not but notice his extreme agitation. And some days after the fatal affair I was fishing with Mr. Renald [Antoine Raynall] (who was present during the whole difficulty), and he assured me most solemnly that G. was quite intoxicated. I do not vouch for this; at the same time I cannot doubt its truth.

The awful consequences of the whole occurrence, with the existing state of things and the unknown future results, I conceive to be the effects and the cause of culpability. That cause is to be traced to the fact of the garrison being left under the command of inexperienced and rash boys.

"Behold, how great a matter a little fire kindleth!"

William Vaux, chaplain, Fort Laramie, N. T. [Nebraska Territory], to Maj. William Hoffman, Fort Laramie, Oct. 4, 1855, in *Senate Executive Documents*, No. 91. Adjutant General Cooper may have had the last word with his November 13, 1855, endorsement that accompanied this letter: "Had he [Hoffman] furnished with his first report the facts which are now disclosed by Mr. Vaux, I should have been saved the necessity of making the endorsement I did make, and this correspondence [and this controversy!] would not have taken place."

79. War Department Report, October 5, 1855
the same who massacred Grattan

The Battle of Blue Water Creek occurred on September 3, 1855, a surprise attack on and rout of Little Thunder's Brulé Lakota village by the U.S. Army expeditionary force commanded by Col. William Selby Harney. The Lakota losses of people and property were devastating: at least eighty-six men, women, and children killed, dozens captured, and an entire tipi village stocked with winter provisions destroyed. The totals of soldier killed and wounded were minimal. Grattan had been avenged.

Later would come the justification that this particular village had housed the killers of Grattan's command, and the victors provided that damning "evidence" to their Washington superiors. The items in question mentioned in this newspaper article have never turned up.

The War Department has received a package of the papers taken from the Sioux at the recent battle of the Bluewater. Among them is a Postmaster's blank—evidently taken from some one of the mail agents, whom they have robbed and murdered—and is covered with Indian hieroglyphics, apparently intended to detail some of the bloody deeds of the tribe. The massacre of Lieutenant Grattan and his party is evidently one of the subjects of this symbolic history. It is also believed to describe the murder of an emigrating party, composed in part of women.

Among the articles captured were: two scalps of white women; a small memorandum book in which some neat penman had noted the incidents of an overland journey; a letter from B. W. Leonard, dated Hermon [?], July 6, 1855, doubtless taken from a captured mail; several rather good sketches of Indians fighting; and a portion of the clothing which had belonged to the soldiers of Grattan's party. There can be no doubt that the Indians from whom these things were taken are the same who massacred Grattan and his command.

"Latest Intelligence by Telegraph," dateline Washington, D.C., Oct. 5, 1855, in *New York Times*, Oct. 6, 1855.

80. Ed Johnson, October 10, 1855

Make such use of this letter as you may think proper.

He was a Kentucky native, an 1838 West Point graduate, and a veteran of the Seminole and Mexican-American wars, but how reliable was Ed Johnson as a source? His modern biographer provided a priceless description of a character "parodied for his careless dress and homely appearance, for his deafness, nervous eye tics, marked profanity, booming voice, gruff countenance, and enormous ears that 'would brush the flies off the back of his head.'" Aside from this, Johnson's approach to the issue came off as well-reasoned, experienced, and professional, and unlike his earlier contribution, he had abandoned terseness. His lengthy analysis of October 10, 1855, disputed Winship's initial analysis that "the whole affair was a deeply matured scheme of treachery on the part of the Indians." Johnson concluded the Hoffman-generated testimony—and this volume of Grattan-related accounts—but it did not end the row between the major and his superiors, nor settle the question of blame. That debate would continue for decades.

I have the honor herewith to present my views in regard to the difficulties which occurred between the Sioux Indians and the troops near this post some fourteen months since. My opinions have been formed after diligent inquiry and upon evidence, oral and written, of eye and ear witnesses. As many contradictory statements have gone forth relative to this affair, and many erroneous ones, upon which public opinion has been formed, it may be well briefly to state what is now received and considered as the true state of the case. It appears that the difficulty had its origin in the act of one individual of the Mineconjou band of Sioux Indians, who killed a lame cow belonging to a Mormon emigrant. This Indian, we are informed, was a Missouri Indian, who, when he came over to the Platte, said that he intended to do something bad before he left. An opportunity, as he conceived, offered, and he killed the emigrant's cow. He carried out his threat.

Immediately after this occurrence, the Bear chief [Conquering Bear], who was a Wazahgie, one of the bands of Sioux Indians, came up to the fort and informed the commanding officer of the affair, stating that the Indian was not a Wazahgie, but a Mineconjou, and that, if the commanding officer would send for him, he thought he would be given up or that he, the Bear, would endeavor to have him given up. This occurred on the day on which the cow was killed. The commanding officer, it is confidently affirmed by those who were here, declined sending on that day for the offender and had definitely postponed any action in the matter until the arrival of the Indian agent, who was expected daily. He appears to have come to the conclusion that it was a matter for adjustment between the Indians and the agent. The Indians considered it as the act of an individual and did not wish to be implicated in the affair. The Bear chief, in order to anticipate any action in the matter, reported it promptly. The day after this occurrence, and the report of it by the Bear at dinner, the commanding officer decided to send an officer and twenty men for the offender. He appears to have come to this decision suddenly and then, in consequence of the repeated and urgent solicitations of Lieutenant Grattan, that he might be sent. Lieutenant Grattan, we are told, urged the commanding officer to send and earnestly requested that he might go. He is said to have entertained for the Sioux Indians a great contempt. He had frequently said that with ten men he could whip any number of them and had expressed a desire to have an opportunity of chastising them.

He appears to have been a young officer of courage but rash and impulsive almost beyond belief. The commanding officer detailed him for this service, with twenty men and two pieces of artillery, with instructions "to bring in the Indian, if practicable without unnecessary risks." Volunteers were called for from the company for dangerous service. Instead of twenty men, as the official reports show, thirty went. The party did not leave the post until 3 o'clock P.M. on the day after the killing of the cow. When preparations were making for the service the ordnance sergeant [Leodegar Schnyder], an old and faithful soldier, was requested by Lieutenant Grattan to go along, which he declined doing, because, as he says, he believed the lieutenant to be rash, that there would be a difficulty and that he had no confidence in his judgment.

At that time there was a Mr. [J. H.] Reed of St. Louis, staying at the post and occupying the same room with Lieutenant Grattan. He says that he heard Lieutenant Grattan say that he would not go unless he had orders to bring the Indian. Mr. Reed says that he advised him not to come back without the Indian. Lieutenant Grattan had jeered some citizens who had on a certain occasion pursued a party of Indians without accomplishing anything, although they had overtaken the party. He had been very severe upon them in his remarks concerning the affair.

There is a matter connected with and bearing in some degree upon this affair, which has not been mentioned. The summer before, a Mineconjou had fired at a soldier who was crossing the Platte in a boat. Lieutenant Fleming was sent at night with a detachment across the river to bring in the offender, or some others, as hostages. He went to their encampment and made the demand, but the offender and nearly all the warriors were absent at the time. The Indians became alarmed and fled, firing as they ran; as they did so, they were fired upon by the troops and three or four killed. The next day the band came in and talked the matter over with the commanding officer, and the affair was amicably adjusted. They did not seek summary vengeance and kill the herd party, the hay party, or the party at the farm, some fifteen miles distant. They came in and talked the matter over and said that perhaps the whites were right, after their manner of thinking or after their way; there the matter ended. It was after this occurrence that Lieutenant Grattan solicited, and had the promise made him that, on the occurrence of any other difficulties, he, Lieutenant Grattan, should be sent against the Indians. It is said that he considered that the officer in command on this occasion had distinguished himself, and he was anxious for a like occasion. The occasion, as he conceived, presented itself, and he urged his claim. He earnestly and strongly urged it, and he was sent as above stated.

These were the influences operating upon him; the advice of others urging him to bring the Indian, regardless, it appears, of his instructions, which were "to bring in the Indian, if practicable, without unnecessary risks," the fear of his being laughed at in case he did not accomplish the object of his mission, and his eager desire to chastise the Indians and thereby distinguish himself.

He was heard to say on leaving the post that he would "conquer them or die," or words to that effect. He requested Mr. Reed, in case he did not return, to pay his man [his "striker" or enlisted man who works voluntarily as a paid servant] a sum of money due him. He is reported by all to have left the post in a state of unusual excitement. A Mr. [Obridge] Allen, who had just arrived the day before, accompanied the command. The "Man-that-is-afraid-of-his-horses," head chief of the Ogalahlas, and the post interpreter [Auguste Lucien], also went along. Arrived at Mr. Gratiot's, about four miles from the post, the party halted, and the interpreter got some liquor, which, together with what he had already taken, made him quite drunk. Just before this, as the party ascended the bluffs which overhang the Platte valley, from which point the Indian encampment was distinctly visible, stretching along the [North] Platte and around Mr. Bordeau's houses, Mr. Allen remarked, "Lieutenant, do you see how many lodges there are?" "Yes," was his reply, "but I don't care how many there are; with thirty men I can whip all the Indians this side of the Missouri." There were at least six hundred lodges visible at the time this remark was made. Soon after, at the suggestion of Mr. Allen, he halted his command, ordered them to load, and gave them the necessary orders as to how they should conduct themselves in the event of a fight, concluding by saying, "Men, I don't believe we shall have a fight, but I hope to God we may have one." Mr. Allen states that the interpreter became quite drunk and was charging over the plain at a furious pace, uttering threats of defiance against the Indians, towards whom he is represented to have long entertained a very bitter hatred. Mr. Allen told him he had better not run his horse down and suggested the probability of having need of his speed before night, but the interpreter did not heed him. The party arrived at Bordeau's trading houses, some eight miles from the post, and three or four from Gratiot's. The Indians came out to see who had come—men, women and children. They were met by the interpreter, who exclaimed with insulting gestures, "We have come to fight, not to talk. Last summer we killed some of you, but now we have come to wipe you out; you are women. If you want to fight, come on; we have come to drink your blood and eat your liver raw," and much in the same strain. Mr. Bordeau came out at the request of Lieut. Grattan and hearing the outrageous and insulting language of the interpreter told Lieut. Grattan to shut his (the interpreter's) mouth; if he did not, there would certainly be a difficulty. He further told him that, if he would make his interpreter hush, he (Bordeau) would settle the matter in thirty minutes. The Bear chief was sent for. He was the chief of the Wazahzies but had been made by Colonel [David D.] Mitchell chief of the Sioux nation. His influence was very great among his own band and mainly attributable to his great personal courage. But over individuals of the other bands into which the Sioux nation is divided, his influence was not so great as that of the various chiefs of those bands. Lieut. Grattan demanded the Indian who had killed the cow. The Bear, we are told, said that the Indian would not be taken or that he could not make him deliver himself up. The cow killer was prepared for the worst, had armed himself, and was waiting the result in his lodge some distance from Bordeau's houses. Lieut. Grattan said he "would have the man or die" and started to go into the midst of the village. Mr. Bordeau advised him not to go in and said that he was going into "a bad place." The lieutenant replied that "he was not afraid, that he had two revolvers." "Draw one then," said Bordeau, "and be on your guard." During all this time the drunken interpreter was bullying and insulting the Indians by the most offensive language and gestures. In vain had Mr. Bordeau and his employes endeavored to make him desist; in vain had Mr. Bordeau appealed to Lieut Grattan and requested him to shut the interpreter's mouth, urging as a reason, that, unless he did so, there would certainly be a difficulty, and volunteering his own services as interpreter to settle the difficulty in thirty minutes. Lieut. Grattan marched his command into the heart of the village and halted it about sixty yards from the lodge occupied by the cow killer and his adherents. There a further conversation ensued between the Bear and the lieutenant. What transpired we do not know, except that from Indian testimony.

The Ogalahla chief, the Man-that-is-afraid-of-his-horses, who came with the party from the fort and who had been with them up to this time, says that the Bear urged the lieutenant to go home and defer the matter until the arrival of the agent. He further states that the Bear offered the lieutenant a mule in place of the cow if the lieutenant would "cover up" the trouble until the arrival of the agent. This much we do know certainly, that twice during the conversation the Ogalahla chief came in great haste to Bordeau from the Bear, requesting him to come out immediately and prevent a difficulty. The message was "To come quick and talk; that the interpreter was drunk, and did not talk straight; that all his talk was about fighting." Mr. Bordeau says that the Ogalahla chief came to him twice with this message and that he started to go but turned back. The Ogalahla chief states that he went twice with the above message. He states further that he went twice with the Bear to the lodge of the cow killer to see if he would give himself up and that his only reply was "Tell the white chief I am ready to die," or "I wish to die." Soon after this the firing commenced, as all say, on the right of the detachment. I believe the troops fired first. The firing was heard and seen from the top of Bordeau's house, and immediately all was confusion. The Indians were attacked, and they defended themselves. Lieutenant Grattan had put himself into their power. He did not think they would fight, or, if they did, he thought that he could with his party whip all the Indians this side of the Missouri river. The Indians were numerous, numbering from ten to fifteen hundred men. The result is known.

We can but lament the fate of Lieutenant Grattan. He appears to have been a young officer of courage and exhibited much zeal in the discharge of the duties of his profession, but he appears to have acted under improper influences. He was ambitious and regardless of his instructions hazarded the safety of his command by his rashness. I believe firmly that he was desirous of having a difficulty with the Indians and that he anxiously awaited an opportunity of making them feel the power of the military. I do not say that this was the sole motive that prompted him. He was doubtless desirous of getting possession of the Indian but not in the least averse to a resort to arms should any obstacle, however slight, present itself to the immediate accomplishment of his mission. If not desirous of a difficulty, why did he allow his mouthpiece, his drunken interpreter, to bully, insult, and dare the Indians to a fight? Why did he not check him, or tie him, when urged by Mr. Bordeau to "shut his mouth?" Why did he allow him to go with his party into the village and there continue to upbraid the Indians with the most opprobrious language? He was warned at the outset of the consequences, but he heedlessly disregarded them. He seems to have had an overweening confidence in himself and his handful of men and a thorough contempt for the foe with whom he had to contend.

This affair has been termed an ambuscade, a deeply laid scheme to entrap the troops and massacre them in consequence of the weakness of the garrison of Fort Laramie. The garrison was weak, and its weakness was well known at headquarters. You, sir, are aware that repeated calls had been made for more troops at the frontier posts. But there is not a shadow of evidence to show that the Indians desired a difficulty; on the contrary, it is very evident that they did not wish to come in collision with the troops. The Bear was heard to say that he was indebted to the whites for all that he was and all that he had. He is known to have killed two or three Indians in defence of the rights of the whites; he has been known to return stolen property at great personal risk, and yet it is sought to make it appear that his coming and reporting the affair was done to ensnare the troops. He did not know that the troops were coming; the commanding officer had decided not to send the troops. Besides would the Indians have allowed thirty men and two pieces of artillery to enter the heart of their village as they prepared for an ambuscade? Their women and children were all present, and, when they saw the troops approach, they ran out, expecting to meet the agent. The failure of the Bear to deliver up the Indian is nothing more than might have been expected, for we all know how feeble the authority of a single chief of one band is over the individuals of other bands. Lieutenant Grattan had orders to bring in the Indian if practicable but to run no unnecessary risks. Did he obey these instructions when, in spite of advice and heralded by a drunken interpreter bullying and insulting the Indians, he rashly went into the midst of six hundred lodges?

You were sent out to investigate this sad affair, and in the discharge of a delicate duty thus confided to you, after collecting all the evidence possible, and after maturely weighing every circumstance connected with the affair, you came to the conclusion that it was no ambuscade, but that it was the result of rashness on the part of the officer in command of the party and inexperience on the part of the commanding officer of the post. A post in the heart of the Indian country was left in command of a second lieutenant of a little more than a year's service, and the duty of taking with only thirty men an Indian from a village of six hundred lodges was assigned to a brevet second lieutenant who had not been a year in service.

I fully concur with you in the views entertained by you relative to the origin of the Sioux difficulties. You have been, I concur, unjustly censured for your reports relative to the difficulty, your motives impugned, and the views you have taken attributed to bias, prejudice, and selfish motives.

You did not wish, nor do I, to reflect upon the character of the dead, but justice to the living renders it necessary that the truth, and the whole truth, should be told; "justicia fiat coelum ruat" should be our motto; yes, let justice be done, though the heavens fall.

I have of late conversed with many officers on the subject of the Grattan difficulty, and all say that the version of the affair, as given by those who have collected all the testimony and who have been here since the occurrence, differs very materially from what they had heard in the States, and I believe they now concur in the views entertained of the origin of the difficulty by those who have been stationed at the post.

You are at liberty to make such use of this letter as you may think proper.

Capt. Ed. Johnson, Sixth Infantry, Fort Laramie, N. T. [Nebraska Territory], to Maj. William Hoffman, commanding Fort Laramie, N. T., Oct. 10, 1855, in *Senate Executive Documents,* No. 91. See also O. F. [Oscar F.] Winship, St. Louis, Mo., to Jno. W. [John W.] Whitfield, "Present," Oct. 12, 1854, Upper Platte Agency, Microfilm Publication No. 234, roll 889, NARA. Maybe it is fitting that Johnson, our concluding narrator, helped wrap up one loose end of the Grattan affair; later in the fall he commanded the twenty-man military escort that took Spotted Tail and the Lakota hostages to their Fort Leavenworth imprisonment. *Missouri Democrat,* Dec. 14, 1855.

Bibliography

Manuscript Collections

American Heritage Center, University of Wyoming, Laramie
    Grace Raymond Hebard Papers
    Owen Wister Collection: Owen Wister's Diary. Frontier Notes, May–Aug. 1894
    Paul and Helen Henderson Collection: "Diary Kept by Mrs. Maria H. (Parsons) Belshaw, 1853."
Church History Library, Church of Jesus Christ of Latter-day Saints, Salt Lake City
    Brigham Young Office Files, 1832–1878.
    General Correspondence, Incoming, Letters from Church Leaders and Others, 1840–1877.
Fort Laramie Collections, Fort Laramie National Historic Site, Fort Laramie, Wyo.
    Burns, John C. "Dick Garnett's Boy," in *Looking Back: Footnotes from an Old Fort,* Jan. 3, 1986, item C12–184;
    "Chaplain Vaux." *Wyoming Churchman,* n.d., 20–21.
    Claudey, Edward, et al. Statement, Fort Laramie.
    Colemen, Martha L. Larson. Obituary.
    Fire Thunder, Edgar. Interview by Merrill Mattes, Oct. 20, 1942.
    Murray, Robert A. "Military Firearms at Fort Laramie, 1849–1890." Typescript. April 1977.
    Nolan, James P. Interview by David L. Hieb, n.d.
    Robinson, Daniel. "Reminiscences of Fort Laramie." Typescript.
    White, Tom. "Post Sutlers/Traders at Fort Laramie." Research file CSUT-8.
Huntington Library, San Marino, Calif.
    "Orville A. Nixon Journal, Fort Laramie to Westport, Kansas [*sic*], 29 August to 28 September 1854," HM 17012. Typescript of Nixon journal, "Book Second of My Trip to the Rocky Mountains, up the South Platte and North Platte Rivers," from Miscellaneous Manuscripts Collection, Kansas State Archives, Kansas Historical Society, Topeka.
J. Willard Marriott Library, University of Utah, Salt Lake City
    William Athol MacMaster Papers

John D. McDermott, Rapid City, S.Dak.
    McDermott Collection: Letter of Peter Grattan to Harry Hibbard, Dec. 5, 1854;
        Interview of the Rev. Sidney Hoadley, July 1992; Basil Nelson Longsworth,
        "The Diary of Basil N. Longsworth, Oregon Pioneer," Division of Women's
        Professional Projects, Works Progress Administration, Portland, 1938.
Lee Library, Brigham Young University, Provo, Utah
    Walter M. Camp Manuscripts: Interviews of Antoine Bordeaux and Thunder Bear.
Lilly Library, Indiana University, Bloomington
    Walter Mason Camp Papers: Interview of Antoine Bordeaux.
Missouri History Museum, St. Louis
    Chouteau Miscellany, Pierre Chouteau Collection: John B. Didier depositions of
        Mar. 13 and Aug. 3, 1855.
National Archives and Records Administration, Washington, D.C.
    Claim of Leon F. Pallardy, no. 8266; John Soissons, Oct. 23, 1889, Seth Ward, Nov.
        28, 1885, and Dec. 5, 1889, and George T. Tackett, Nov. 29, 1889, statements
        in claim of Ward and Guerrier, no. 712, Indian Depredation Claims. Records
        of the U.S. Court of Claims, RG 123.
    Letters Received, Department of the West. Records of the U.S. Army Continental
        Commands, RG 393.
    Letters Received, Office of the Adjutant General, Main Series, 1822–1860. Records
        of the Office of the Adjutant General, RG 94. Microfilm Publication 567, roll
        498.
    Letters Received by the Office of Indian Affairs from the Upper Platte Agency,
        1846–1870. Records of the Bureau of Indian Affairs, RG 75. Microfilm Publica-
        tion 234, roll 889.
    Letters Sent, Letters Received, and Orders, Fort Laramie Post Records. Records
        of the U.S. Army Continental Commands, RG 393.
    Post Returns, Fort Laramie. Returns from U.S. Military Posts, 1800–1916. Records
        of the Office of the Adjutant General, RG 94.
    "Report of an Inspection of Forts Ripley, Ridgely, Snelling, Laramie, Kearney,
        Riley, Leavenworth, and Atkinson; Made by Brevet Major O. F. Winship, Asst.
        Adjutant General, U.S. Army, in the Months of May, June, July, August and
        September, 1854." Letters Received, Office of the Adjutant General, 1822–1860.
        Main Series, RG 94. Microfilm Publication 567, roll 508.
    Returns of the Regular Army, Sixth U.S. Infantry, 1849–1854. Records of the
        Office of the Adjutant General, RG 94. Microfilm Publication 665, roll 67.
    William Garnett File, HRG7A D26. Records of the U.S. House of Representatives,
        RG 233.
Nebraska State Historical Society, Lincoln
    Addison E. Sheldon Collection: Interviews of American Horse and Francis Salway.
    Hall-Kinney Family Collection: "Crossing the Plains in 1854 as Told by Elle Kinney
        Ware," typescript.
    Paul D. Riley Collection

Newberry Library, Chicago
  Elmo Scott Watson Papers: George Colhoff winter count.
U.S. Army Military History Institute, Carlisle Barracks, Pa.
  Luther P. Bradley Papers
Wyoming State Archives, Cheyenne
  Coutant Collection

Government Publications

Annual Report of the Commissioner of Indian Affairs, Transmitted with the Message of the President at the Opening of the Second Session of the Thirty-Third Congress, 1854. Washington, D.C.: A. O. P. Nicholson, 1855.
"The Committee on Pensions, to Whom Was Referred the Bill (H.R. 1830) Granting a Pension to Peter Grattan." *Senate Reports,* No. 931, Mar. 3, 1881, 46th U.S. Congress, 3rd session. Serial 1948.
Heitman, Francis B. *Historical Register and Dictionary of the United States Army from Its Organization, September 29, 1789, to March 2, 1903.* 2 vols. Washington, D.C.: Government Printing Office, 1903.
Kappler, Charles J., ed. *Indian Affairs: Laws and Treaties.* 4 vols. Washington, D.C.: Government Printing Office, 1904–1929.
"Letter from the Secretary of War, Transmitting Information Relating to an Engagement between the United States Troops and the Sioux Indians near Fort Laramie." *House of Representatives Reports,* No. 63, 33rd U.S. Congress, 2nd session, 1854–55. Serial 788.
Official Army Register for 1853. Washington, D.C.: Adjutant General's Office, Jan. 1, 1853.
Official Army Register for 1854. Washington, D.C.: Adjutant General's Office, Jan. 1, 1854.
"Report of the Secretary of War." In *House Executive Documents,* No. 1, 33rd U.S. Congress, 2nd session, 1854–55. Serial 778.
"Report of the Secretary of War, in Compliance with a Resolution of the Senate of the 1st Instant, Calling for Copies of the Correspondence Respecting the Massacre of Lieutenant Grattan and His Command by Indians." *Senate Executive Documents,* No. 91, 34th U.S. Congress, 1st session, 1855–56. Serial 823.

Newspapers

Congressional Globe (Washington, D.C.), 1855, 1860
Council Bluffs Bugle (Council Bluffs, Iowa), 1854
Deseret News (Salt Lake City, Utah), 1854
Fremont County Journal (Sidney, Iowa), 1854
Goshen County News and Fort Laramie Scout (Torrington, Wyo.), 1928
Guide-Review (Lingle, Wyo.), 1951
Herald of Freedom (Lawrence, Kans.), 1854, 1855
Liberty Weekly Tribune (Liberty, Mo.), 1854, 1855

Littleton Courier (Littleton, N.H.), 1901

Missouri Democrat (St. Louis), 1854, 1855

Missouri Republican (St. Louis), 1851, 1854, 1855

National Intelligencer (Washington, D.C.), 1854

National Tribune (Washington, D.C.), 1885

New York Daily Tribune (New York, N.Y.), 1854

New York Herald (New York, N.Y.), 1854, 1855

New York Times (New York, N.Y.), 1854, 1855

North American and United States Gazette (Philadelphia, Pa.), 1854

Omaha Arrow (Omaha, Neb.), 1854

Omaha Nebraskian (Omaha, Neb.), 1856

Sheridan Enterprise (Sheridan, Wyo.), 1907

St. Joseph Cycle (St. Joseph, Mo.), 1854

St. Joseph Gazette (St. Joseph, Mo.), 1853, 1854

Vermont Patriot & State Gazette (Montpelier, Vt.), 1854.

Weekly Brunswicker (Brunswick, Mo.), 1854

Western Reserve Chronicle (Warren, Ohio), 1855

Books and Articles

Adams, George Rollie. *General William Selby Harney: Prince of Dragoons.* Lincoln: University of Nebraska Press, 2001.

Ahmad, Diana L. "'I Fear the Consequences to Our Animals': Emigrants and Their Livestock on the Overland Trails." *Great Plains Quarterly* 32 (Summer 2012): 165–82.

Alder, Lydia D. "The Massacre at Fort Laramie." *Improvement Era* 12 (June 1909): 636–38.

Allen, O. [Obridge]. *Allen's Guide Book and Map to the Gold Fields of Kansas & Nebraska and Great Salt Lake City.* Washington, D.C.: R. A. Waters, 1859. Facsimile edition by Nolie Mumey. Denver: privately published, 1953.

Anderson, Harry H. "The Controversial Sioux Amendment to the Fort Laramie Treaty of 1851." *Nebraska History* 37 (Sept. 1956): 201–20.

———. "Fur Traders as Fathers: The Origins of the Mixed-Blooded Community Among the Rosebud Sioux." *South Dakota History* 3 (Summer 1973): 233–70.

Ball, Durwood. *Army Regulars on the Western Frontier, 1848–1861.* Norman: University of Oklahoma Press, 2001.

Bandel, Eugene. *Frontier Life in the Army, 1854–1861.* Edited by Ralph P. Bieber. Glendale, Calif.: Arthur H. Clark, 1932.

Barry, Louise. *The Beginning of the West: Annals of the Kansas Gateway to the American West, 1540–1854.* Topeka: Kansas State Historical Society, 1972.

Beck, Paul N. *The First Sioux War: The Grattan Fight and Blue Water Creek, 1854–1856.* Lanham, Md.: University Press of America, 2004.

Benson, Ezra T. "Latest News from Our Immigration." *Deseret News* (Salt Lake City), Sept. 28, 1854. Pratt-Benson-Eldredge Company. Mormon Pioneer

Overland Travel, 1847–1868 (database). Church of Jesus Christ of Latter-day Saints, Salt Lake City. https://history.lds.org/overlandtravel/sources/7283/latest-news-from-our-immigration-deseret-news-28-sept-1854-3.

Bratt, John. *Trails of Yesterday*. Lincoln: University Publishing, 1921.

Bray, Kingsley M. *Crazy Horse: A Lakota Life*. Norman: University of Oklahoma Press, 2006.

———. "The Oglala Lakota and the Establishment of Fort Laramie." *Museum of the Fur Trade Quarterly* 36 (Winter 2000): 3–18.

———. "Teton Sioux Population History, 1655–1881." *Nebraska History* 75 (Summer 1994): 165–88.

Brooks, Juanita, ed. *On the Mormon Frontier: The Diary of Hosea Stout*. 2 vols. Salt Lake City: University of Utah Press, 1964.

Buecker, Thomas R. and R. Eli Paul, eds. *The Crazy Horse Surrender Ledger*. Lincoln: Nebraska State Historical Society, 1994.

Chappell, Gordon S. "The Fortifications of Old Fort Laramie." *Annals of Wyoming* 34 (Oct. 1962): 145–62.

Clemmer, Gregg S. *Old Alleghany: The Life and Wars of General Ed Johnson*. Staunton, Va.: Hearthside, 2004.

Croghan, George. *Army Life on the Western Frontier: Selections from the Official Reports Made between 1826 and 1845 by Colonel George Croghan*. Edited by Francis Paul Prucha. Norman: University of Oklahoma Press, 1958.

Cullum, George W. *Biographical Register of the Officers and Graduates of the U.S. Military Academy at West Point, N.Y.* 2 vols. New York: D. Van Nostrand, 1868.

Davies, John Johnson. "Historical Sketch of My Life." *Utah Historical Quarterly* 9 (July–Oct. 1941): 155–67.

DeMallie, Raymond J. "Teton." In *Handbook of North American Indians*, vol. 13, *Plains*, edited by Raymond J. DeMallie, 794–820. Washington, D.C.: Smithsonian Institution, 2001.

Dorris, J. T. "Federal Aid to Oregon Trail Prior to 1850." *Oregon Historical Quarterly* 30 (Dec. 1929): 305–25.

Dougherty, William Wallace. *Doctor on the Western Frontier: The Diaries of Dr. William Wallace Dougherty, 1854–1880, Practicing in Liberty, Clay County, Missouri, and Iatan, Platte County, Missouri*. Liberty, Mo.: Clay County Archives and Historical Library, 2004.

Ewers, John C. *The Blackfeet: Raiders on the Northwestern Plains*. Norman: University of Oklahoma Press, 1958.

Faust, Patricia L., ed. *Historical Times Illustrated Encyclopedia of the Civil War*. New York: Harper and Row, 1986.

Ford, Dixon, and Lee Kreutzer. "Oxen: Engines of the Overland Migration." *Overland Journal* 33 (Spring 2015): 4–29.

Frazer, Robert W., ed. *Mansfield on the Condition of the Western Forts, 1853–54*. Norman: University of Oklahoma Press, 1963.

————. *New Mexico in 1850: A Military View by Colonel George Archibald McCall.* Norman: University of Oklahoma Press, 1968.

Garavaglia, Louis A., and Charles G. Worman. *Firearms of the American West, 1803–1865.* Albuquerque: University of New Mexico Press, 1984.

Glass, Jefferson. *Reshaw: The Life and Times of John Baptiste Richard, Extraordinary Entrepreneur and Scoundrel of the Western Frontier.* Glendo, Wyo.: High Plains Press, 2014.

Gray, John S. "The Salt Lake Hockaday Mail, Part 1." *Annals of Wyoming* 56 (Fall 1984): 12–19.

————. "The Story of Mrs. Picotte-Galpin, a Sioux Heroine: Eagle Woman Learns about White Ways and Racial Conflict, 1820–1868." *Montana: The Magazine of Western History* 36 (Spring 1986): 2–21.

Grinnell, George Bird. *The Fighting Cheyennes.* Norman: University of Oklahoma Press, 1956.

Haddock, Edith Parker, and Dorothy Hardy Matthews. *History of Bear Lake Pioneers.* Paris, Idaho: Daughters of Utah Pioneers, 1968.

Hafen, LeRoy R., and Francis Marion Young. *Fort Laramie and the Pageant of the West, 1834–1890.* Glendale, Calif.: Arthur H. Clark, 1938.

Hafen, LeRoy R., and Ann W. Hafen, eds. *The Mountain Men and the Fur Trade of the Far West.* 10 vols. Glendale, Calif.: Arthur H. Clark, 1965–1972.

Hale, Edward H. *Kansas and Nebraska: The History, Geographical and Physical Characteristics, and Political Position of Those Territories.* Boston: Phillips, Samson, 1854.

Hanson, Charles E., Jr. "James Bordeaux." *Museum of the Fur Trade Quarterly* 2 (Spring 1966): 2–12.

————. "James Bordeaux—Chapter Two." *Museum of the Fur Trade Quarterly* 27 (Winter 1991): 2–7.

————. "Sefroy Iott." *Museum of the Fur Trade Quarterly* 7 (Winter 1971): 4–6.

Hanson, Charles E., Jr., and Veronica Sue Walters. "The Early Fur Trade in Northwestern Nebraska." *Nebraska History* 57 (Fall 1976): 291–314.

Hanson, James A. *Little Chief's Gatherings: The Smithsonian Institution's G. K. Warren 1855–1856 Plains Indian Collection and The New York State Library's 1855–1857 Warren Expeditions Journals.* Chadron, Neb.: Fur Press, 1996.

Hedren, Paul L., foreword, and Carroll Friswold, introduction. *The Massacre of Lieutenant Grattan and His Command by Indians.* Glendale, Calif.: Arthur H. Clark, 1983.

Herman, Eddie. "Couple Credited With Heroism Lie Buried in Unmarked Graves." *Rapid City Journal* (S.Dak.), Nov. 26, 1950.

Holt, Marilyn Irvin. "Joined Forces: Robert Campbell and John Daugherty as Military Entrepreneurs." *Western Historical Quarterly* 30 (Summer 1999): 183–202.

Hyde, George E. *Red Cloud's Folk: A History of the Oglala Sioux Indians.* Norman: University of Oklahoma Press, 1957.

————. *Spotted Tail's Folk: A History of the Brulé Sioux.* Norman: University of Oklahoma Press, 1961.

"Intelligence." In vol. 8 of *The Spirit of Missions,* 141. New York: Board of Missions of the Protestant Episcopal Church, 1843.

Jensen, Richard E., ed. *Voices of the American West*, vol. 1, *The Indian Interviews of Eli S. Ricker, 1903–1919*. Lincoln: University of Nebraska Press, 2005.

Jordan, David M. *"Happiness Is Not My Companion": The Life of General G. K. Warren*. Bloomington: Indiana University Press, 2001.

Kauffman, Kyle D., and Jonathan J. Liebowitz. "Draft Animals on the United States Frontier." *Overland Journal* 15 (Summer 1997): 13–26.

Kelly, Mark William. *Lost Voices on the Missouri: John Dougherty and the Indian Frontier*. Leavenworth, Kans.: Sam Clark, 2013.

Larsen, Christian J. "Journal 1851–1914." Hans Peter Olsen Company. Mormon Pioneer Overland Travel, 1847–1868 (database). Church of Jesus Christ of Latter-day Saints, Salt Lake City. https://history.lds.org/overlandtravelsources/10254605260248933418 -englarsen-christian-john-journal-1851-1914-vol-5-translation-198-202.

Lavender, David. *Fort Laramie and the Changing Frontier*. Washington, D.C.: National Park Service, 1983.

Lecompte, Janet. *Pueblo, Hardscrabble, Greenhorn: The Upper Arkansas, 1832–1856*. Norman: University of Oklahoma Press, 1978.

Lewis, Emily H. "Shadow of the Brave." *True West* 10 (Sept. 1962): 28–29, 55–57. In item RGD949, S1.543, Clifford Family, Paul D. Riley Collection, Nebraska State Historical Society.

Longacre, Edward G. *General John Buford*. Conshohocken, Pa.: Combined Books, 1995.

Mattes, Merrill J. *The Great Platte River Road: The Covered Wagon Mainline via Fort Kearny to Fort Laramie*. Lincoln: Nebraska State Historical Society, 1969.

———. *Platte River Road Narratives: A Descriptive Bibliography of Travel over the Great Central Overland Route to Oregon, California, Utah, Colorado, Montana, and Other Western States and Territories, 1812–1866*. Urbana: University of Illinois Press, 1988.

McCann, Lloyd E. "The Grattan Massacre." *Nebraska History* 37 (Mar. 1956): 1–26.

McChristian, Douglas C. *Fort Laramie: Military Bastion of the High Plains, 1849–1890*. Norman, Okla.: Arthur H. Clark, 2008.

McClellan, Carolyn Minnette. "The Sioux Expedition, 1854–1856." Master's thesis, Washington University in St. Louis, 1945.

McDermott, John D. "Crime and Punishment in the United States Army: A Phase of Fort Laramie History." *Journal of the West* 7 (Apr. 1968): 246–55.

———. "Fort Laramie's Silent Soldier, Leodegar Schnyder." *Annals of Wyoming* 36 (Apr. 1964): 4–18.

———. *A Guide to the Indian Wars of the West*. Lincoln: University of Nebraska Press, 1998.

———. "James Bordeaux." In *The Mountain Men and the Fur Trade of the Far West*, vol. 5, edited by LeRoy R. Hafen and Ann W. Hafen. Glendale, Calif.: Arthur H. Clark, 1968: 65–80.

———. "Joseph Bissonette." In *The Mountain Men and the Fur Trade of the Far West*, vol. 4, edited by LeRoy R. Hafen and Ann W. Hafen. Glendale, Calif.: Arthur H. Clark, 1966: 49–60.

———. *Red Cloud's War: The Bozeman Trail, 1866–1868*. 2 vols. Norman, Okla.: Arthur H. Clark, 2010.

MacKinnon, William P. "The Buchanan Spoils System and the Utah Expedition: Careers of W. M. F. Magraw and John M. Hockaday." *Utah Historical Quarterly* 31 (Spring 1963): 127–50.

MacMaster, William Athol. "Diary, 1848–1887." Daniel Garn Company. Mormon Pioneer Overland Travel, 1847–1868 (database). Church of Jesus Christ of Latter-day Saints, Salt Lake City. https://history.lds.org/overlandtravel/sources/5171/ mac-master-william-athole-diary-1848-1887-fd-1-351-63.

Mitchell, Hezekiah. "Journal, June–Sept. 1854." James Brown Company. Mormon Pioneer Overland Travel, 1847–1868 (database). Church of Jesus Christ of Latter-day Saints, Salt Lake City. https://history.lds.org/overlandtravel/sources/4861/ mitchell-hezekiah-journal-1854-june-sept.

Mitchell, Sidney F. "Chronology of the Life of Hezekiah Mitchell and Sarah Mallinson Mitchell." Darrin and Andrea Lythgoe's Genealogy Pages. http://lythgoes.net/ genealogy/history/HezekiahMitchell2.php.

Morrison, W. W. "Grattan Massacre." *Annals of Wyoming* 27 (Oct. 1955): 168–74.

———. "Grattan Massacre." *Annals of Wyoming* 42 (Apr. 1970): 83–86.

Mullis, Randy. *Peacekeeping on the Plains: Army Operations in Bleeding Kansas.* Columbia: University of Missouri Press, 2004.

Nadeau, Remi. *Fort Laramie and the Sioux Indians.* Englewood Cliffs, N. J.: Prentice-Hall, 1967.

Obray, Thomas Lorenzo. "Latest News from Our Immigration." *Deseret News* (Salt Lake City), Sept. 28, 1854. Pratt-Benson-Eldredge Company. Mormon Pioneer Overland Travel, 1847–1868 (database). Church of Jesus Christ of Latter-day Saints, Salt Lake City. https://history.lds.org/overlandtravel/sources/7283/ latest-news-from-our-immigration-deseret-news-28-sept-1854-3.

"Orville A. Nixon." Biographies of Hickman County, Tennessee. Genealogy Trails History Group. http://genealogytrails.com/tenn/hickman/biographies_n.html.

Ostler, Jeffrey. *The Plains Sioux and U.S. Colonialism from Lewis and Clark to Wounded Knee.* Cambridge, U.K.: Cambridge University Press, 2004.

Paine, Bayard H. *Pioneers, Indians and Buffaloes.* Curtis, Neb.: Curtis Enterprise, 1935.

Paul, R. Eli., ed. *Autobiography of Red Cloud: War Leader of the Oglalas.* Helena: Montana Historical Society Press, 1997.

———. *Blue Water Creek and the First Sioux War, 1854–1856.* Norman: University of Oklahoma Press, 2004.

———. "Counting Indians." *Wild West* 18 (Dec. 2005): 27.

———. "First Shots in the First Sioux War." *Wild West* 18 (Dec. 2005): 22–26, 28.

Penner, Kristl Knudsen. "John Wilkins Whitfield." Handbook of Texas Online, Texas State Historical Association, Denton. Modified Nov. 17, 2011. https://tshaonline. org/handbook/online/articles/fwh38.

Peterson, Lawrence K. *Confederate Combat Commander: The Remarkable Life of Brigadier General Alfred Jefferson Vaughan Jr.* Knoxville: University of Knoxville Press, 2013.

Peterson, Lulla Hansen. "The Life of Johanna Marie (Domgaard) Hansen." 2013 digitization of 1938 typescript. FamilySearch. https://familysearch.org/photos/stories/3754570.

Powell, W. H. "Fort Laramie's Early History." *Collections of the Wyoming Historical Society.* Vol. 1. Cheyenne: Wyoming Historical Society, 1897: 176–78.

Powers, Thomas. *The Killing of Crazy Horse.* New York: Alfred A. Knopf, 2010.

Price, Catherine. *The Oglala People, 1841–1879: A Political History.* Lincoln: University of Nebraska Press, 1996.

Rickey, Don, Jr. *Forty Miles a Day on Beans and Hay: The Enlisted Soldier Fighting the Indian Wars.* Norman: University of Oklahoma Press, 1963.

Riley, Paul D. "John B. Didier." In *The Mountain Men and the Fur Trade of the Far West,* vol. 9, edited by LeRoy R. Hafen and Ann W. Hafen, 137–38. Glendale, Calif.: Arthur H. Clark, 1972.

Roberts, B. H. *A Comprehensive History of the Church of Jesus Christ of Latter-day Saints.* 6 vols. Salt Lake City: Deseret News Press, 1930.

Rodenbough, Theophilus F. *From Everglade to Canyon with the Second United States Cavalry: An Authentic Account of Service in Florida, Mexico, Virginia, and the Indian Country, 1836–1875.* Norman: University of Oklahoma Press, 2000.

Sandoz, Mari. "The Look of the West—1854." *Nebraska History* 35 (Dec. 1954): 243–54.

Sill, James. "Necrology—Hugh Brady Fleming." in *Twenty-Sixth Annual Reunion of the Association of Graduates of the United States Military Academy at West Point, New York, June 10th, 1895.* Saginaw, Mich.: Seemann and Peters, 1895: 92–97.

Simonin, Louis L. *The Rocky Mountain West in 1867.* Translated and annotated by Wilson O. Clough. Lincoln: University of Nebraska Press, 1966.

Sutherland, Thomas. "Robert Campbell Company Report, 1854 August 22." Robert L. Campbell Company. Mormon Pioneer Overland Travel, 1847–1868 (database). Church of Jesus Christ of Latter-day Saints, Salt Lake City. https://history.lds.org/overlandtravel/sources/4931/.

Tate, Michael L. *Indians and Emigrants: Encounters on the Overland Trails.* Norman: University of Oklahoma Press, 2006.

Taylor, Emerson Gifford. *Gouverneur Kemble Warren: The Life and Letters of an American Soldier, 1830–1882.* Boston and New York: Houghton Mifflin, 1932.

Thompson, Jerry, ed. *Texas and New Mexico on the Eve of the Civil War: The Mansfield and Johnstown Inspections, 1859–1861.* Albuquerque: University of New Mexico Press, 2001.

Thrapp, Dan L. *Encyclopedia of Frontier Biography.* 2 vols. Glendale, Calif.: Arthur H. Clark, 1988.

Townsend, Edward D. "Necrology—William Hoffman." In *Sixteenth Annual Reunion of the Association of Graduates of the United States Military Academy at West Point, New York, June 12th, 1885,* 36–39. East Saginaw, Mich.: Evening News, 1885.

Unruh, John D., Jr. *The Plains Across: The Overland Emigrants and the Trans-Mississippi West, 1840–60.* Urbana: University of Illinois Press, 1979.

Utley, Robert M. *Frontiersmen in Blue: The United States and the Indian, 1846–1865*. New York: Macmillan, 1967.

Van Kirk, Sylvia. *Many Tender Ties: Women in Fur-Trade Society, 1670–1870*. Norman: University of Oklahoma Press, 1980.

Vaux, William. "Report from Fort Laramie, Oct. 1, 1854." In vol. 20 of *The Spirit of Missions*, 40–41. New York: Board of Missions of the Protestant Episcopal Church, 1855.

Waggoner, Josephine. *Witness: A Hunkpapa Historian's Strong-Heart Song of the Lakotas*. Edited by Emily Levine. Lincoln: University of Nebraska Press, 2013.

Walker, James R. *Oglala Society*. Edited by Raymond J. DeMallie. Lincoln: University of Nebraska Press, 1982.

Ware, Eugene F. *Indian War of 1864*. Introduction to the Bison Book edition by John D. McDermott. Lincoln: University of Nebraska Press, 1994.

Warren, G. K. [Gouverneur Kemble]. *Preliminary Report of Explorations in Nebraska and Dakota, in the Years 1855-'56-'57*. Washington, D.C.: Government Printing Office, 1875.

"Washington L. Jolley Company (1854)." Mormon Pioneer Overland Travel, 1847–1868 (database). Church of Jesus Christ of Latter-day Saints, Salt Lake City. https://history.lds.org/overlandtravel/companies/173/washington-l-jolley-company-1854.

Watkins, Albert, ed. "Notes of the Early History of the Nebraska Country." In vol. 20 of *Publications of the Nebraska State Historical Society*, 1–400. Lincoln: Nebraska State Historical Society, 1922.

White, David A., ed. *News of the Plains and Rockies, 1803–1865*. Vol. 4, *Scientists, Artists, 1835–1859: Original Narratives of Overland Travel and Adventure Selected from the Wagner-Camp and Becker Bibliography of Western Americana*. Spokane: Arthur H. Clark, 1998.

Williamson, John P. *An English-Dakota School Dictionary*. Yankton Agency, Dakota Territory: Iapi Oaye Press, 1886.

Wilson, Frederick T. "Old Fort Pierre and Its Neighbors." In vol. 1 of *South Dakota Historical Collections*, 257–379. Aberdeen, S.Dak.: News Printing, 1902.

Wissler, Clark. "The Enigma of the Squaw-Man." *Natural History* 41 (Mar. 1938): 185–89.

Withers, Ethel Massie, ed. "Experiences of Lewis Bissell Dougherty on the Oregon Trail." Parts 1–5, *Missouri Historical Review* 24 (April 1930): 359–78; 24 (July 1930): 550–67; 25 (October 1930): 102–15; 25 (January 1931): 306–21; 25 (April 1931): 474–89.

Woods, Fred E. "The 1854 Mormon Emigration at the Missouri-Kansas Border." *Kansas History: A Journal of the Central Plains* 32 (Winter 2009–10): 226–45.

———. "A Gifted Gentleman in Perpetual Motion: John Taylor as an Emigration Agent." In *Champion of Liberty: John Taylor*, edited by Mary Jane Woodger, 177–92. Provo, Utah: Brigham Young University Religious Studies Center, 2009.

Woolson, A. A. *Reminiscences of Lisbon, N. H.* Littleton, N.H.: Courier Printing, 1912.

Young, Otis E. *The West of Philip St. George Cooke, 1809–1895*. Glendale, Calif.: Arthur H. Clark, 1955.

Index

Unless otherwise noted, names in parentheses indicate incorrect or alternative spellings as found in the documents.